REEDS MARINA GUIDE 2019

GW00759595

Section 1

The Marinas and Services Section has been fully updated for the 2019 season. These useful pages provide chartlets and facility details for some 200 marinas around the shores of the UK and Ireland, including the Channel Islands, the perfect complement to any Reeds Nautical Almanac.

Section 2

The Marine Supplies & Services section lists more than 1000 services at coastal and other locations around the British Isles. It provides a quick and easy reference to manufacturers and retailers of equipment, services and supplies both nationally and locally together with emergency services.

Advertisement Sales
Enquiries about advertising space should be addressed to:
adlardcoles@bloomsbury.com

Printed by Bell and Bain Ltd, Glagow

Section 1
Marinas and Services Section

Area Guide
Showing Coastal Divisions

Area 1 .....South West England.. Isles of Scilly to Anvil Point

Area 2 .....Central Southern England..Anvil Point to Selsey Bill

Area 3 .....South East England .... Selsey Bill to North Foreland

Area 4 .....East England .... North Foreland to Great Yarmouth

Area 5 .....North East England... Great Yarmouth to Berwick-upon-Tweed

Area 6 .....South East Scotland... Eyemouth to Rattray Head

Area 7 .....North East Scotland................... Rattray Head to Cape Wrath including Orkney & Shetland Is

Area 8 .....North West Scotland ....Cape Wrath to Crinan Canal

Area 9 .....South West Scotland..Crinan Canal to Mull of Galloway

Area 10 ...North West England.......................... Isle of Man & N Wales, Mull of Galloway to Bardsey Is

Area 11 ...South Wales & Bristol Channel... Bardsey Island to Land's End

Area 12 ...South Ireland ....Malahide, clockwise to Liscannor Bay

Area 13 ...North Ireland...Liscannor Bay, clockwise to Lambay Island

Area 14 ...Channel Islands...Guernsey and Jersey

SOUTH WEST ENGLAND – Isles of Scilly to Anvil Point

Key to Marina Plans symbols

	Bottled gas	P	Parking
	Chandler		Pub/Restaurant
	Disabled facilities		Pump out
	Electrical supply		Rigging service
	Electrical repairs		Sail repairs
	Engine repairs		Shipwright
	First Aid		Shop/Supermarket
	Fresh Water		Showers
D	Fuel - Diesel		Slipway
P	Fuel - Petrol	WC	Toilets
	Hardstanding/boatyard		Telephone
@	Internet Café		Trolleys
	Laundry facilities	V	Visitors berths
	Lift-out facilities		Wi-Fi

Area 1 - South West England

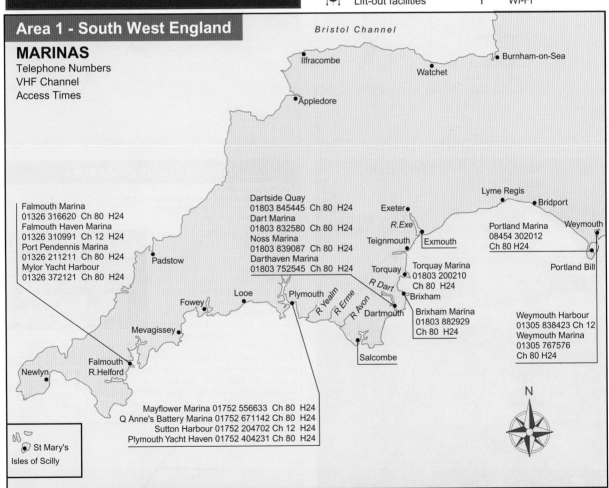

MARINAS
Telephone Numbers
VHF Channel
Access Times

Bristol Channel

Ilfracombe

Watchet

Burnham-on-Sea

Appledore

Falmouth Marina
01326 316620 Ch 80 H24
Falmouth Haven Marina
01326 310991 Ch 12 H24
Port Pendennis Marina
01326 211211 Ch 80 H24
Mylor Yacht Harbour
01326 372121 Ch 80 H24

Dartside Quay
01803 845445 Ch 80 H24
Dart Marina
01803 832580 Ch 80 H24
Noss Marina
01803 839087 Ch 80 H24
Darthaven Marina
01803 752545 Ch 80 H24

Exeter

R.Exe

Teignmouth

Exmouth

Lyme Regis

Bridport

Portland Marina
08454 302012
Ch 80 H24

Weymouth

Padstow

Torquay

Torquay Marina
01803 200210
Ch 80 H24

R Dart

Brixham

Portland Bill

Fowey

Looe

Plymouth

R Yealm

R Erme

R Avon

Dartmouth

Brixham Marina
01803 882929
Ch 80 H24

Weymouth Harbour
01305 838423 Ch 12
Weymouth Marina
01305 767576
Ch 80 H24

Mevagissey

Salcombe

Newlyn

Falmouth
R.Helford

Mayflower Marina 01752 556633 Ch 80 H24
Q Anne's Battery Marina 01752 671142 Ch 80 H24
Sutton Harbour 01752 204702 Ch 12 H24
Plymouth Yacht Haven 01752 404231 Ch 80 H24

N

St Mary's
Isles of Scilly

FALMOUTH MARINA

Falmouth Marina
North Parade, Falmouth, Cornwall, TR11 2TD
Tel: 01326 316620 Fax: 01326 313939
Email: falmouth@premiermarinas.com
www.premiermarinas.com

VHF	Ch 80
ACCESS	H24

Falmouth Marina lies tucked away in sheltered waters at the southern end of the Fal Estuary. Welcoming to both visiting and residential yachts, its comprehensive facilities include a restaurant, convenience store and hairdresser, while just a 20-minute walk away

is Falmouth's town centre where you will find no shortage of shops and eating places. Comprising more than 70 sq miles of navigable water, the Fal Estuary is an intriguing cruising area full of hidden creeks and inlets.

FACILITIES AT A GLANCE

Key
a Marina office
b Waste oil and bin compound
c Under cover boat storage

FALMOUTH HAVEN MARINA

Falmouth Haven Marina
44 Arwenack Street
Tel: 01326 310991
Email: welcome@falmouthhaven.co.uk

VHF	Ch 12
ACCESS	H24

Run by Falmouth Harbour Commissioners (FHC), Falmouth Haven Marina has become increasingly popular since its opening in 1982, enjoying close proximity to the amenities and entertainments of Falmouth town centre. Sheltered by a breakwater, Falmouth Haven caters for 50 boats and offers petrol and diesel supplies as well as good shower and laundry facilities.

Falmouth Harbour is considered by some to be the cruising capital of Cornwall and its deep water combined with easily navigable entrance – even in the severest conditions – makes it a favoured destination for visiting yachtsmen.

FACILITIES AT A GLANCE

PORT PENDENNIS MARINA

Port Pendennis Marina
Challenger Quay, Falmouth, Cornwall, TR11 3YL
Tel: 01326 211211 Fax: 01326 311116
www.portpendennis.com

VHF	Ch 80
ACCESS	H24

Easily identified by the tower of the National Maritime Museum, Port Pendennis Marina is a convenient arrival or departure point for trans-Atlantic or Mediterranean voyages. Lying adjacent to the town centre, Port Pendennis is divided into an outer marina, with full tidal access, and inner marina, accessible three hours either side of HW. Among

its impressive array of marine services is Pendennis Shipyard, one of Britain's most prestigious yacht builders, while other amenities on site include car hire, tennis courts and a yachtsman's lounge, from where you can send faxes or e-mails. Within walking distance of the marina are beautiful sandy beaches, an indoor swimming pool complex and castle.

FACILITIES AT A GLANCE

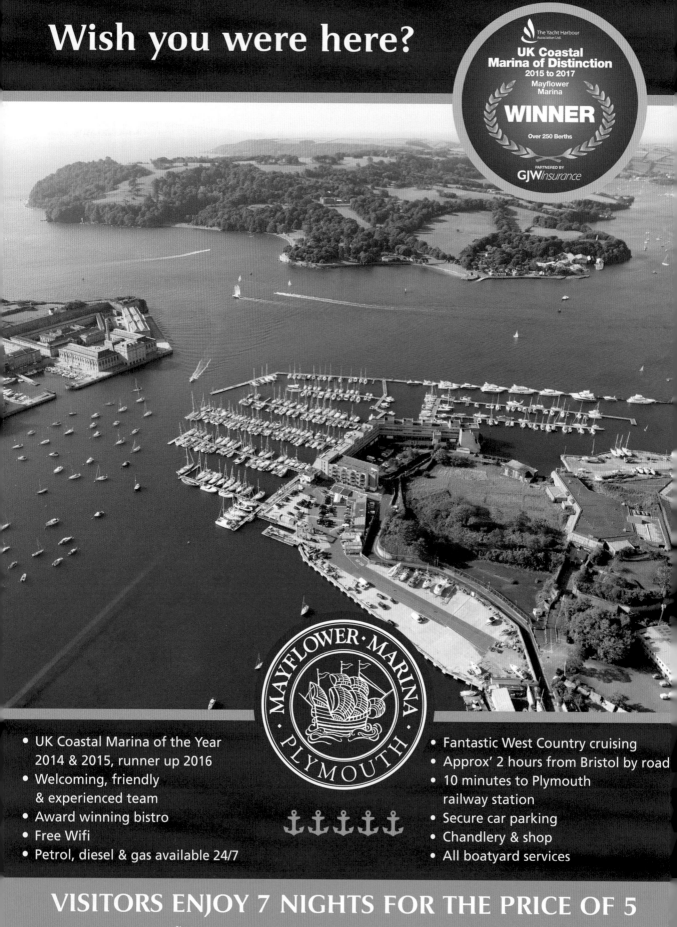

MYLOR YACHT HARBOUR

Mylor Yacht Harbour Marina
Mylor, Falmouth, Cornwall, TR11 5UF
Tel: 01326 372121
Email: enquiries@mylor.com

| VHF | Ch M, 80 |
| ACCESS | H24 |

Situated on the western shore of Carrick Roads in the beautiful Fal Estuary, Mylor Yacht Harbour has been improved and expanded in recent years, comprising two substantial breakwaters, three inner pontoons with 180 berths and 240 swinging moorings. With a large visitor pontoon, H24 access, good shelter and excellent facilities, it ranks among the most popular marinas on the SW coast of England.

Formerly the Navy's smallest dockyard, established in 1805, Mylor is today a thriving yachting centre and full service boatyard. On site there is a cafe and restaurant overlooking stunning local scenery. Falmouth just 10 mins away, with attractions such as Pendennis Castle and the National Maritime Museum in Falmouth.

FACILITIES AT A GLANCE

Key
a Harbour cafe and shops
b Showers/toilets
c Kingsmoor Cottage and
   Castaways Wine Bar
d Marina office
e Rigging pontoon
f New public slipway
g Fueling pontoon
h Marine services and
   Harbour office
i Water taxi pick up
j Yacht club/laundry
k Holiday accommodation

Not Dredged

34

B *Dredged to 2m below CD*

This is the life...

A welcoming yacht harbour anchored by the country's finest sailing waters.

Image © Aerial Cornwall

- Contemporary marina & safe moorings
- One of the largest visitor pontoons in the south west
- Full service boatyard
- Boat lifting & shore storage
- 1st class shore side facilities
- All tides access & prime sailing location

VHF ch. 37/80

Mylor Yacht Harbour | **Marine Team** | **HARBOURSIDE** *Holidays*

mylor.com 01326 372 121 enquiries@mylor.com

MAYFLOWER MARINA

⚓⚓⚓⚓

Mayflower International Marina
Ocean Quay, Richmond Walk, Plymouth, PL1 4LS
Tel: 01752 556633 Fax: 01752 606896
Email: info@mayflowermarina.co.uk

| VHF | Ch 80 |
| ACCESS | H24 |

Sitting on the famous Plymouth Hoe, with the Devon coast to the left and the Cornish coast to the right, Mayflower Marina is a friendly, well-run marina. Facilities include 24 hour access to fuel, gas and a launderette, full repair and maintenance services as well as an on site bar and brasserie. The marina is located only a short distance from Plymouth's town centre, where there are regular train services to and from several major towns and cities.

FACILITIES AT A GLANCE

Northern approach

Key
a Marina office
b Brokerage,
   chandlery
c Cafe
d Bar
e Brasserie
f Berth holders toilets
   and showers
g Ocean Court Flats

Southern approach

QUEEN ANNE'S BATTERY

⚓⚓⚓⚓

Queen Anne's Battery
Plymouth, Devon, PL4 0LP
Tel: 01752 671142
Email: qab@mdlmarinas.co.uk www.queenannesbattery.co.uk

| VHF | Ch 80 |
| ACCESS | H24 |

Plymouth, a vibrant and fast growing city, is home to Queen Anne's Battery, a 235 resident berth marina with outstanding facilities for yachtsmen and motor cruisers alike. Located just south of Sutton Harbour, QAB promises a welcoming stay with alongside pontoon berthing protected by the surrounding breakwater. While on the city's doorstep, the marina is a short walk away from the historical Barbican, providing peace and tranquility to visitors.

The marina is often frequented by crowds of people marveling the many prestigious international yacht and powerboat races Plymouth Sound facilitates.

QAB is an exposed treasure along a beautiful historic coastline, at times resembling a mini 'Cowes' with its vibrancy.

FACILITIES AT A GLANCE

Key
a Toilets and showers
b Royal Western Yacht Club
c Marina office and provisions shop
d Bar/restaurant
e Cafe

1

PLYMOUTH YACHT HAVEN

Plymouth Yacht Haven Ltd
Shaw Way, Mount Batten, Plymouth, PL9 9XH
Tel: 01752 404231 Fax: 01752 484177
Email: plymouth@yachthavens.com www.yachthavens.com

♏ ♏ ♏ ♏
VHF Ch 80
ACCESS H24

Situated minutes from Plymouth sound, Plymouth Yacht Haven enjoys a tranquil setting, yet is just a five minute water taxi ride from the bustling barbican with all its restaurants and attractions. The Yacht Haven offers excellent protection from the prevailing SW winds and is within easy reach of some of the most fantastic cruising grounds.

This 450-berth marina can accommodate vessels up to 45m in length and 7m in draught. Members of staff are on site 24/7 to welcome you as a visitor and to serve diesel. With an on site 75T travel hoist and storage, a restaurant, chandlery, and extensive range of marine service, Plymouth Yacht Haven has plenty to offer both on and off the water.

FACILITIES AT A GLANCE
🔌 ♒ ♿ ⚓ ⛽ 🔧
✚ ⚓ 🛟 ♻ @ 🖥
🖥 P ✕ 🅰 ♟ ✂
Ⓥ 🏳 WC 🚿 ♟

Key
a Houses
b Berth holders car park
c Washdown area
d Shipwright, etc
e Snacks and takeaway
f Mountbatten Watersports Centre and bar/restaurant
g Main reception - toilets, showers, phones, launderette and disabled facilities
h The Bridge restaurant

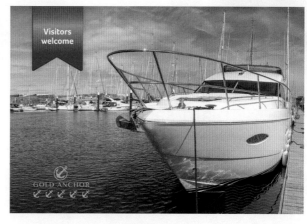
SUTTON HARBOUR

Sutton Harbour
The Jetty, Sutton Harbour, Plymouth, PL4 0DW
Tel: 01752 204702 Fax: 01752 204693
Email: marina@sutton-harbour.co.uk
www.suttonharbourmarina.com

♏ ♏ ♏ ♏
VHF Ch 12
ACCESS H24

Sutton Harbour Marina, located in the heart of Plymouth's historic Barbican area and a short stroll from the city centre, offers 5-star facilities in a sheltered location, surrounded by boutique waterfront bars and restau

a minimum 3.5m depth, the harbour has 24hr lock access on request with free flow approx 3hrs either side of high tide. The marina of choice for international yacht races such as The Transat and Fastnet. Visitors are invited to come and enjoy the unrivalled shelter, facilities, atmosphere and location that Sutton harbour offers.

FACILITIES AT A GLANCE
🔌 ♒ ♿ ⚓ ⛽ 🔧
✚ ⚓ 🛟 @ 🖥 P
✕ 🅰 ♟ ✂ 🏳
🏳 WC 🚿 Ⓥ 🏳 ♟

Key
a Fish market
b National Marine Aquarium
c Customs House
d The Cove
e Marina office
f Lock tower

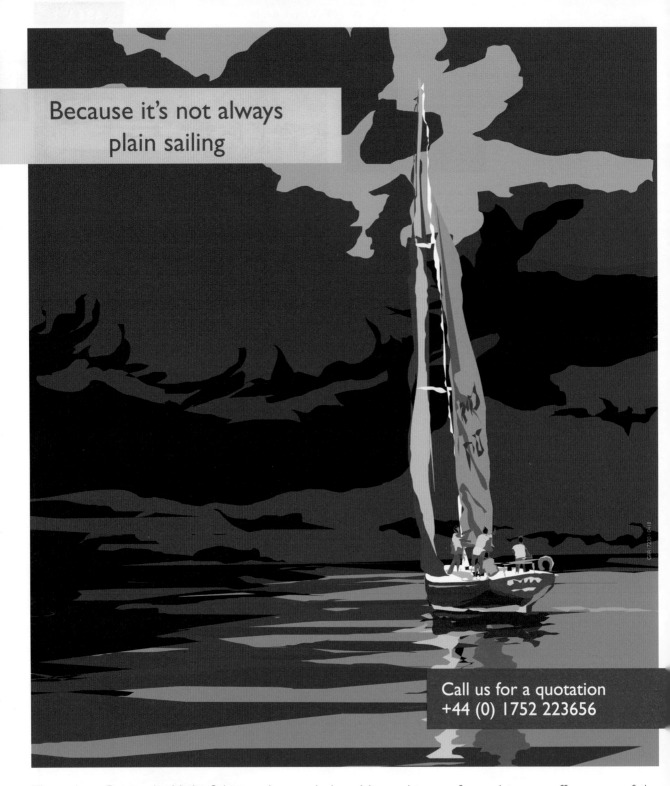

Because it's not always plain sailing

Call us for a quotation
+44 (0) 1752 223656

The unique Pantaenius Yacht Scheme clauses, designed by yachtsmen for yachtsmen, offer some of the broadest cover available. Why not join the 100,000 boat owners worldwide who enjoy the peace of mind a Pantaenius policy provides.

PANTAENIUS
Sail & Motor Yacht Insurance

Plymouth · pantaenius.co.uk

DARTHAVEN MARINA

Darthaven Marina
Brixham Road, Kingswear, Devon, TQ6 0SG
Tel: 01803 752242
Email: admin@darthaven.co.uk
www.darthaven.co.uk

VHF	Ch 80
ACCESS	H24

Darthaven Marina is a family run business situated in the village of Kingswear on the east side of the River Dart. Within half a mile from Start Bay and the mouth of the river, it is the first marina you come to from seaward and is accessible at all states of the tide. Darthaven prides itself on being more than just a marina, offering a high standard of marine services with both electronic and engineering experts plus wood and GRP repairs on site. A shop, post office and three pubs are within a walking distance of the marina, while a frequent ferry service takes passengers across the river to Dartmouth.

FACILITIES AT A GLANCE

Key
a Main office
  Chandlery
  Electricians
b Shipwrights
c Engineers
d Yacht taxi pontoon
e Berthing office
f Welding workshop

DART MARINA

Dart Marina
Sandquay Road, Dartmouth, Devon, TQ6 9PH
Tel: 01803 837161 Fax: 01803 835040
Email: yachtharbour@dartmarina.com
www.dartmarinayachtharbour.com

VHF	Ch 80
ACCESS	H24

Dart Marina Yacht Harbour, in one of the most stunning locations on the UK coastline, is a peaceful spot for simply sitting on deck relaxing and perfectly positioned for day sailing or more ambitious cruising. With visitor berths, 110 annual berths, all accessible at any tide, the Yacht Harbour is sought after for its intimate atmosphere and stylish setting.

Professional, knowledgeable and helpful, the marina team is on-site all year round and there are impeccable facilities including showers, bathrooms and laundry.

In Dartmouth there are restaurants, bistros, cafes, delis, independent shops, galleries, a cinema, chandlers, antique and lifestyle shops in abundance.

FACILITIES AT A GLANCE

NOSS MARINA

Noss Marina
Bridge Road, Kingswear, Devon, TQ6 0EA
Tel: 01803 839087 Fax: 01803 835620
Email: info@nossmarina.co.uk
www.nossmarina.co.uk

VHF	Ch 80
ACCESS	H24

Upstream of Dartmouth on the east shore of the River Dart is Noss Marina. Enjoying a peaceful rural setting, this marina is well suited to those who prefer a quieter atmosphere. Besides 180 fully serviced berths, 50 fore-and-aft moorings in the middle reaches of the river are also run by the marina, with mooring holders entitled to use all the facilities available to berth holders. During summer, a passenger ferry service runs regularly between Noss-on-Dart and Dartmouth, while a grocery service to your boat can be provided on request.

FACILITIES AT A GLANCE

Key
a Marina office
b Amenities

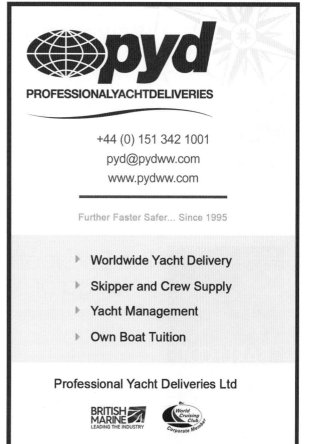

DARTSIDE QUAY

Dartside Quay
Galmpton Creek, Brixham, Devon, TQ5 0EH
Tel: 01803 845445
Email: dartsidequay@mdlmarinas.co.uk
www.dartsidequay.co.uk

VHF	Ch 80
ACCESS	H24

Located at the head of Galmpton Creek, Dartside Quay lies three miles upriver from Dartmouth.

In a sheltered position and with beautiful views across to Dittisham, it offers extensive boatyard facilities. The seven-acre dry boat storage area has space for over 300 boats and is serviced by a 65-ton hoist operating from a purpose-built dock, plus a 16-ton trailer hoist operating on a slipway.

There are also a number of summer mud moorings available and a well stocked chandlery, in fact if the item you want is not in stock we can order it in for you.

FACILITIES AT A GLANCE

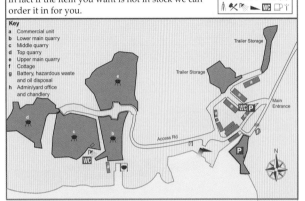

Key
a Commercial unit
b Lower main quarry
c Middle quarry
d Top quarry
e Upper main quarry
f Cottage
g Battery, hazardous waste and oil disposal
h Admin/yard office and chandlery

BRIXHAM MARINA

Brixham Marina
Berry Head Road, Brixham, Devon, TQ5 9BW
Tel: 01803 882929
Email: brixham@mdlmarinas.co.uk
www.brixhammarina.co.uk

VHF	Ch 80
ACCESS	H24

Home to one of Britain's largest fishing fleets, Brixham Harbour is located on the southern shore of Torbay, which is well sheltered from westerly winds and where tidal streams are weak. Brixham Marina, housed in a separate basin to the work boats, provides easy access in all weather conditions and at all states of the tide. Provisions and diesel are available and there is a bar and restaurant, ideal for when you've worked up an appetite out on the water.

Local attractions include a walk out to Berry Head Nature Reserve and a visit to the replica of Sir Francis Drake's *Golden Hind.*

FACILITIES AT A GLANCE

Key
a Dock manager's office
b Information centre
c Boat sales and Sea School

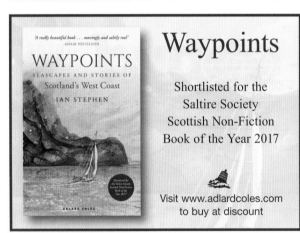
TORQUAY MARINA

Torquay Marina
Torquay, Devon, TQ2 5EQ
Tel: 01803 200210
Email: torquaymarina@mdlmarinas.co.uk
www.torquaymarina.co.uk

VHF	Ch 80
ACCESS	H24

Tucked away in the north east corner of Torbay, Torquay Marina is well sheltered from the prevailing SW'ly winds, providing safe entry in all conditions and at any state of the tide. Located in the centre of Torquay, the marina enjoys easy access to the town's numerous shops, bars and restaurants.

Torquay is ideally situated for either exploring Tor Bay itself, with its many delightful anchorages, or else for heading further west to experience several other scenic harbours such as Dartmouth and Salcombe. It also provides a good starting point for crossing to Brittany, Normandy or the Channel Islands.

FACILITIES AT A GLANCE

Key
a Dock manager's office
b Dockmaster offices
c Restaurant, cafe and newsagents

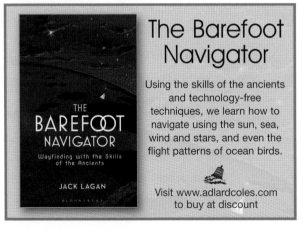

PORTLAND MARINA

Portland Marina
Osprey Quay, Portland, Dorset, DT5 1DX
Tel: 08345 430 2012
www.deanreddyhoff.co.uk
Email: berths@portlandmarina.co.uk

⚓⚓⚓⚓

| VHF | Ch 80 |
| ACCESS | H24 |

Portland Marina is an ideal location for both annual berthing and weekend stopovers. The marina offers first class facilities including washrooms, on-site bar and restaurant, lift out and storage up to 50T, dry stacking up to 9m, 24-hour manned security, fuel berth, sewage pump out, extensive car parking and a full range of marine services including a chandlery.

The marina is within walking distance of local pubs and restaurants on Portland with Weymouth's bustling town centre and mainline railway station just a short bus or ferry ride away.

FACILITIES AT A GLANCE

Key
a Admin Office, washrooms, showers and laundry
b Bar and Restaurant
c Business/retail units
d Refuse and recycling bins
e Commercial units
f Dry stack storage building
g Sunseeker

Berthing guide
From low at hammerheads
Odds outside
Evens inside

WEYMOUTH HARBOUR

Harbour Office
13 Custom House Quay, Weymouth, Dorset, DT4 8BG
Tel: 01305 838423
Email: weymouthharbour@dorset.gov.uk
www.weymouth-harbour.co.uk

| VHF | Ch 12 |
| ACCESS | H24 |

Weymouth Harbour, situated on the Jurassic Coast, lays NE of Portland in the protected waters of Weymouth Bay. Located in the heart of the old town and accessible at any state of tide, the Georgian harbour has numerous overnight berths. Pontoons on both quays have electricity and fresh water, as well as modern shower facilities. Restaurants and shops abound within walking distance and visitors are also welcome in the Royal Dorset YC and Weymouth SC, both situated on the quayside.

Vessels are advised to call *Weymouth Harbour* on Ch12 on approach, and vessels over 15m are recommended to give prior notification of intended arrival.

FACILITIES AT A GLANCE

Key
a Waiting pontoon for bridge
b Lifeboat
c Weymouth Sailing Club
d Royal Dorset Yacht Club

WEYMOUTH MARINA

Weymouth Marina
70 Commercial Road, Dorset, DT4 8NA
Tel: 01305 767576 Fax: 01305 767575
www.weymouth-marina.co.uk
Email: sales@weymouth-marina.co.uk

| VHF | Ch 80 |
| ACCESS | H24 |

With more than 280 permanent and visitors' berths, Weymouth is a modern, purpose-built marina ideally situated for yachtsmen cruising between the West Country and the Solent. It is also conveniently placed for sailing to France or the Channel Islands. Accessed via the town's historic

lifting bridge, which opens every even hour 0800–2000 (plus 2100 Jun–Aug), the marina is dredged to 2.5m below chart datum. It provides easy access to the town centre, with its abundance of shops, pubs and restaurants, as well as to the traditional seafront where an impressive sandy beach is overlooked by an esplanade of hotels.

FACILITIES AT A GLANCE

2

CENTRAL SOUTHERN ENGLAND – Anvil Point to Selsey Bill

Reeds PDF ebooks

In response to popular demand, all the Reeds Almanacs are now available as searchable, highlightable PDF ebooks. (All ebooks incorporate the Marina Guide.)

Visit www.reedsnauticalalmanac.co.uk for further information

Key to Marina Plans symbols

Bottled gas		P	Parking
Chandler			Pub/Restaurant
Disabled facilities			Pump out
Electrical supply			Rigging service
Electrical repairs			Sail repairs
Engine repairs			Shipwright
First Aid			Shop/Supermarket
Fresh Water			Showers
Fuel - Diesel			Slipway
Fuel - Petrol		WC	Toilets
Hardstanding/boatyard			Telephone
@ Internet Café			Trolleys
Laundry facilities		V	Visitors berths
Lift-out facilities			Wi-Fi

Area 2 - Central Southern England

MARINAS
Telephone Numbers
VHF Channel
Access Times

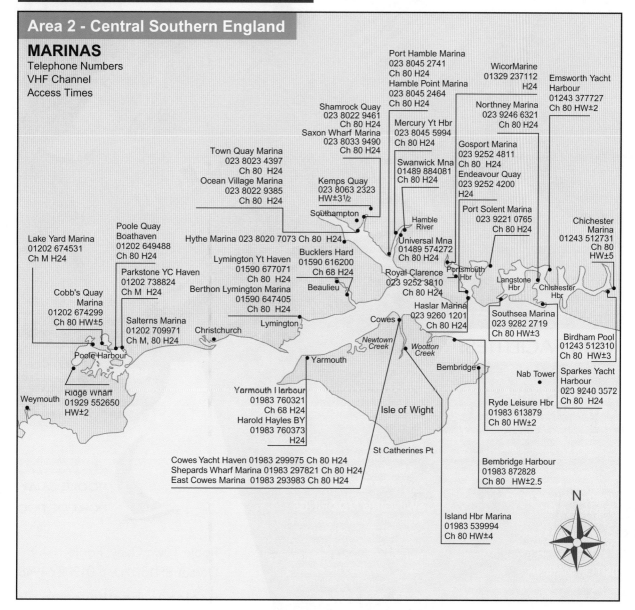

Port Hamble Marina 023 8045 2741 Ch 80 H24
Hamble Point Marina 023 8045 2464 Ch 80 H24
WicorMarine 01329 237112 H24
Emsworth Yacht Harbour 01243 377727 Ch 80 HW±2
Shamrock Quay 023 8022 9461 Ch 80 H24
Saxon Wharf Marina 023 8033 9490 Ch 80 H24
Mercury Yt Hbr 023 8045 5994 Ch 80 H24
Northney Marina 023 9246 6321 Ch 80 H24
Town Quay Marina 023 8023 4397 Ch 80 H24
Ocean Village Marina 023 8022 9385 Ch 80 H24
Swanwick Mna 01489 884081 Ch 80 H24
Gosport Marina 023 9252 4811 Ch 80 H24
Endeavour Quay 023 9252 4200 H24
Kemps Quay 023 8063 2323 HW±3½
Southampton
Hamble River
Port Solent Marina 023 9221 0765 Ch 80 H24
Chichester Marina 01243 512731 Ch 80 HW±5
Lake Yard Marina 01202 674531 Ch M H24
Poole Quay Boathaven 01202 649488 Ch 80 H24
Hythe Marina 023 8020 7073 Ch 80 H24
Universal Mna 01489 574272 Ch 80 H24
Bucklers Hard 01590 616200 Ch 80 H24
Royal Clarence 023 9252 3810 Ch 80 H24
Portsmouth Hbr
Langstone Hbr
Chichester Hbr
Parkstone YC Haven 01202 738824 Ch M H24
Lymington Yt Haven 01590 677071 Ch 80 H24
Berthon Lymington Marina 01590 647405 Ch 80 H24
Beaulieu
Cobb's Quay Marina 01202 674299 Ch 80 HW±5
Salterns Marina 01202 709971 Ch M, 80 H24
Christchurch
Lymington
Cowes
Haslar Marina 023 9260 1201 Ch 80 H24
Southsea Marina 023 9282 2719 Ch 80 HW±3
Birdham Pool 01243 512310 Ch 80 HW±3
Poole Harbour
Newtown Creek
Wootton Creek
Bembridge
Nab Tower
Sparkes Yacht Harbour 023 9240 3572 Ch 80 H24
Weymouth
Ridge Wharf 01929 552650 HW±2
Yarmouth
Yarmouth Harbour 01983 760321 Ch 68 H24
Harold Hayles BY 01983 760373 H24
Isle of Wight
Ryde Leisure Hbr 01983 613879 Ch 80 HW±2
St Catherines Pt
Cowes Yacht Haven 01983 299975 Ch 80 H24
Shepards Wharf Marina 01983 297821 Ch 80 H24
East Cowes Marina 01983 293983 Ch 80 H24
Bembridge Harbour 01983 872828 Ch 80 HW±2.5
Island Hbr Marina 01983 539994 Ch 80 HW±4

N

Poole...

The next page in your adventure

- The Jurassic Coast
- Brownsea Island
- Dining out
- Enterainment
- Fireworks

Plus much more!

HOME OF THE
**POOLE HARBOUR
BOAT SHOW**

OUR FACILITIES:

PERMANENT BERTHS
It's in a private position that makes the most of the views and gorgeous sunsets, yet it's still close to Poole's historic quay, old town and vibrant shopping centre.

- 75 permanent berths
- Superyacht berths
- Floating docks for jet skis and RIBs up to 6.1m
- 24 hour security
- Deep water: 2.5 - 6m
- Water taxi service, parking

VISITOR MARINA
Use your boat as a holiday home; entertain family, friends, colleagues or customers onboard; sail the stunning Jurassic Coast.

Enjoy all the attractions of Poole, Bournemouth and beautiful Dorset. A warm welcome always awaits!

- 125 visitor berths all year for vessels up to 70m in length and up to 4.5m draft
- Swinging moorings

SWINGING MOORINGS
Relax with a glass of wine, on a sunny afternoon, on your own swinging mooring in Poole Harbour overlooking Brownsea Island. Away from the madding crowd, these offer you ultimate privacy, peace & tranquillity.

POOLE QUAY
Boat Haven
PORT OF POOLE
Marina

Poole Town Quay, Poole,
Dorset BH15 1HJ t: 01202 649488

poolequayboathaven.co.uk
VHF Channel 80 call sign "Poole Quay Boat Haven"

RIDGE WHARF YACHT CENTRE

Ridge Wharf Yacht Centre
Ridge, Wareham, Dorset, BH20 5BG
Tel: 01929 552650 Fax: 01929 554434
Email: office@ridgewharf.co.uk www.ridgewharf.co.uk

VHF	
ACCESS	HW±2

On the south bank of the River Frome, which acts as the boundary to the North of the Isle of Purbeck, is Ridge Wharf Yacht Centre. Access for a 1.5m draught is between one and two hours either side of HW, with berths drying out to soft mud. The Yacht Centre cannot be contacted on VHF, so it is best to phone up ahead of time to inquire about berthing availability.

A trip upstream to the ancient market town of Wareham is well worth while, although owners of deep-draughted yachts may prefer to go by dinghy. Tucked between the Rivers Frome and Trent, it is packed full of cafés, restaurants and shops.

FACILITIES AT A GLANCE

LAKE YARD MARINA

Lake Yard Marina
Lake Drive, Hamworthy, Poole, Dorset BH15 4DT
Tel: 01202 674531
Email: office@lakeyard.com www.lakeyard.com

VHF	Ch M
ACCESS	H24

Lake Yard is situated towards the NW end of Poole Harbour, just beyond the SHM No 73. The entrance can be easily identified by 2FR (vert) and 2FG (vert) lights. Enjoying 24 hour access, the marina has no designated visitors' berths, but will accommodate visiting yachtsmen if resident berth holders are away. Its on site facilities include full maintenance and repair services as well as hard standing and a 50 ton boat hoist, although for the nearest fuel go to Corralls (Tel 01202 674551), opposite the Town Quay. Lake Yard's Waterfront Club, offering spectacular views across the harbour, opens seven days a week for lunchtime and evening meals.

FACILITIES AT A GLANCE

COBB'S QUAY MARINA

Cobb's Quay Marina
Hamworthy, Poole, Dorset, BH15 4EL
Tel: 01202 674299
Email: cobbsquay@mdlmarinas.co.uk
www.cobbsquaymarina.co.uk

VHF	Ch 80
ACCESS	HW±5

Lying on the west side of Holes Bay in Poole Harbour, Cobb's Quay is accessed via two lifting bridges, which operate simultaneously. The hourly lifting schedule which runs from 0530 to 2330 (except for weekday rush hours) marks the entrance into Holes Bay accessible

HW±5. With fully serviced pontoons for yachts up to 20m LOA, visitors can enjoy the facilities including the highly reputable Cobb's YC. The marina also offers a convenient 240-berth dry stack area for motorboats up to 10m. Offering increased security and lower maintenance costs, the service includes unlimited launching on demand 24/7. Poole Harbour is the second largest natural harbour in the world and is rich in wildlife, water sports and secret hideaways.

FACILITIES AT A GLANCE

Key
a Dock manager's office
b Information point
c Yacht club
d Convenience store

POOLE QUAY BOAT HAVEN

Poole Quay Boat Haven
Poole Town Quay, Poole, Dorset, BH15 1HJ
Tel: 01202 649488 Fax: 01202 785619
Email: info@poolequayboathaven.co.uk

VHF	Ch 80
ACCESS	H24

Once inside the Poole Harbour entrance small yachts heading for Poole Quay Boat Haven should use the Boat Channel running parallel south of the dredged Middle Ship Channel, which is primarily used by ferries sailing to and from the Hamworthy terminal. The marina can be accessed via the Little Channel and is easily identified by the large breakwater alongside the Quay. With deep water at all states of the tide the marina has berthing available for 125 yachts up to 60m, but due to its central location the marina can get busy so it is best to reserve a berth.

There is easy access to all of Poole Quay's facilities including restaurants, bars, Poole Pottery and the Waterfront Museum.

FACILITIES AT A GLANCE

Key
a Berthing office
b Showers/Toilets
c The Quay Hotel
d Fish landing area

Even nos - port side of pontoon
Odd nos - starboard side of pontoon

PORT OF POOLE MARINA

Port of Poole Marina
Poole Town Quay, Poole, Dorset, BH15 1HJ
Tel: 01202 649488 Fax: 01202 785619
Email: info@poolequayboathaven.co.uk

VHF	Ch 80
ACCESS	H24

Beware of the chain ferry operating at the entrance to Poole harbour. Once inside small yachts heading for the marina should use the Boat Channel running parallel south of the Middle Ship Channel. The marina is to the east of the main ferry terminals and can be identified by a large floating breakwater at the entrance.

The marina has deep water at all tides and berthing for 60 permanent vessels. It is also used as an overflow for visitors from Poole Quay Boat Haven, subject to availability.

A water taxi is available during daylight hours to access the quay for restaurants and shops, also accessible with a 10–15min walk round the quays.

FACILITIES AT A GLANCE

PARKSTONE YACHT HAVEN

Parkstone Yacht Club
Pearce Avenue, Parkstone, Poole, Dorset, BH14 8EH
Tel: 01202 738824 Fax: 01202 716394
Email: office@parkstoneyc.co.uk

VHF	Ch M
ACCESS	H24

Situated on the north side of Poole Harbour between Salterns Marina and Poole Quay Boat Haven, Parkstone Yacht Haven can be entered at all states of the tides. Its approach channel has been dredged to 2.0m and is clearly marked by buoys. Run by the Parkstone Yacht Club, the Haven provides 200 deep water berths for members and visitors' berths. Other services include a new office facility with laundry and WCs, bar, restaurant, shower/changing rooms and wi-fi. With a busy sailing programme for over 2,500 members, the Yacht Club plays host to a variety of events including Poole Week, which is held towards the end of August. Please phone for availability.

FACILITIES AT A GLANCE

SALTERNS MARINA

Salterns Marina
40 Salterns Way, Lilliput, Poole
Dorset, BH14 8JR
Tel: 01202 709971 Fax: 01202 700398
Email: marina@salterns.co.uk www.salterns.co.uk

VHF	Ch M, 80
ACCESS	H24

Holding the Five Gold Anchor award, Salterns Marina provides a service which is second to none. Located off the North Channel, it is approached from the No 31 SHM and benefits from deep water at all states of the tide. Facilities include 220 alongside pontoon berths as well as 75 swinging moorings with a free launch service. However, with very few designated visitors' berths, it is best to contact the marina ahead of time for availability.

Fuel, diesel and gas can all be obtained 24/7 and the well-stocked chandlery, incorporating a coffee shop, stays open seven days a week.

FACILITIES AT A GLANCE

YARMOUTH HBR/HAROLD HAYLES BY

Yarmouth Harbour
Yarmouth, Isle of Wight, PO41 0NT
Tel: 01983 760321 Fax: 01983 761192
info@yarmouth-harbour.co.uk
www.yarmouth-harbour.co.uk

VHF	Ch 68
ACCESS	H24

Harold Hayles Ltd
The Quay, Yarmouth, Isle of Wight, PO41 0RS
Tel: 01983 760373 Fax: 01983 760666
Email: info@haroldhayles.co.uk
www.haroldhayles.co.uk

VHF	
ACCESS	H24

The most western harbour on the Isle of Wight, Yarmouth is not only a convenient passage stopover but a very desirable destination in its own right, with virtually all weather and tidal access, although strong N to NE'ly winds can produce a considerable swell. The HM launch patrols the harbour entrance and will direct visiting yachtsmen to a walkashore or standalone pontoon berths; call *Yarmouth Harbour* on Ch 68 prior to entering the harbour. The pretty harbour and town offer plenty of fine restaurants and amenities.

Walkashore pontoon moorings are also available from the Harold Hayles and River Yar BYs in the SW corner of the harbour, the latter S of the bridge. Pre-booking is preferred for both individuals or rallies.

FACILITIES AT A GLANCE

LYMINGTON YACHT HAVEN

Lymington Yacht Haven
King's Saltern Road, Lymington, S041 3QD
Tel: 01590 677071
Email: lymington@yachthavens.com www.yachthavens.com

VHF	Ch 80
ACCESS	H24

Lymington Yacht Haven has the enviable position of being the first marina that comes into sight on your port hand side as you make your way up the well-marked Lymington river channel. Nestled between the 500 acre Lymington to Keyhaven nature reserve and the famous Georgian market town of Lymington, there is something for everyone.

Lymington Yacht Haven is manned 24/7 for fuel and berthing and boasts the most modern luxury shore side facilities you will find in the UK. Bike and electric bike hire are available through the marina office to explore the beautiful New Forest.

FACILITIES AT A GLANCE

Key
a Royal Lymington Yacht Club
b Lymington Town Sailing Club
c Owners store
d LYH office, brokerage, showers and laundry
e Haven Bar Bistro
f Yacht charter and sales
g Rigger
h Power boat sales
i Electronics

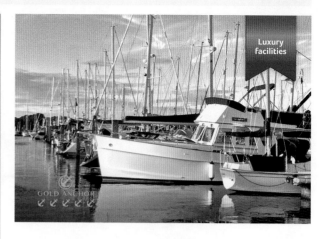

Luxury facilities

GOLD ANCHOR

Lymington Yacht Haven
Visitors welcome

- Perfectly situated at the mouth of Lymington River
- Sheltered pontoon berths fully serviced with water, electricity and FREE Wi-Fi
- 24 hour access, service and fuel
- Luxury shoreside facilities and Haven Restaurant
- An easy 10 minute walk to Lymington High Street
- Special Winter Visitor Rates (Nov–Feb inclusive)

Call **01590 677071** or **VHF Ch 80** or visit **yachthavens.com**

Lymington Yacht Haven

BERTHON LYMINGTON MARINA

Berthon Lymington Marina Ltd
The Shipyard, Lymington, Hampshire, SO41 3YL
Tel: 01590 647405 Fax: 01590 647446
www.berthon.co.uk Email: marina@berthon.co.uk

VHF	Ch 80
ACCESS	H24

Situated approximately half a mile up river of Lymington Yacht Haven, on the port hand side, is Lymington Marina. Easily accessible at all states of the tide, it offers between 60 to 70 visitors' berths, with probably the best washrooms in the Solent. Its close proximity to the town centre and first rate services mean that booking is essential on busy weekends. Lymington Marina's parent, Berthon Boat Co, has state of the art facilities and a highly skilled work force of 100+ to deal with any repair, maintenance or refit.

Lymington benefits from having the New Forest on its doorstep and the Solent Way footpath provides an invigorating walk to and from Hurst Castle.

FACILITIES AT A GLANCE

Key
a Dockmaster's office
b Berthon International
c Yacht maintenance & repair
d Building refit shed
e Anchor House
f Seaforth House
g Refueller

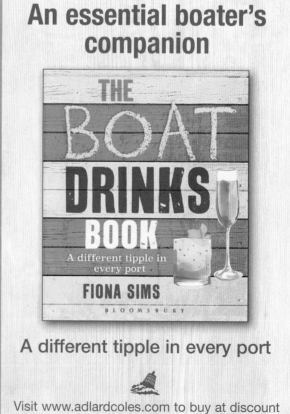

2

LYMINGTON HARBOUR

Lymington Harbour Commisioner
Bath Road, Lymington, SO41 3SE
Tel: 01590 672014
Email: info@lymingtonharbour.co.uk

| VHF | Ch 66 |
| ACCESS | H24 |

Lymington Harbour Commission provides berths at Dan Bran Pontoon and Lymington Town Quay in addition to the river moorings. Dan Bran is accessible at all states of the tide inside the wave screen. Power is available along its 650' length with use of the facilities at Lymington Town SC and walk ashore access to the town. It is sited between the marinas a short walk from Town Quay, and ideal for club rallies or events as it can accommodate up to 50 boats together.

Town Quay provides shelter up river at the foot of the cobbles, which lead directly to the town centre. 20 boats (up to 2m draft) raft up to 4 deep on a walk ashore pontoon. 40 fore and aft moorings lie just off the quay.

FACILITIES AT A GLANCE

Key
a   Royal Lymington Yacht Club
b   Lymington Town Sailing Club
c   Yacht charter and sales
d   Power boat sales

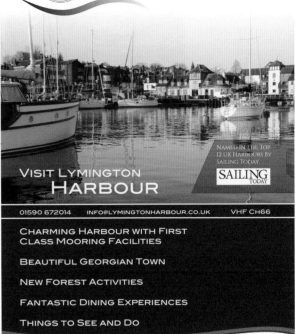
BUCKLERS HARD MARINA

Bucklers Hard
Beaulieu, New Forest, Hampshire, SO42 7XB
Tel: 01590 616200
www.beaulieuriver.co.uk harbour.office@beaulieu.co.uk

| VHF | Ch 68 |
| ACCESS | H24 |

Situated on the Beaulieu River, Buckler's Hard Yacht Harbour is the ideal location from which to sail in the Solent or visit for a short stay to explore the surrounding New Forest. Recent investment in the TYHA 5 Gold Anchor marina offers improved facilities and technology to keep pace with modern demands, while preserving the unique character and charm of the unspoilt natural haven. Both permanent marina berths and river moorings are available. Visiting boats are welcome and advised to book in advance or radio Beaulieu River Radio on CH68 before entering the river.

FACILITIES AT A GLANCE

NB
Pontoon numbering runs from low inside with even numbers on the north side of pontoons and odd on the south.

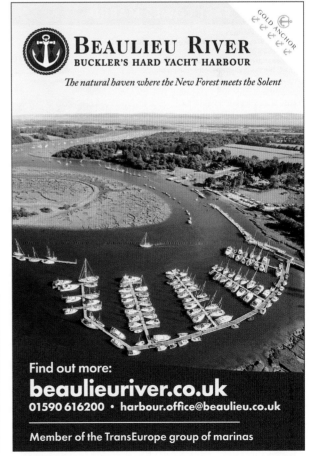

COWES YACHT HAVEN

Cowes Yacht Haven
Vectis Yard, Cowes, Isle of Wight, PO31 7BD
Tel: 01983 299975 Fax: 01983 200332
www.cowesyachthaven.com
Email: info@cowesyachthaven.com

VHF Ch 80
ACCESS H24

Situated virtually at the centre of the Solent, Cowes is best known as Britain's premier yachting centre and offers all types of facilities to yachtsmen. Cowes Yacht Haven, operating 24 hours a day, has very few permanent moorings and is dedicated to catering for visitors and events. At peak times it can become very crowded and for occasions such as Aberdeen Asset Management Cowes Week you need to book up in advance.

FACILITIES AT A GLANCE

COWES HARBOUR SHEPARDS MARINA

Cowes Harbour Shepards Marina
Medina Road, Cowes, Isle of Wight, PO31 7HT
Tel: 01983 297821 Email: shepards.chc@cowes.co.uk
www.cowesharbourshepardsmarina.co.uk

VHF Ch 80
ACCESS H24

Shepards Marina is one of Cowes Harbour's main marina facilities offering a full range of services and amenities for yacht racing events, rallies, and catering also to the cruising sailor and powerboater. The marina has capacity for 130 visiting boats, 40 resident berth holders.

Visitor berths can be booked in advance, subject to availability. All berths benefit from water and electricity, free Wi-Fi, inclusive showers, and site-wide CCTV. Discounted rates are available for rallies of six or more boats, sailing schools, and winter berthing.

On site you will also find the Basque Kitchen restaurant, Girls for Sail, Island Divers, and Solent Sails. Fuel can be obtained from the fuel berth located 200m south of the chain ferry.

FACILITIES AT A GLANCE

EAST COWES MARINA

East Cowes Marina
Britannia Way, East Cowes, Isle of Wight, PO32 6UB
Tel: 01983 293983
www.eastcowesmarina.co.uk
Email: berths@eastcowesmarina.co.uk

VHF Ch 80
ACCESS H24

Accommodating around 235 residential yachts and 150 visiting boats at all states of the tide, East Cowes Marina is situated on the quiet and protected east bank of the Medina River, about a quarter mile above the chain ferry. A small convenience store is just five minutes walk away. The new centrally heated shower and toilet facilities ensure the visitor a warm welcome at any time of the year, as does the on-site pub and restaurant.

Several water taxis provide a return service to Cowes, ensuring a quick and easy way of getting to West Cowes.

FACILITIES AT A GLANCE

Key
a Marina office
b Showers, toilets & laundry
c Pub and restaurant
d RNLI, Inshore Lifeboat Centre
e Yacht stores

2

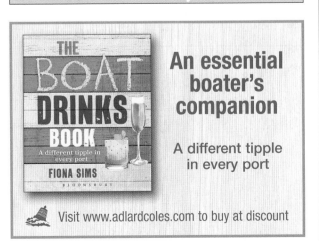
ISLAND HARBOUR MARINA

Island Harbour Marina
Mill Lane, Binfield, Newport, Isle of Wight, PO30 2LA
Tel: 01983 539994 Fax: 01983 523401
Email: info@island-harbour.co.uk

VHF Ch 80
ACCESS HW±4

Situated in beautiful rolling farmland about half a mile south of Folly Inn, Island Harbour Marina provides around 200 visitors' berths. Protected by a lock that is operated daily from 0800 – 2100 during the summer and from 0800 – 1730 during the winter, the marina is accessible for about three hours either side of HW for draughts of 1.5m.

Due to its secluded setting, the marina's on site chandlery also sells essential provisions and newspapers. A half hour walk along the river brings you to Newport, the capital and county town of the Isle of Wight.

FACILITIES AT A GLANCE

Key
a Control tower
b Bin store
c Chandlery
d Restaurant

HYTHE MARINA VILLAGE

Hythe Marina Village
Shamrock Way, Hythe, Southampton, SO45 6DY
Tel: 023 8020 7073
Email: hythe@mdlmarinas.co.uk
www.hythemarinavillage.co.uk

VHF Ch 80
ACCESS H24

Situated on the western shores of Southampton Water, Hythe Marina Village is approached by a dredged channel leading to a lock basin. The lock gates are controlled H24 throughout the year with a waiting pontoon south of the approach basin.

Hythe Marina Village incorporates full marine services as well as on-site restaurants and a selection of shops can be found in the town centre, a 5 minute walk away. Forming an integral part of the New Forest Waterside, Hythe is the perfect base from which to explore Hampshire's pretty inland villages and towns, or alternatively you can catch the ferry to Southampton's Town Quay.

FACILITIES AT A GLANCE

Key
a Restaurants and bars
b Lock building
c Boat storage and Trailer park

TOWN QUAY

Associated British Ports
Town Quay, Southampton, SO14 2AQ
Tel: 02380 234397 Mobile: 07764 293588
Email: info@townquay.com www.townquay.com

VHF Ch 80
ACCESS H24

In the heart of Southampton, Town Quay is walking distance from the City's cultural quarter, West Quay Shopping Centre and a variety of restaurants, bars and theatres making the marina a vibrant place to stay all year round.

The marina is accessible at all states of the tide and the reception is open 24 hours a day with free drinks and wi-fi. Free cycle hire and use of a gas BBQ on the 'chill out' deck is available.

Located on the eastern shores of Southampton Water, Town Quay offers unrivalled views of Southampton's busy maritime activity and direct access to the world famous cruising and racing waters of the Solent.

FACILITIES AT A GLANCE

OCEAN VILLAGE MARINA

Ocean Village Marina
2 Channel Way, Southampton, SO14 3TG
Tel: 023 8022 9385
Email: oceanvillage@mdlmarinas.co.uk
www.oceanvillagemarina.co.uk

VHF Ch 80
ACCESS H24

The entrance to Ocean Village Marina lies on the port side of the River Itchen, just before the Itchen Bridge. With the capacity to accommodate large yachts and tall ships, the marina, accessible 24 hours a day, is a renowned home for international yacht races.

Situated at the heart of an exciting new waterside development incorporating shops, cinemas, restaurants and a £50m luxury spa hotel complex, as well as the Royal Southampton Yacht Club, Ocean Village offers a vibrant atmosphere for all visitors.

FACILITIES AT A GLANCE

Key
a Marina office, WC, showers, launderette
b RSYC
c Pitcher & Piano
d Banana Wharf
e Ocean Rooms Beauty
f Steak of the Art
g Maritimo Lounge
h Dock office
i Harbour Hotel & Spa
j Harbour Lights Cinema

SHAMROCK QUAY

Shamrock Quay
William Street, Northam, Southampton, Hants, SO14 5QL
Tel: 023 8022 9461
Email: shamrockquay@mdlmarinas.co.uk
www.shamrockquay.co.uk

VHF Ch 80
ACCESS H24

Shamrock Quay, lying upstream of the Itchen Bridge on the port hand side, offers excellent facilities to yachtsmen. It also benefits from being accessible and manned 24 hours a day. On-site there is a 75-ton travel hoist and a 47-ton boat mover,

and for dining out there is a choice of restaurants and bars.

The city centre is about two miles away, where among the numerous attractions are the Medieval Merchant's House in French Street, the Southampton City Art Gallery and the SeaCity Museum in the Civic Centre.

FACILITIES AT A GLANCE

Key
a Offices, shops and COVE restaurant
b Marina office
c Café

2

KEMPS QUAY

Kemp's Shipyard Ltd
Quayside Road, Southampton, SO18 1BZ
Tel: 023 8063 2323 Fax: 023 8022 6002
Email: enquiries@kempsquay.com

VHF
ACCESS HW±3.5

At the head of the River Itchen on the starboard side is Kemps Quay, a family-run marina with a friendly, old-fashioned feel. Accessible only 3½ hrs either side of HW, it has a limited number of deep water berths, the rest being half tide, drying out to soft mud. Its restricted access is, however, reflected in the lower prices.

Although situated on the outskirts of Southampton, a short bus or taxi ride will soon get you to the city centre. Besides a nearby BP Garage selling bread and milk, the closest supermarkets can be found in Bitterne Shopping Centre, which is five minutes away by bus.

FACILITIES AT A GLANCE

SAXON WHARF

Saxon Wharf
Lower York Street, Northam, Southampton, SO14 5QF
Tel: 023 8033 9490
Email: saxonwharf@mdlmarinas.co.uk
www.saxonwharfmarina.co.uk

VHF Ch 80
ACCESS H24

Placed on the River Itchen in Southampton, Saxon Wharf is a marine service centre specifically designed for the superyacht market. With a 200-ton boat hoist and heavy duty pontoons, Saxon Wharf is the ideal location for large vessels in need of secure, quick turnaround lift-outs, repair work or even full-scale refits.

With a Dry Stack facility boasting the largest capacity forklift truck in the UK, Saxon Wharf can now dry stack boats of up to 13m LOA. There is also ample storage ashore and 24-hour security. Shamrock Quay, where there are bars and restaurants, is within 300 metres of this location.

FACILITIES AT A GLANCE

Key
a Office
b Security gate
c Oyster Yacht Services
d Offices

HAMBLE POINT MARINA

Hamble Point Marina
School Lane, Hamble, Southampton, SO31 4NB
Tel: 023 8045 2464
Email: hamblepoint@mdlmarinas.co.uk
www.hamblepointmarina.co.uk

VHF Ch 80
ACCESS H24

Situated virtually opposite Warsash, this is the first marina you will come to on the western bank of the Hamble. Accommodating yachts and power boats up to 30m in length, it offers easy access to the Solent.

The marina boasts extensive facilities including 137 dry stack berths for motorboats up to 10 metres and over 50 tenants who provide boat-owners with a wide range of marine services from boat repairs to electrical work. Hamble Point is within a 20-minute walk of Hamble Village, where there are a plethora of pubs and restaurants on offer.

FACILITIES AT A GLANCE

Key
a Information
b First aid point
c Marina office
d Administration office
e Chandlery
f Ketch Rigger Bar and Restaurant
g Sailmakers

PORT HAMBLE MARINA

Port Hamble Marina
Satchell Lane, Hamble, Southampton, SO31 4QD
Tel: 023 8045 2741
Email: porthamble@mdlmarinas.co.uk
www.porthamblemarina.co.uk

VHF Ch 80
ACCESS H24

Port Hamble Marina is situated on the River Hamble right in the heart of the South Coast's sailing scene. With thousands of visitors every year, this busy marina is popular with racing enthusiasts and cruising vessels looking for a vibrant atmosphere. The picturesque Hamble village, with its inviting pubs and restaurants, is only a few minutes walk away.

On site, Port Hamble also offers excellent amenities including luxurious all-new male and female facilities, alongside boutique style extension shower rooms. Banana Wharf bar and restaurant provides the perfect spot to meet, eat and drink by the water whilst petrol and diesel is available seven days a week. Locally there are several companies on hand who cater for every boating need.

FACILITIES AT A GLANCE

Key
a Dock manager's office
b Boat sales
c Royal Air Force YC
d Banana Wharf Bar & Restaurant

MERCURY YACHT HARBOUR

Mercury Yacht Harbour
Satchell Lane, Hamble, Southampton, SO31 4HQ
Tel: 023 8045 5994
Email: mercury@mdlmarinas.co.uk
www.mercuryyachtharbour.co.uk

VHF Ch 80
ACCESS H24

Mercury Yacht Harbour is the third marina from seaward on the western bank of the River Hamble, tucked away in a picturesque, wooded site adjacent to Badnam Creek. Enjoying deep water at all states of the tide, it accommodates yachts up to 24m LOA and boasts an extensive array of facilities.

The on-site chandlery stocks a plethora of essential items, and for a good meal look no further than The Waters Edge Bar and Restaurant whose balcony offers striking views over the water. Hamble Village is only a 20-minute walk away.

FACILITIES AT A GLANCE

Key
a Toilets and showers
b Launderette
c Chandlery
d Waters Edge
  Bar & Restaurant
e Dockmaster,
  marina manager's office
f Waste disposal
g Recycling area

P and Boat storage

UNIVERSAL MARINA

Universal Marina
Crableck Lane, Sarisbury Green, Southampton, SO31 7ZN
Tel: 01489 574272 Fax: 01489 574273
Email: info@universalmarina.co.uk

VHF Ch 80
ACCESS H24

Universal Marina is one of the few remaining independent marinas offering south coast moorings. Universal Marina's unique location is unbeatable, tucked in between the oak trees on the East Bank of the Hamble where 68 acres of natural wildlife and marshlands surrounds the busy and friendly marina. Positioned only minutes off the M27, it is one of the most accessible marinas on the south coast. The 250 berth complex, features all the latest facilities required by the modern day boat owner, recently upgraded pontoons, power, water and wifi available to each berth. Visitors are welcome & although there are no dedicated visitor berths these are available by prior arrangement.

FACILITIES AT A GLANCE

Key
a Marina Office and Chandlery
b Bar & restaurant
c Showers, WC
d Laundry room and WC
e Workshops
f Boatyard

SWANWICK MARINA

Swanwick Marina
Swanwick, Southampton, Hampshire, SO31 1ZL
Tel: 01489 884081 Fax: 01489 579073
Email: swanwick@premiermarinas.com
www.premiermarinas.com

VHF Ch 80
ACCESS H24

Situated on the east bank of the River Hamble next to Bursledon Bridge, Swanwick Marina is accessible at all states of the tide and can accommodate yachts up to 20m LOA.

The marina's fully-licensed bar and bistro, The Boat House, overlooking the river, is open for breakfast, lunch and dinner all year round. Alternatively, just a short row or walk away is the celebrated Jolly Sailor pub in Bursledon on the west bank, made famous for being the local watering hole in the British television series *Howard's Way*.

FACILITIES AT A GLANCE

Key
a Marina office
b Pub/restaurant
c Chandlery
d Boat sales offices

RYDE LEISURE HARBOUR

Ryde Harbour
The Esplanade, Ryde, Isle of Wight, PO33 1JA
Tel: 01983 613879 Fax: 01983 613903
www.rydeharbour.com Email: ryde.harbour@iow.gov.uk

VHF Ch 80
ACCESS HW±2

Known as the 'gateway to the Island', Ryde, with its elegant houses and abundant shops, is among the Isle of Wight's most popular resorts. Its well-protected harbour is conveniently close to the exceptional beaches as well as to the town's restaurants and amusements.

Drying to 2.5m and therefore only accessible to yachts that can take the ground, the harbour accommodates 90 resident boats as well as up to 75 visiting yachts. Fin keel yachts may dry out on the harbour wall.

Ideal for family cruising, Ryde offers a wealth of activities, ranging from ten pin bowling and ice skating to crazy golf and tennis.

Ice rink and ten pin bowling complex

2

BEMBRIDGE HARBOUR

Bembridge Harbour
Harbour Office, The Duver, St Helens, Ryde
Isle of Wight, PO33 1YB
Tel: 01983 872828 Fax: 01983 872922
Email: thorpemalcolm@btconnect.com
www.bembridgeharbour.co.uk

VHF	Ch 80
ACCESS	HW±2.5

Bembridge is a compact, pretty harbour whose entrance, although restricted by the tides (recommended entry for a 1.5m draught is 2½hrs before HW), is well sheltered in all but north north easterly gales. Offering excellent sailing clubs, beautiful beaches and fine restaurants, this Isle of Wight port is a first class haven with plenty of charm. With approximately 120 new visitors' berths on the Duver Marina pontoons, which can now be booked online, the marina at St Helen's Quay at the western end of the harbour is now allocated to annual berth holders only.

FACILITIES AT A GLANCE

HASLAR MARINA

Haslar Marina
Haslar Road, Gosport, Hampshire, PO12 1NU
Tel: 023 9260 1201
www.haslarmarina.co.uk Email: sales@haslarmarina.co.uk

VHF	Ch 80
ACCESS	H24

This modern, purpose-built marina lies to port on the western side of Portsmouth Harbour entrance and is easily recognised by its prominent lightship incorporating a bar and restaurant. Accessible at all states of the tide, Haslar's extensive facilities do not however include fuel, the nearest being at the Gosport Marina only a few cables north.

Within close proximity is the Royal Navy Submarine Museum and the Museum of Naval Firepower 'Explosion' both worth a visit.

FACILITIES AT A GLANCE

Key
a Admin. offices, security, toilets, showers, weather,
b Rubbish skips, security gate
c Bistro/bar and independent operators, trolleys
d Security, car park
e Superloo: toilets, showers, trolleys
f Bar, restaurant, toilets, shower, laundry
g Sealift
h Public slipway

Berth numbering
High numbers outermost.
Even numbers on south side of pontoons, odds on the north.

GOSPORT MARINA

Premier Gosport Marina
Mumby Road, Gosport, Hampshire, PO12 1AH
Tel: 023 9252 4811 Fax: 023 9258 9541
Email: gosport@premiermarinas.com
www.premiermarinas.com

VHF	Ch 80
ACCESS	H24

A few cables north of Haslar Marina, again on the port hand side, lies Gosport Marina. Boasting 519 fully-serviced, visitors' and 80 dry stack berths, its extensive range of facilities incorporates a fuel barge on its southern breakwater as well as shower and laundry amenities. Numerous boatyard and engineering specialists are also located in and around the premises.

Within easy reach of the marina is Gosport town centre, offering a cosmopolitan selection of restaurants along with several supermarkets and shops.

FACILITIES AT A GLANCE

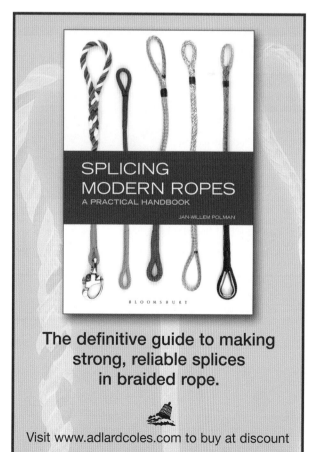

ROYAL CLARENCE MARINA

Royal Clarence Marina, Royal Clarence Yard
Weevil Lane, Gosport, Hampshire PO12 1AX
Tel: 02392 523523 Fax: 02392 523523
Email: mikebraidley@castlemarinas.co.uk
www.royalclarencemarina.org

VHF | Ch 80
ACCESS | H24

Royal Clarence Marina enjoys a unique setting, with the former Royal Navy victualling yard as its backdrop and views across to Gunwharf Quays on the opposite side of the harbour. The remarkably peaceful and calm marina lies within a deep water basin with 5.25m draught and offers berths up to 18m in length. RCM also has over 150m of alongside berthing making it the ideal location for rallies and other maritime events. Only five minutes from the entrance to Portsmouth Harbour, the marina is ideally located for cruising and racing in the Solent and beyond.

FACILITIES AT A GLANCE

WICORMARINE YACHT HAVEN

WicorMarine Yacht Haven
Cranleigh Road, Portchester, Hampshire, PO16 9DR
Tel: 01329 237112 Fax: 01329 248595
Email: inbox@wicormarine.co.uk

VHF |
ACCESS | H24

WicorMarine Yacht Haven is situated in the picturesque upper reaches of Portsmouth Harbour away from the hustle and bustle. Their deepwater pontoons offer an affordable alternative to busy marinas and are only 30 mins from the harbour entrance.

An excellent range of boatyard facilities including a 12T boat hoist, undercover storage, H24 showers and toilets, diesel, fresh water, on site repair services and a well-stocked chandlery complete with Calor Gas and Camping Gaz exchange. A water taxi operates at peak times during the sailing season but they also offer dinghy storage and owners' store. The popular, licensed Salt Café is open to visitors all year round where you can take in the stunning views of the harbour from the waterfront deck.

FACILITIES AT A GLANCE

Key
a Long pontoon
b Main dinghy pontoon
c Lower dinghy pontoon
d Scrubbing grid
e Slip
– Moorings
l Pontoon moorings

US 1-4

PORT SOLENT MARINA

Port Solent Marina
South Lockside, Portsmouth, PO6 4TJ
Tel: 023 9221 0765 Fax: 023 9232 4241
www.premiermarinas.com
Email: portsolent@premiermarinas.com

VHF | Ch 80
ACCESS | H24

Port Solent Marina is located to the north east of Portsmouth Harbour, not far from the historic Portchester Castle. Accessible via a 24-hour lock, this purpose built marina offers a full range of facilities. The Boardwalk comprises an array of shops and restaurants, while close by is a David Lloyd Health Centre and a large Odeon cinema.

No visit to Portsmouth Harbour is complete without a trip to the Historic Dockyard, home to Henry VIII's *Mary Rose*, Nelson's HMS *Victory* and the first iron battleship, HMS *Warrior*, built in 1860.

FACILITIES AT A GLANCE

Key | a Laundry, berth holders showers, toilets and baby change
b Portsmouth Harbour YC
c Chandlery, marine engineers
d Under cover boat shed
e Berth holders showers, toilets and public toilets, baby change
f David Lloyd Health and Fitness Club
g The Boardwalk - bars/restaurants
h Odeon cinema
i Marina control and Port Solent reception
j Residential building

SOUTHSEA MARINA

Southsea Marina
Fort Cumberland Road, PO4 9RJ
Tel: 02392 822719 Fax: 02392 822220
Email: southsea@premiermarinas.com
www.premiermarinas.com

VHF | Ch 80
ACCESS | HW±3

Southsea Marina is a small and friendly marina located on the western shore of Langstone Harbour, an expansive tidal bay situated between Hayling Island and Portsmouth. The channel is clearly marked by seven starboard and nine port hand markers. A tidal gate allows unrestricted movement in and out of the marina up to 3 hours either side of HW operates the entrance. The minimum depth in the marina entrance during this period is 1.6m and a waiting pontoon is available. There are excellent on site facilities including a bar, restaurant and chandlery.

FACILITIES AT A GLANCE

SPARKES MARINA

Sparkes Marina
38 Wittering Road, Hayling Island, Hampshire, PO11 9SR
Tel: 023 9246 3572
Email: sparkes@mdlmarinas.co.uk   www.sparkesmarina.co.uk

VHF Ch 80
ACCESS H24

Just inside the entrance to Chichester Harbour, on the eastern shores of Hayling Island, lies Sparkes Marina. Its facilities include 24-hour showers and toilets, a laundry room, an office/reception, and Drift: Hayling Island bar and restaurant.

In addition to its berthing and marina services, Sparkes has many skilled professionals on site, including specialists in engineering, outboard engines, glass fibre repairs, rigging, sails and covers, marine carpentry, electrical, boat management and valeting. There is storage ashore for over 200 boats and a 40 ton mobile crane (lifting capacity 15 tons).

FACILITIES AT A GLANCE

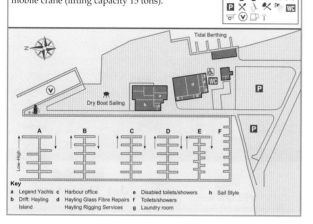

Key
a Legend Yachts
b Drift: Hayling Island
c Harbour office
d Hayling Glass Fibre Repairs
   Hayling Rigging Services
e Disabled toilets/showers
f Toilets/showers
g Laundry room
h Sail Style

NORTHNEY MARINA

Northney Marina
Northney Road, Hayling Island, Hampshire, PO11 0NH
Tel: 023 9246 6321
Email: northney@mdlmarinas.co.uk
www.northneymarina.co.uk

VHF Ch 80
ACCESS H24

Situated in Chichester Harbour, Northney Marina is set on the northern shore of Hayling Island in the well-marked Sweare Deep Channel, which branches off to port almost at the end of Emsworth Channel. This 228-berth marina offers excellent boatyard facilities, a provisions store and laundry area, diesel, a slipway, Salt Shack Café, wi-fi and 24/7 staff cover. There is also an events area for rallies.

FACILITIES AT A GLANCE

Key
a Marina office and provisions store
b Recycling facilities

EMSWORTH YACHT HARBOUR

Emsworth Yacht Harbour Ltd
Thorney Road, Emsworth, Hants, PO10 8BP
Tel: 01243 377727   Fax: 01243 373432
Email: info@emsworth-marina.co.uk
www.emsworth-marina.co.uk

VHF
ACCESS HW±2

Accessible about one and a half to two hours either side of high water, Emsworth Yacht Harbour is a sheltered site, offering good facilities to yachtsmen.

Created in 1964 from a log pond, the marina is within easy walking distance of the pretty little town of Emsworth, which boasts at least 10 pubs, several high quality restaurants and two well-stocked convenience stores.

FACILITIES AT A GLANCE

Key
a Ground floor - toilets and showers
   1st floor - harbour office
b Home Marine - outboard engine repairs

CHICHESTER MARINA

Chichester Marina
Birdham, Chichester, West Sussex, PO20 7EJ
Tel: 01243 512731   Fax: 01243 513472
Email: chichester@premiermarinas.com
www.premiermarinas.com

VHF Ch 80
ACCESS HW±5

Chichester Marina, nestling in an enormous natural harbour, has more than 1,000 berths, making it one of the largest in the UK. Its approach channel can be easily identified by the CM SHM pile. The channel was dredged to 0.5m below CD in 2004, giving access of around five hours either side of HW at springs. Besides the wide ranging marine facilities, there are also a restaurant and small convenience store on site. Chichester, which is only about a five minute bus or taxi ride away, has several places of interest, the most notable being the cathedral.

FACILITIES AT A GLANCE

Key
a Brush washing facility
b Toilets, showers, baby change, telephone
c Trailer sailer storage
d BA Peters offices
e Launderette
f Toilets, showers, baby change, telephone, disabled facilities
g Restaurant/bar, chandlery, shop
h Reception car park
i CYC boat park
j Marina control building
k Security checkpoint

BIRDHAM POOL MARINA

Birdham Pool Marina
Birdham Pool, Chichester, Sussex
Tel: 01243 512310 Fax: 01243 513163
Email: mikebraidley@castlemarinas.co.uk

| VHF | Ch 80 |
| ACCESS | HW±3·5 |

Birdham Pool is the UK's oldest marina, with a charm not found elsewhere. A recent programme of improvements sees 28 new berths, a new 30-ton crane to lift out boats up to 50ft long and 2m draft, brand new facilities block and new Marine Trades Centre showcasing traditional skilled craftsmen. Visitors will not be disappointed by the unique and picturesque setting, with views across the South Downs as well as Chichester Harbour. Access is HW±3·5, via a dredged channel marked by starboard hand piles.

FACILITIES AT A GLANCE

SOUTH EAST ENGLAND – Selsey Bill to North Foreland

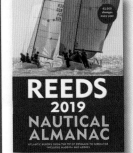
Key to Marina Plans symbols

Bottled gas		P	Parking
Chandler			Pub/Restaurant
Disabled facilities			Pump out
Electrical supply			Rigging service
Electrical repairs			Sail repairs
Engine repairs			Shipwright
First Aid			Shop/Supermarket
Fresh Water			Showers
Fuel - Diesel			Slipway
Fuel - Petrol		WC	Toilets
Hardstanding/boatyard			Telephone
@	Internet Café		Trolleys
Laundry facilities		V	Visitors berths
Lift-out facilities			Wi-Fi

Area 3 - South East England

MARINAS
Telephone Numbers
VHF Channel
Access Times

N. Foreland

Margate

Ramsgate

Ramsgate Royal Harbour Marina
01843 572100
Ch 14, 80 H24

S. Foreland

Dover

Folkestone

Dover Marina
01304 241663
Ch 80 H24

Lady Bee Marina
01273 593801
Ch 14 H24

Brighton Marina
01273 819919
Ch M, 80 H24

Rye

Harbour of Rye
01797 225225
Ch 14 HW±2

Shoreham

Brighton

Littlehampton

Littlehampton Marina
01903 713553
Ch 80
HW-3 to +2.5
Hillyards
01903 713327
HW-3 to +2.5

Newhaven
Newhaven Marina
01273 513881
Ch 80 H24

Eastbourne

Sovereign Harbour Marina
01323 470099
Ch 17 H24

N

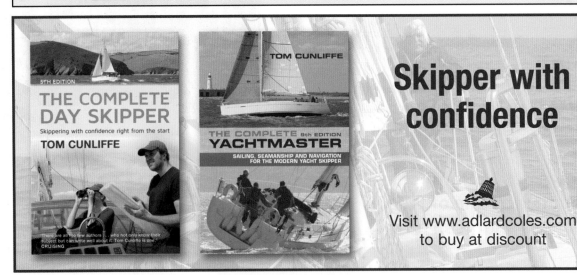

3

LITTLEHAMPTON MARINA

Littlehampton Marina
Ferry Road, Littlehampton, W Sussex
Tel: 01903 713553 Fax: 01903 732264
Email: sales@littlehamptonmarina.co.uk

VHF | Ch 80
ACCESS | HW-3 to +2.5

A typical English seaside town with funfair, promenade and fine sandy beaches, Littlehampton lies roughly midway between Brighton and Chichester at the mouth of the River Arun. It affords a convenient stopover for yachts either east or west bound, providing you have the right tidal conditions to cross the entrance bar with its charted depth of 0.7m. The marina lies about three cables above Town Quay and Fisherman's Quay, both of which are on the starboard side of the River Arun, and is accessed via a retractable footbridge that opens on request to the HM (note that you should contact him by 1630 the day before you require entry).

FACILITIES AT A GLANCE

Key
a Marina offices
b Cafe

LADY BEE MARINA

Lady Bee Marina
138-140 Albion Street, Southwick
West Sussex, BN42 4EG
Tel: 01273 593801 Fax: 01273 870349

VHF | Ch 14
ACCESS | H24

Shoreham, only five miles west of Brighton, is one of the South Coast's major commercial ports handling, among other products, steel, grain, tarmac and timber. On first impressions it may seem that Shoreham has little to offer the visiting yachtsman, but once through the lock and into the eastern arm of the River Adur, the quiet Lady Bee Marina, with its Spanish waterside restaurant, can make this harbour an interesting alternative to the lively atmosphere of Brighton Marina. Run by the Harbour Office, the marina meets all the usual requirements, although fuel is available in cans from Southwick garage or from Corral's diesel pump situated in the western arm.

FACILITIES AT A GLANCE

Key
a Sussex Yacht Club
b Riverside Boatyard

BRIGHTON MARINA

Brighton Marina
West Jetty, Brighton, East Sussex, BN2 5UP
Tel: 01273 819919 Fax: 01273 675082
Email: brighton@premiermarinas.com
www.premiermarinas.com

VHF | Ch M, 80
ACCESS | H24

Brighton Marina is the largest marina in the country and with its extensive range of shops, restaurants and facilities, is a popular and convenient stopover for east and west-going passagemakers. Note, however, that it is not advisable to attempt entry in strong S to SE winds.

Only half a mile from the marina is the historic city of Brighton itself, renowned for being a cultural centre with a cosmopolitan atmosphere. Among its numerous attractions are the exotic Royal Pavilion, built for King George IV in the 1800s, and the Lanes, with its multitude of antiques shops.

FACILITIES AT A GLANCE

Key
a David Lloyd Heath & Fitness Club
b Bowling alley
c Casino/night club
d Multiplex cinema
e Yacht club
f Petrol station
g Mariners Quay
h Marina reception

NEWHAVEN MARINA

Newhaven Marina
The Yacht Harbour, Fort Road, Newhaven
East Sussex, BN9 9BY
Tel: 01273 513881
Email: john.stirling@newhavenmarina.co.uk

VHF	Ch 80
ACCESS	H24

Some seven miles from Brighton, Newhaven lies at the mouth of the River Ouse. With its large fishing fleet and regular ferry services to Dieppe, the harbour has over the years become progressively commercial, therefore care is needed to keep clear of large vessels under manoeuvre.

The marina lies approximately quarter of a mile from the harbour entrance on the west bank and was recently dredged to allow full tidal access except on LWS.

FACILITIES AT A GLANCE

Coastguard

SOVEREIGN HARBOUR MARINA

Sovereign Harbour Marina
Pacific Drive, Eastbourne, East Sussex, BN23 5BJ
Tel: 01323 470099
Email: eastbourne@premiermarinas.com
www.premiermarinas.com

VHF	Ch 17
ACCESS	H24

Opened in 1993 and taken over by Premier Marinas in 2007, Sovereign Harbour is accessible at all states of the tide and weather except for in strong NE to SE'ly winds. Entered via a lock H24, the Five Gold Anchor Award marina is part of one of the largest waterfront complexes in the UK, enjoying close proximity to shops, restaurants and a multiplex cinema. The Sovereign Harbour YC is on site and welcomes visitors to its bar and galley.

A short bus or taxi ride takes you to Eastbourne, where you will find shops and eating places to suit all tastes and budgets.

FACILITIES AT A GLANCE

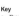

Key
a The Waterfront, shops, restaurants, pubs and offices
b Harbour office - weather information and visitor's information
c Cinema
d Retail park - supermarket and post office
e Restaurant
f Toilets, showers, launderette and disabled facilities
g 24 hr fuel pontoon (diesel, petrol and holding tank pump out)
h Recycling centre
i Boatyard, boatpark, marine engineers, riggers and electricians
NB Berth numbering runs from low outer to high inner

HARBOUR OF RYE

Harbour of Rye
New Lydd Road, Camber, E Sussex, TN31 7QS
Tel: 01797 225225
Email: rye.harbour@environment-agency.gov.uk
www.environment-agency.gov.uk/harbourofrye

VHF	Ch 14
ACCESS	HW±2

The Strand Quay moorings are located in the centre of the historic town of Rye with all of its amenities a short walk away. The town caters for a wide variety of interests with the nearby Rye Harbour Nature Reserve, a museum, numerous antique shops and plentiful pubs, bars and restaurants. Vessels, up to a length of 15 metres, wishing to berth in the soft mud in or near the town of Rye should time their arrival at the entrance for not later than one hour after high water. Larger vessels should make prior arrangements with the Harbour Master. Fresh water, electricity, shower and toilet facilities are available.

FACILITIES AT A GLANCE

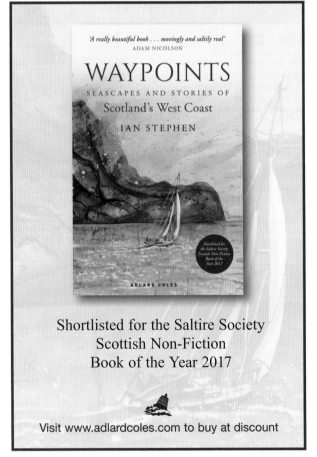

DOVER MARINA

Dover Harbour Board
Harbour House, Dover, Kent, CT17 9TF
Tel: 01304 241663 Fax: 01304 242549
Email: marina@doverport.co.uk www.doverport.co.uk/marina

VHF Ch 80
ACCESS H24

Nestling under the famous White Cliffs, Dover sits between South Foreland to the NE and Folkestone to the SW. Boasting a maritime history stretching back as far as the Bronze Age, Dover is today one of Britain's busiest commercial ports, with a continuous stream of ferries and cruise liners plying to and from their European destinations. However, over the past years the harbour has made itself more attractive to the cruising yachtsman, with the marina, set well away from the busy ferry terminal, offering three sheltered berthing options in the Tidal Harbour, Granville Dock and Wellington Dock.

FACILITIES AT A GLANCE

Key
a Marina office
b Storage
c Waste oil disposal
d Scrubbing berth (tidal)

ROYAL HARBOUR MARINA

Royal Harbour Marina, Ramsgate
Harbour Office, Military Road, Ramsgate, Kent, CT11 9LQ
Tel: 01843 572100 Fax: 01843 590941
Email: portoframsgate@thanet.gov.uk
www.portoframsgate.co.uk

VHF Ch 14, 80
ACCESS H24

Steeped in maritime history, Ramsgate was awarded 'Royal' status in 1821 by George IV in recognition of the warm welcome he received when sailing from Ramsgate. Offering good shelter and modern facilities, including both red and white diesel, the Royal Harbour comprises an outer marina accessible H24 and an inner marina, entered approximately HW±2. Permission to enter or leave the Royal Harbour must be obtained from Port Control on channel 14 and berthing instructions can be obtained from the Dockmaster on channel 80. Full information may be found on the website.

FACILITIES AT A GLANCE

Key
a Harbour office
b Port Control (VHF 14)
c Dock office
d Showers/toilets
   laundry
e RNLI
f Dockmasters office
g Fuel barge (VHF 14)
h Museum

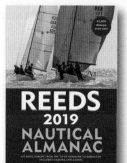
Key to Marina Plans symbols

🛢	Bottled gas	P	Parking
♿	Chandler	✕	Pub/Restaurant
♿	Disabled facilities		Pump out
🔌	Electrical supply		Rigging service
	Electrical repairs		Sail repairs
🔧	Engine repairs	✂	Shipwright
✚	First Aid	🛒	Shop/Supermarket
	Fresh Water		Showers
D	Fuel - Diesel		Slipway
P	Fuel - Petrol	WC	Toilets
	Hardstanding/boatyard	☎	Telephone
@	Internet Café		Trolleys
▣	Laundry facilities	V	Visitors berths
	Lift-out facilities	Ϋ	Wi-Fi

Area 4 - East England

MARINAS

Telephone Numbers, VHF Channel, Access Times

Gallions Pt Marina
020 7476 7054
Ch M, 80 HW±5
South Dock Marina
020 7252 2244
Ch M HW-2½ to +1½
Poplar Dock Marina
020 7308 9930
Ch 13 HW±1
St Katharine Haven
020 7264 5312
Ch 80 HW-2 to +1½
Chelsea Harbour
020 7225 9157
Ch 80 HW±1½
Brentford Dock Marina
020 8232 8941 HW±2½
Penton Hook Marina
01932 568681
Ch 80 H24
Windsor Marina
01753 853911
Ch 80 H24
Bray Marina
01628 623654
Ch 80 H24

Suffolk Yacht Hbr 01473 659240 Ch 80 H24
Royal Harwich YC Marina 01473 780319 Ch 77 H24
Woolverstone Marina 01473 780206 Ch 80 H24
Fox's Marina 01473 689111 Ch 80 H24
Neptune Marina 01473 215204 Ch M, 80 H24
Ipswich Haven Marina 01473 236644 Ch M, 80 H24

Burnham Yacht Harbour 01621 782150 Ch 80 H24
Essex Marina 01702 258531 Ch 80 H24
Bridgemarsh Marina 01621 740414 Ch 80 HW±4
Fambridge Yacht Haven 01621 740370 Ch 80 H24
Fambridge Yacht Station 01621 742911 Ch 80 H24

Limehouse Marina
020 7308 9930
Ch 80 HW±3

Port Werburgh 01634 225107 Ch 80 HW±3

Chatham Maritime Marina
01634 899200

Gt Yarmouth
Lowestoft
Royal Norfolk & Suffolk YC
01520 566726 Ch 14, 80 H24
Lowestoft Haven Marina
01520 580300 Ch M, 80 H24
Lowestoft Cruising Club
07913 391950, H24
Southwold

Shotley Marina
01473 788982
Ch 80 H24
Orford
Ipswich

Titchmarsh Marina   Walton Yacht Basin
01255 672185   01255 675873
Ch 80 HW±5   Ch 80 HW-¾ to +¼
Harwich

Bradwell Marina 01621 776235 Ch M, 80 HW±4½
Blackwater Marina 01621 740264 Ch M HW±2
Tollesbury Marina 01621 869202 Ch 80 HW±2
Heybridge Basin 01621 853506 Ch 80 HW±1

R Thames

N. Foreland

Gillingham Marina
01634 280022   Ramsgate
Ch 80 HW±4½

N

GILLINGHAM MARINA

Gillingham Marina
173 Pier Road, Gillingham, Kent, ME7 1UB
Tel: 01634 280022 Fax: 01634 280164
Email: berthing@gillingham-marina.co.uk
www.gillingham-marina.co.uk

VHF Ch 80
ACCESS HW±4.5

Gillingham Marina comprises a locked basin, accessible four and a half hours either side of high water, and a tidal basin upstream which can be entered approximately two hours either side of high water. Deep water moorings in the river cater for yachts arriving at other times.

Visiting yachts are usually accommodated in the locked basin, although it is best to contact the marina ahead of time. Lying on the south bank of the River Medway, the marina is approximately eight miles from Sheerness, at the mouth of the river, and five miles downstream of Rochester Bridge. Facilities include a well-stocked chandlery, brokerage and an extensive workshop.

FACILITIES AT A GLANCE

Key
a Workshop
b Showers & toilets
c Shop
d Laundry
e Play area
f Reception & club
g Tender storage
h Lead in pontoon
i Petrol & diesel
j Leisure centre

PORT WERBURGH

Port Werburgh
Vicarage Lane, Hoo, Rochester, Kent, ME3 9TW
Tel: 01634 252107 Fax: 01634 253477
Email: jillswann@wanttoliveafloat.com

VHF Ch 80
ACCESS HW±3

Hoo Marina has been purchased by Residential Marine Ltd and is now incorporated into Port Werburgh. The port, some eight miles upriver from Sheerness, can be approached either straight across the mud flats at HW or via the creek, which has access HW±3 for shallow draught boats. The path of the creek is marked by withies, which must be kept to port.

The port accommodates residential and leisure boats from 20–200ft and has a lifting service available for craft up to 17 tons; a dry dock is available for larger boats. There are no workshop facilities but boat owners are encouraged to work on their own boats. Security is provided by H24 CCTV coverage.

All berths are supplied with water and electricity and the onsite amenity block has showers, toilets and a laundry room. There is a grocery store adjacent and shops in Hoo village approximately half a mile distant. There is a frequent bus service to nearby Rochester.

FACILITIES AT A GLANCE

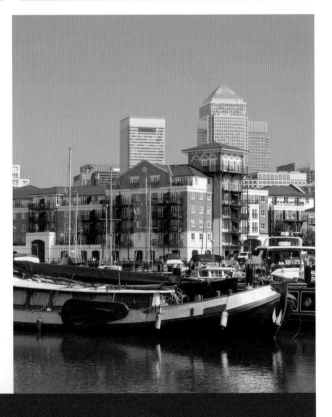

BWML

Limehouse Basin Marina
London

An oasis of calm in the heart of London

Fully serviced pontoons
Visitors welcome

020 7308 9930   bwml.co.uk   phil.cotman@bwml.co.uk

CHATHAM MARITIME MARINA

Chatham Maritime Marina, The Lock Building,
Leviathan Way, Chatham Maritime, Chatham, Medway, ME4 4LP
Tel: 01634 899200
Email: chatham@mdlmarinas.co.uk
www.chathammaritimemarina.co.uk

VHF Ch 80
ACCESS H24

Chatham Maritime Marina is situated on the banks of the River Medway in Kent, providing an ideal location from which to explore the surrounding area. There are plenty of secluded anchorages in the lower reaches of the Medway Estuary, while the river is navigable for some 13 miles from its mouth at Sheerness right up to Rochester, and even beyond for those yachts drawing less than 2m. Only 45 minutes from London by road, the marina is part of a multi-million pound leisure and retail development, accommodating 412 boats following a recent expansion.

FACILITIES AT A GLANCE

Key
a Fuel berth
b Pontoon access gate
c Crane pad
d Boat storage
e Facilities building
f Events berthing
g Waiting pontoon
h Lock control building
i Pump House No.5
j Pub, restaurant, hotel and convenience store

LIMEHOUSE MARINA

BWML Limehouse Marina
46 Goodhart Place, London, E14 8EG
Tel: 020 7308 9930 Fax: 020 7363 0428
Email: limehouse.marina@bwml.co.uk www.bwml.co.uk

VHF Ch 80
ACCESS HW±3

Limehouse Marina, situated where the canal system meets the Thames, is now considered the 'Jewel in the Crown' of the British inland waterways network. With complete access to 2,000 miles of inland waterway systems and with access to the Thames at most stages of the tide except around low water, the marina provides a superb location for river, canal and sea-going pleasure craft alike. Boasting a wide range of facilities and up to 90 berths, Limehouse Marina is housed in the old Regent's Canal Dock.

FACILITIES AT A GLANCE

Key
a Cruising Association
b Chemical toilet disposal

4

GALLIONS POINT MARINA

Gallions Point Marina, Gate 14, Royal Albert Basin
Woolwich Manor Way, North Woolwich
London, E16 2QY. Tel: 020 7476 7054 Fax: 020 7474 7056
Email: info@gallionspointmarina.co.uk
www.gallionspointmarina.co.uk

VHF Ch M, 80
ACCESS HW±5

Gallions Point Marina lies about 500 metres down-stream of the Woolwich Ferry on the north side of Gallions Reach. Accessed via a lock at the entrance to the Royal Albert Basin, the marina offers deep water pontoon berths as well as hard standing. Future plans to improve facilities include the development of a bar/restaurant, a chandlery and an RYA tuition school.

FACILITIES AT A GLANCE

☞ Dock Edge Moorings

SOUTH DOCK MARINA

South Dock Marina
Rope Street, Off Plough Way
London, SE16 7SZ
Tel: 020 7252 2244 Fax: 020 7237 3806
Email: christopher.magro@southwark.gov.uk

VHF	Ch M
ACCESS	HW-2.5 to +1.5

South Dock Marina is housed in part of the old Surrey Dock complex on the south bank of the River Thames. Its locked entrance is immediately downstream of Greenland Pier, just a few miles down river of Tower Bridge. For yachts with a 2m draught, the lock can be entered HW-2½ to HW+1½ London Bridge, although if you arrive early there is a holding pontoon on the pier. The marina can be easily identified by the conspicuous arched rooftops of Baltic Quay, a luxury waterside apartment block. Once inside this secure, 200-berth marina, you can take full advantage of all its facilities as well as enjoy a range of restaurants and bars close by or visit historic maritime Greenwich.

FACILITIES AT A GLANCE

Key
a Marina office
b Conspic building

CHELSEA HARBOUR MARINA

Chelsea Harbour Marina
Estate Managements Office
C2-3 The Chambers, London, SW10 0XF
Tel: 07770 542783 Fax: 020 7352 7868
Email: harboumaster@chelsea-harbour.co.uk

VHF	
ACCESS	HW±1.5

Chelsea Harbour is widely thought of as one of London's most significant maritime sites. It is located in the heart of SW London, therefore enjoying easy access to the amenities of Chelsea and the West End. On site is the Chelsea Harbour Design Centre, where 80 showrooms exhibit the best in British and International interior design, offering superb waterside views along with excellent cuisine in the Wyndham Grand.

The harbour lies approximately 48 miles up river from Sea Reach No 1 buoy in the Thames Estuary and is accessed via the Thames Flood Barrier in Woolwich Reach. With its basin gate operating one and a half hours either side of HW (+ 20 minutes at London Bridge), the marina welcomes visiting yachtsmen.

FACILITIES AT A GLANCE

Key
a Belvedere Tower
b Harbour Yard
c Wyndham Grand Hotel
d Kings Quay
e Chelsea Crescent
f Thames Quay
   Showers, toilets & laundry

ST KATHARINE DOCKS

St Katharine's Marina Ltd
50 St Katharine's Way, London, E1W 1LA
Tel: 020 7264 5312 Fax: 020 7702 2252
Email: marina.reception@skdocks.co.uk
www.skdocks.co.uk/marina

VHF	Ch 80
ACCESS	HW -2 to +1.5

St Katharine Docks Marina has been recently refurbished and offers 185 berths equipped for boats up to 40m in three separate, secure and calm basins. The historic docks are located next to Tower Bridge.

This is a unique marina benefiting from waterside dining, boutique shops and excellent transport links to the West End. Visitors are welcomed all year round and the marina provides its own calendar of events details of which can be found on the website and social media pages.

The marina is ideally situated for visiting the Tower of London, Tower Bridge, *HMS Belfast* and the City of London all of which can be reached on foot. A short river bus service away is Greenwich and the Cutty Sark and to the west the Shard and London Eye.

FACILITIES AT A GLANCE

Key
a Ivory House
b Dickens Inn
c Marina office
d Tower Hotel

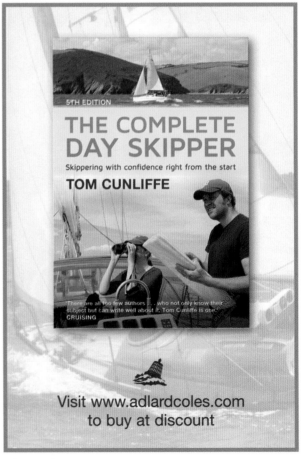

BRENTFORD DOCK MARINA

Brentford Dock Marina
2 Justin Close, Brentford, Middlesex, TW8 8QE
Tel: 020 8232 8941 Mob: 07970 143 987
E-mail: brentforddockmarina@gmail.com

VHF
ACCESS HW±2.5

Brentford Dock Marina is situated on the River Thames at the junction with the Grand Union Canal. Its hydraulic lock is accessible for up to two and a half hours either side of high water, although boats over 9.5m LOA enter on high water by prior arrangement. There is a grocery store on site. The main attractions within the area are the Royal Botanic Gardens at Kew and the Kew Bridge Steam Museum at Brentford.

FACILITIES AT A GLANCE

Key
a   Shop
b   Rubbish disposal
c   Recycling bins
d   Marina office and first aid
e   Toilets, showers and slop out facilities

PENTON HOOK MARINA

Penton Hook Marina
Staines Road, Chertsey, Surrey, KT16 8PY
Tel: 01932 568681
Email: pentonhook@mdlmarinas.co.uk
www.pentonhookmarina.co.uk

VHF
ACCESS H24

Penton Hook, the largest inland marina in Europe, is situated on what is considered to be one of the most attractive reaches of the River Thames; close to the vibrant town of Staines-on-Thames and about a mile downstream from Runnymede.

Providing unrestricted access to the River Thames through a deep water channel below Penton Hook Lock, the marina can accommodate ocean-going craft of up to 30m LOA and is ideally placed for a visit to Thorpe Park, reputedly one of the country's most popular family leisure attractions.

FACILITIES AT A GLANCE

Key
a   Information point
b   Dock manager's office
c   Yacht club
d   Repairs and under cover storage

4

WINDSOR MARINA

Windsor Marina
Maidenhead Road, Windsor
Berkshire, SL4 5TZ
Tel: 01753 853911
Email: windsor@mdlmarinas.co.uk www.windsormarina.co.uk

VHF
ACCESS H24

Situated on the outskirts of Windsor town on the south bank of the River Thames, Windsor Marina enjoys a peaceful garden setting. On site is the Windsor Yacht Club and fuel (diesel and petrol), enabling you to fill up as and when you need.

A trip to the town of Windsor, comprising beautiful Georgian and Victorian buildings, would not be complete without a visit to Windsor Castle. With its construction inaugurated over 900 years ago by William the Conqueror, it is the oldest inhabited castle in the world and accommodates a priceless art and furniture collection.

FACILITIES AT A GLANCE

Key
a   Boat sales & engineers
b   Recycling bins
c   Dock office
d   Trimmers
e   Yacht club

BRAY MARINA

Bray Marina
Monkey Island Lane, Bray
Berkshire, SL6 2EB
Tel: 01628 623654
Email: bray@mdlmarinas.co.uk www.braymarina.co.uk

VHF
ACCESS H24

Bray Marina is situated in a country park setting among shady trees, providing berth holders with a tranquil mooring. From the marina there is direct access to the Thames and there are extensive well-maintained facilities available for all boat owners. The 400-berth marina boasts an active club, which holds social functions as well as boat training lessons and handling competitions, a small chandlery and engineering services.

Upstream is the National Trust property, Cliveden House, with its extensive gardens and woodlands. Cookham is home of the Queen's Swan Keeper, who can sometimes be seen in his traditional costume. Further on still is Hambledon Mill; from here the river is navigable as far as Lechlade.

FACILITIES AT A GLANCE

Key
a   Boat storage
b   Boat sales office
c   Marina office, small chandlery, toilets, showers, repairs and engineering
d   Battery, hazardous waste, oil and fuel disposal

BURNHAM YACHT HARBOUR MARINA

Burnham Yacht Harbour Marina Ltd
Burnham-on-Crouch, Essex, CM0 8BL
Tel: 01621 782150 HM: 01621 786832
Email: admin@burnhamyachtharbour.co.uk

VHF	Ch 80
ACCESS	H24

Boasting four major yacht clubs, each with comprehensive racing programmes, Burnham-on-Crouch has come to be regarded by some as 'the Cowes of the East Coast'. At the western end of the town lies Burnham Yacht Harbour, dredged 2.2m below datum. Offering a variety of on site facilities, its entrance can be easily identified by a yellow pillar buoy with an 'X' topmark.

The historic town, with its 'weatherboard' and early brick buildings, elegant quayside and scenic riverside walks, exudes plenty of charm. Among its attractions are a sports centre, a railway museum and a two-screen cinema.

FACILITIES AT A GLANCE

Key
a Workshop
b Yacht sales
c Marina office
d Shower block
e The Swallowtail
f RNLI shore station
g Country park

Burnham Yacht Harbour Marina limited

Burnham Yacht harbour provides all the facilities you require from a modern secure marina with 24 hour tidal access, 350 fully serviced berths, Swallowtail restaurant and bar, chandlery, workshop, yacht brokerage and friendly staff.

For a full list of incentives and deals please visit our website www.burnhamyachtharbour.co.uk or call 01621 782150

ESSEX MARINA

Essex Marina
Wallasea Island, Essex, SS4 2HF
Tel: 01702 258531 Fax: 01702 258227
Email: info@essexmarina.co.uk
www.essexmarina.co.uk

VHF	Ch 80
ACCESS	H24

Surrounded by beautiful countryside, Essex Marina is situated in Wallasea Bay, about half a mile up river of Burnham on Crouch. Boasting 500 deep water berths, including 50 swinging moorings, the marina can be accessed at all states of the tide. On site are a 70 ton boat hoist, a chandlery and brokerage service as well as the Essex Marina Yacht Club.

Essex Marina is the home of Boats.co.uk. There is a ferry service which runs from Easter until the end of September, taking passengers across the river 6 days a week to Burnham, where you will find numerous shops and restaurants.

FACILITIES AT A GLANCE

Key
a Marina office & chandlery
b Essex Marina Yacht Club
c Brokerage & boat sales
d Licenced bar & restaurant

BRIDGEMARSH MARINA

Bridgemarsh Marine
Fairholme, Bridge Marsh Lane, Althorne, Essex
Tel: 01621 740414 Mobile: 07968 696815 Fax: 01621 742216

VHF	Ch 80
ACCESS	HW±4

On the north side of Bridgemarsh Island, just beyond Essex Marina on the River Crouch, lies Althorne Creek. Here Bridgemarsh Marine accommodates over 100 boats berthed alongside pontoons supplied with water and electricity. A red beacon marks the entrance to the creek, with red can buoys identifying the approach channel into the marina. Accessible four hours either side of high water, the marina has an on site yard with two docks, a slipway and crane. The village of Althorne is just a short walk away, from where there are direct train services (taking approximately one hour) to London.

FACILITIES AT A GLANCE

HEYBRIDGE BASIN

Heybridge Basin
Lock Hill, Heybridge Basin, Maldon, Essex, CM9 4RY
Tel: 07712 079764
Email: grant.everiss@waterways.org.uk
www.essexwaterways.com

VHF	Ch 80
ACCESS	HW±1

Towards the head of the River Blackwater and not far from Maldon, lies Heybridge Basin sea lock. It is situated at the lower end of the 14M Chelmer and Blackwater Navigation Canal and can be entered approximately 1-1.5hrs before HW for vessels drawing up to 2m. There is good holding ground in the river just outside the lock. There are in excess of 300 permanent moorings along the navigation and room for up to 20 rafting visiting vessels in the Basin, which has a range of facilities, including shower and laundry amenities. Please book at least 24hrs in advance especially during the summer months. The manned lock is operational for tides between 0600 and 2000.

FACILITIES AT A GLANCE

BRADWELL MARINA

Bradwell Marina, Port Flair Ltd, Waterside
Bradwell-on-Sea, Essex, CM0 7RB
Tel: 01621 776235 Fax: 01621 776393
Email: info@bradwellmarina.com
www.bradwellmarina.com

VHF	Ch M, 80
ACCESS	HW±4.5

Opened in 1984, Bradwell is a privately-owned marina situated in the mouth of the River Blackwater, serving as a convenient base from which to explore the Essex coastline or as a departure point for cruising further afield to Holland and Belgium.

The yacht basin can be accessed four and a half hours either side of HW and offers plenty of protection from all wind directions. With a total of 300 fully serviced berths, generous space has been allocated for manoeuvring between pontoons. Overlooking the marina is Bradwell Club House, incorporating a bar, restaurant, launderette and ablution facilities.

FACILITIES AT A GLANCE

Key
a Clubhouse
b Tower office

FAMBRIDGE YACHT HAVEN

Fambridge Yacht Haven
Church Road, North Fambridge, Essex, CM3 6LU
Tel: 01621 740370 www.yachthavens.com
Email: fambridge@yachthavens.com

VHF	Ch 80
ACCESS	H24

The Haven is split over two sites in the village of North Fambridge. The marina is located just under a mile upstream of its 'Yacht Station' facility with access via Stow Creek, which branches N off the R Crouch. The channel is straight and clearly marked to the ent of the Yacht Haven. Home to the West Wick Yacht Club, the marina has 220 berths to accommodate vessels up to 20m LOA. North Fambridge features the 500 year-old Ferry Boat Inn, a favourite haunt with the sailing fraternity. Burnham-on-Crouch is six miles down river, while the Essex and Kent coasts are within easy sailing distance. Excellent repair facilities can be found ashore together with undercover storage for vessels up to 19m LOA with a maximum weight of 40 tons.

FACILITIES AT A GLANCE

Key
a Marina reception
b Waste
c West Wick YC
d Boat Shed Essex
e Marina maintenance, workshop & stores
f Under cover storage
g Chandler

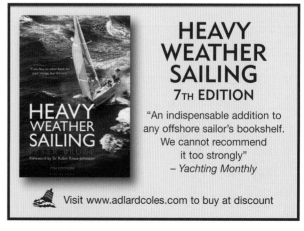

FAMBRIDGE YACHT STATION

Fambridge Yacht Station
Church Road, North Fambridge, Essex, CM3 6LU
Tel: 01621 742911 www.yachthavens.com
Email: fambridge@yachthavens.com

VHF	Ch 80
ACCESS	H24

The Yacht Station is located just under a mile downstream of Fambridge Yacht Haven and is set within the sheltered River Crouch directly between the rural villages of North and South Fambridge. Home to the North Fambridge Yacht Club, the Yacht Station has a 120m visitor pontoon providing deep water berthing alongside and foot access to mud berths and the village of North Fambridge. There are also 110 deep water swinging moorings in 5 straight E/W trots just off the visitor pontoon. A launch service operates during summer weekends and bank holidays. As with the marina, excellent repair facilities can be found ashore for vessels with a maximum weight of 25t.

FACILITIES AT A GLANCE

Key
a Yacht Station reception
b Crane dock
c N Fambridge YC
d Floating dinghy storage
e IBS Boat Supplies

Mud berths
Fl(3)G.4s   Fl(3)G.4s
Swinging moorings

Visitors welcome

Fambridge Yacht Haven
Full tidal access

– 220 sheltered & fully serviced pontoon berths
– 120 deepwater swinging moorings
– 120m visitor pontoon with full tidal access
– A TransEurope Marina
– FREE Wi-Fi for berth holders & visitors
– Walking distance from the famous Ferry Boat Inn
– Hassle-free Park & Ride Service
– Modern 40t & 25t slipway hoists & 30t mobile crane

Call **01621 740370** or **VHF Ch 80**
or visit **yachthavens.com**

Fambridge Yacht Haven

BLACKWATER MARINA

Blackwater Marina
Marine Parade, Maylandsea, Essex
Tel: 01621 740264
Email: info@blackwater-marina.co.uk

VHF	Ch M
ACCESS	HW±2

Blackwater Marina is a place where families in day boats mix with Smack owners and yacht crews; here seals, avocets and porpoises roam beneath the big, sheltering East Coast skies and here the area's rich heritage of working Thames Barges and Smacks remains part of daily life today.

But it isn't just classic sailing boats that thrive on the Blackwater. An eclectic mix of motor cruisers, open boats and modern yachts enjoy the advantages of a marina sheltered by its natural habitat, where the absence of harbour walls allows uninterrupted views of some of Britain's rarest wildlife and where the 21st century shoreside facilities are looked after by experienced professionals, who are often found sailing on their days off.

FACILITIES AT A GLANCE

Key
a Maylandsea Bay YC
b Harlow (Blackwater) Sailing Club
c Marina office

Flag Station

Marina
Bar

TOLLESBURY MARINA

Tollesbury Marina
The Yacht Harbour, Tollesbury, Essex, CM9 8SE
Tel: 01621 869202 Fax: 01621 868489
email: harbourmaster@tollesburymarina.com

VHF	Ch 80
ACCESS	HW±2

Tollesbury Marina lies at the mouth of the River Blackwater in the heart of the Essex countryside. Within easy access from London and the Home Counties, it has been designed as a leisure centre for the whole family, with on-site activities comprising tennis courts and a covered heated swimming pool as well as a convivial bar and restaurant. Accommodating over 240 boats, the marina can be accessed two hours either side of HW and is ideally situated for those wishing to explore the River Crouch to the south and the Rivers Colne, Orwell and Deben to the north.

FACILITIES AT A GLANCE

Waste oil container

Waste bin

Scrubbing posts

Waste bin

Tollesbury Cruising Club

Key
a Brokerage and Chandlery
b Workshop
c Covered Heated Pool and Tennis

TITCHMARSH MARINA

Titchmarsh Marina Ltd
Coles Lane, Walton on the Naze, Essex, CO14 8SL
Tel: 01255 672185 Fax: 01255 851901
Email: info@titchmarshmarina.co.uk
www.titchmarshmarina.co.uk

VHF Ch 80
ACCESS HW±5

Titchmarsh Marina sits on the south side of The Twizzle in the heart of the Walton Backwaters. As the area is designated a 'wetland of international importance', the marina has been designed and developed to function as a natural harbour. The 420 berths are well-sheltered by the high-grassed clay banks, offering good protection in all conditions. The marina entrance has a depth of 1.3m at LWS but once inside the basin this increases to around 2m; there is a tide gauge at the fuel berth. Among the excellent facilities onsite are the well-stocked chandlery and the Harbour Lights restaurant and bar serving food daily.

FACILITIES AT A GLANCE

Key
a   Harbour master, chandlery (+ cycle hire) marine engineers, marine electronics
b   Hardstanding
c   Harbour Lights - restaurant and bar

4

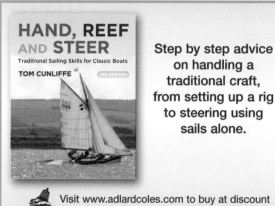
WALTON YACHT BASIN

Walton and Frinton Yacht Trust
Mill Lane, Walton on the Naze, CO14 8PF
Managed by Bedwell & Co Tel: 01255 675873
Mobile: 07957 848031

VHF Ch 80
ACCESS HW-0.75,HW+0.25

Walton Yacht Basin lies at the head of Walton Creek, an area made famous in Arthur Ransome's *Swallows & Amazons* and *Secret Waters*. The creek can only be navigated HW±2, although yachts heading for the Yacht Basin should arrive on a rising tide as the entrance gate is kept shut once the tide turns in order to retain the water inside. Before entering the gate, moor up against the Club Quay to enquire about berthing availability.

A short walk away is the popular seaside town of Walton, full of shops, pubs and restaurants. Its focal point is the pier which, overlooking superb sandy beaches, offers various attractions. Slightly further out of town, the Naze affords pleasant coastal walks with striking panoramic views.

FACILITIES AT A GLANCE

SUFFOLK YACHT HARBOUR

Suffolk Yacht Harbour Ltd
Levington, Ipswich, Suffolk, IP10 0LN
Tel: 01473 659240 Fax: 01473 659632
Email: info@syharbour.co.uk
www.syharbour.co.uk

VHF Ch 80
ACCESS H24

A friendly, independently-run marina on the East Coast of England, Suffolk Yacht Harbour enjoys a beautiful rural setting on the River Orwell, yet is within easy access of Ipswich, Woodbridge and Felixstowe. With approximately 550 berths, the marina offers extensive facilities while the Haven Ports Yacht Club provides a bar and restaurant.

FACILITIES AT A GLANCE

SHOTLEY MARINA

Shotley Marina Ltd
Shotley Gate, Ipswich,Suffolk, IP9 1QJ
Tel: 01473 788982 Fax: 01473 788868
Email: sales@shotleymarina.co.uk
www.shotleymarina.co.uk

VHF	Ch 80
ACCESS	H24

Based in the well protected Harwich Harbour where the River Stour joins the River Orwell, Shotley Marina is only eight miles from the county town of Ipswich. Entered via a lock at all states of the tide, its first class facilities include extensive boat repair and maintenance services as well as a well-stocked chandlery and on site bar and restaurant. The marina is strategically placed for sailing up the Stour to Manningtree, up the Orwell to Pin Mill or exploring the Rivers Deben, Crouch and Blackwater as well as the Walton Backwaters.

FACILITIES AT A GLANCE

Key
a Shotley Marine Services
b Lock control
c Lock waiting pontoons
d SPYC
e Mariners Bar and function rooms
f Baths, showers and toilets
g Launderette
h Shipwreck bar and restaurant
i Shotley Point YC
j HMS Ganges Museum

ROYAL HARWICH YACHT CLUB MARINA

Royal Harwich Yacht Club Marina
Marina Road, Woolverstone, Suffolk, IP9 1AT
Tel: 01473 780319 Fax: 01473 780919 Berths: 07742 145994
www.royalharwichyachtclub.co.uk
Email: office.manager@royalharwich.co.uk

VHF	Ch 77
ACCESS	H24

This 54 berth marina is ideally situated at a mid point on the Orwell between Levington and Ipswich. The facility is owned and run by the Royal Harwich Yacht Club and enjoys a full catering and bar service in the Clubhouse. The marina benefits from full tidal access, and can accommodate yachts up to 14.5m on the hammerhead. Within the immediate surrounds, there are boat repair services, and a well stocked chandlery. The marina is situated a mile's walk from the world famous Pin Mill and is a favoured destination with visitors from Holland, Belgium and Germany. The marina welcomes racing yachts and cruisers, and is able to accommodate multiple bookings.

FACILITIES AT A GLANCE

RIVER ORWELL

FOX'S MARINA

Fox's Marina & Boatyard
The Strand, Ipswich, Suffolk, IP2 8SA
Tel: 01473 689111
Email: foxs@foxsmarina.com www.foxsmarina.com

VHF Ch 80
ACCESS H24

Located on the picturesque River Orwell, Fox's provides good shelter in all conditions and access at all states of tide with 100 pontoon berths and ashore storage for 200 vessels. A 70T hoist is able to handle boats up to 80ft in length.

Fox's Marina & Boatyard offers a full range of in-house services and, with 10,000 sq ft of heated workshop space, are specialists in repairs and refits of sailing/motor yachts and commercial craft. Specific services include coppercoat and osmosis treatment, specialist GRP and gelcoat repairs, spray painting and varnishing, and custom stainless fabrication.

Also on-site, Fox's Chandlery and Marine Store, is the largest stockist of marine chandlery and equipment, sailing, leisure and country clothing in East Anglia.

FACILITIES AT A GLANCE

Key
a Chandlery
b Harbourmaster office
c Yacht Club

WOOLVERSTONE MARINA

Woolverstone Marina
Woolverstone, Ipswich, Suffolk, IP9 1AS
Tel: 01473 780206
Email: woolverstone@mdlmarinas.co.uk
www.woolverstonemarina.co.uk

VHF Ch 80
ACCESS H24

Woolverstone Marina is set in 22 acres of glorious parkland on the picturesque River Orwell. Within easy reach of the sea and a multitude of scenic destinations, this is a great base to start cruising. Walton Backwaters and the

River Deben are only a short distance away. If you prefer longer distance cruising then Belgium and Holland are directly across the North Sea.

Besides boat repair services, an on-site chandlery and ablution facilities, the marina also incorporates a luxurious lodge park, yacht brokerage and an on-site restaurant and bar, which overlooks the river.

FACILITIES AT A GLANCE

Key
a Marina office, toilets, showers, and launderette
b Restaurant and Bar

NEPTUNE MARINA

Neptune Marina Ltd
Neptune Quay, Ipswich, IP4 1QJ
Tel: 01473 215204
Email: enquiries@neptune-marina.com

VHF	Ch M, 80
ACCESS	H±2.5

Neptune Marina is situated at Neptune Quay on the historic waterfront, and ever-increasing shoreside developments. This 26-acre dock is accessible through a H24 lock gate, with a waiting pontoon outside. Onsite facilities include boatyard and lift-out facilities plus superfast wifi for boat owners.

The Neptune Marina building occupies an imposing position in the NE corner of the dock with quality coffee shop and associated retail units. There are a number of excellent restaurants along the quayside and adjacent to the marina.

The modern town centre catering for all needs is just a 10-minute walk away.

FACILITIES AT A GLANCE

Key
a Old Custom House
b Conference centre
c Floating French restaurant
d Bistro
e Bellway apartments
f Neptune Marina office & facilities
g Marina storage yard

IPSWICH HAVEN MARINA

Associated British Ports
New Cut East, Ipswich, Suffolk, IP3 0EA
Tel: 01473 236644 Fax: 01473 236645
Email: ipswichhaven@abports.co.uk

VHF	Ch M, 80
ACCESS	H24

Lying at the heart of Ipswich, the Haven Marina enjoys close proximity to all the bustling shopping centres, restaurants, cinemas and museums that this County Town of Suffolk has to offer. The main railway station is only a 10-minute walk away, where there are regular connections to London, Cambridge and Norwich, all taking just over an hour to get to.

Within easy reach of Holland, Belgium and Germany, East Anglia is proving an increasingly popular cruising ground. The River Orwell, displaying breathtaking scenery, was voted one of the most beautiful rivers in Britain by the RYA.

FACILITIES AT A GLANCE

Key
a Toilets, showers, laundry, office
b Licensed bistro
c R&J Marine Electronics
d Boat sales
e Fairline PDI Shed
f Future restaurant retail
g Burton Waters Repair Shop

See continuation on inset left

LOWESTOFT HAVEN MARINA

Lowestoft Haven Marina
School Road, Lowestoft, Suffolk, NR33 9NB
Tel: 01502 580300
Email: lowestofthaven@abports.co.uk
www.lowestofthavenmarina.co.uk

VHF Ch M, 80
ACCESS H24

Lowestoft Haven Marina is based on Lake Lothing with easy access to both the open sea and the Norfolk Broads. The town centres of both Lowestoft and Oulton Broad are within a short distance of the marina.

The marina's 140 berths can accommodate vessels from 7–20m. Offering a full range of modern facilities the marina welcomes all visitors.

FACILITIES AT A GLANCE

Key
a   Boat storage
b   Marina office

4

ROYAL NORFOLK & SUFFOLK YACHT CLUB

Royal Norfolk and Suffolk Yacht Club
Royal Plain, Lowestoft, Suffolk, NR33 0AQ
Tel: 01502 566726
Email: admin@rnsyc.org.uk   www.rnsyc.net

VHF Ch 14, 80
ACCESS H24

With its entrance at the inner end of the South Pier, opposite the Trawl Basin on the north bank, the Royal Norfolk and Suffolk Yacht Club marina occupies a sheltered position in Lowestoft Harbour. Lowestoft has always been an appealing destination to yachtsmen due to the fact that it can be accessed at any state of the tide, 24 hours a day. Note, however, that conditions just outside the entrance can get pretty lively when the wind is against tide. The clubhouse is enclosed in an impressive Grade 2 listed building overlooking the marina and its facilities include a bar and restaurant as well as a formal dining room.

FACILITIES AT A GLANCE

RNSYC

Key
a   Showers, toilets including disabled   d   Sun lounge
b   Restaurant   e   Bar
c   Reception   f   Marina office

LOWESTOFT CRUISING CLUB

Lowestoft Cruising Club
Off Harbour Road, Oulton Broad, Lowestoft, Suffolk, NR32 3LY
Tel: 07810 522515
www.lowestoftcruisingclub.co.uk

VHF
ACCESS H24

Lowestoft Cruising Club welcomes visitors and can offer a friendly atmosphere, some of the finest moorings and at very competitive rates. Whatever the weather, these moorings provide a calm, safe haven for visiting yachts and with the Mutford lock only 250 metres away, easy access onto the Norfolk and Suffolk Broads. Facilities include electricity and water, plus excellent showers, toilets and secure car parking. These moorings are the nearest ones to the railway stations (to Norwich and Ipswich), bus routes, shops, banks, pubs and restaurants in Oulton Broad.

FACILITIES AT A GLANCE

WORLD CLASS SKIPPERS WANTED

NO PRESSURE

Sir Robin Knox-Johnston
Founder of the Clipper Round the World Yacht Race

Join the elite and take on the world's longest yacht race, crewed exclusively by novice crew embarking on the race of their lives.

Clipper Race Skippers are exceptional. They have the fortitude to take on the toughest of mental challenges, and the physical endurance to successfully lead a team through Mother Nature's extreme environments on a 40,000 mile lap around the globe.

Now we're recruiting for the next edition of the Clipper Race. To qualify you must hold a Yachtmaster Ocean certificate [commercial endorsed] or International Yacht Training Master of Yachts.

↘ **APPLY NOW**

clipperroundtheworld.com/careers
+44 (0) 2392 526000

CLIPPER | **ROUND THE WORLD**

NORTH EAST ENGLAND - Great Yarmouth to Berwick-upon-Tweed

Reeds PDF ebooks

In response to popular demand, all the Reeds Almanacs are now available as searchable, highlightable PDF ebooks. (All ebooks incorporate the Marina Guide.)

Visit www.reedsnauticalalmanac.co.uk for further information

Key to Marina Plans symbols

🔥	Bottled gas	P	Parking
	Chandler	✗	Pub/Restaurant
♿	Disabled facilities		Pump out
	Electrical supply		Rigging service
	Electrical repairs		Sail repairs
	Engine repairs		Shipwright
✚	First Aid		Shop/Supermarket
	Fresh Water		Showers
	Fuel - Diesel		Slipway
	Fuel - Petrol	WC	Toilets
	Hardstanding/boatyard		Telephone
@	Internet Café		Trolleys
	Laundry facilities	Ⓥ	Visitors berths
	Lift-out facilities		Wi-Fi

Area 5 - North East England

MARINAS
Telephone Numbers
VHF Channel
Access Times

5

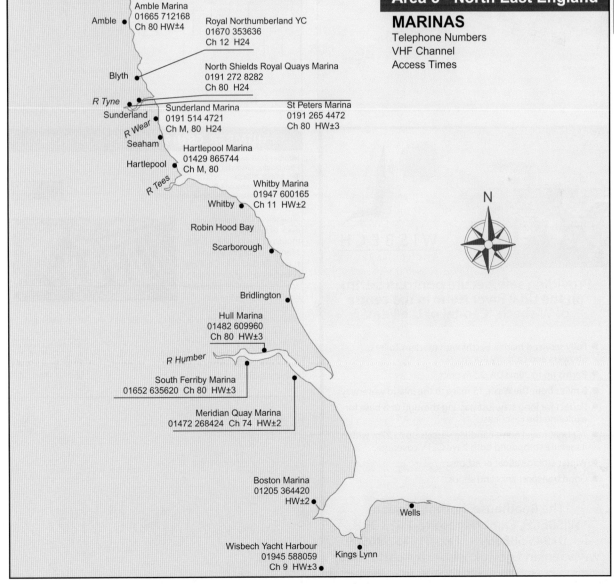

Amble Marina 01665 712168 Ch 80 HW±4
Royal Northumberland YC 01670 353636 Ch 12 H24
North Shields Royal Quays Marina 0191 272 8282 Ch 80 H24
Sunderland Marina 0191 514 4721 Ch M, 80 H24
St Peters Marina 0191 265 4472 Ch 80 HW±3
Hartlepool Marina 01429 865744 Ch M, 80
Whitby Marina 01947 600165 Ch 11 HW±2
Hull Marina 01482 609960 Ch 80 HW±3
South Ferriby Marina 01652 635620 Ch 80 HW±3
Meridian Quay Marina 01472 268424 Ch 74 HW±2
Boston Marina 01205 364420 HW±2
Wisbech Yacht Harbour 01945 588059 Ch 9 HW±3

Amble, Blyth, R Tyne, Sunderland, R Wear, Seaham, Hartlepool, R Tees, Whitby, Robin Hood Bay, Scarborough, Bridlington, R Humber, Wells, Kings Lynn

WISBECH YACHT HARBOUR

Wisbech Yacht Harbour
Harbour Master, Harbour Office, The Boathouse,
Harbour Square, Wisbech, Cambridgeshire PE13 3BH
Tel: 01945 588059 Fax: 01945 580589
Email: afoster@fenland.gov.uk www.fenland.gov.uk

VHF	Ch 9
ACCESS	HW±3

Regarded as the capital of the English Fens, Wisbech is situated about 25 miles north east of Peterborough and is a market town of considerable character and historical significance. Rows of elegant houses line the banks of the River Nene, with the North and South Brink still deemed two of the finest Georgian streets in England.

Wisbech Yacht Harbour, linking Cambridgeshire with the sea, is proving increasingly popular as a haven for small craft, despite the busy commercial shipping. In recent years the facilities have been developed and improved upon and the HM is always on hand to help with passage planning both up or downstream.

FACILITIES AT A GLANCE

BOSTON GATEWAY MARINA

Boston Gateway Marina
Witham Bank East, Boston, Lincs, PE21 9JU
Tel: 07480 525230
Email: enquiries@bostongatewaymarina.co.uk

VHF	
ACCESS	H±2

Located near Boston Grand Sluice Lock on the sunny side of the River Witham, the marina is ideally situated for easy access to The Wash and is suitable for both sea-going and river boats. It is a short walk to the centre of the historic town of Boston, Lincolnshire, but retains a tranquil feel. The marina offers visitor, short-term and longer-term moorings to suit each individual customer. Power and water are available for all boats.

The town centre offers the normal variety of facilities within easy walking distance. Local tourist attractions include the 14th century St Botolph's Church – 'The Stump' – the 1390s Boston Guildhall Musuem and a 450-year old market to name but a few.

FACILITIES AT A GLANCE

HUMBER CRUISING ASSOCIATION

Humber Cruising Association
Fish Docks, Grimsby, DN31 3SD
Tel: 01472 268424
www.hcagrimsby.co.uk
Email: berthmaster@hcagrimsby.co.uk

VHF	Ch 74
ACCESS	HW±2

Situated in the locked fish dock of Grimsby, at the mouth of the River Humber, Meridian Quay Marina is run by the Humber Cruising Association and comprises approximately 200 alongside berths plus 30 more for visitors. Accessed two hours either side of high water via lock gates, the lock should be contacted on VHF Ch 74 (call sign 'Fish Dock Island') as you make your final approach. The pontoon berths are equipped with water and electricity; there is a fully licensed clubhouse. Also available are internet access and laundry facilities.

FACILITIES AT A GLANCE

5

HULL MARINA

Hull Marina
W 13, Kingston Street, Hull, HU1 2DQ
Tel: 01482 609960 Fax: 01482 224148
Email: david.parkinson@bwml.co.uk
www.bwml.co.uk

VHF Ch 80
ACCESS HW±3

Situated on the River Humber, Hull Marina is literally a stone's throw from the bustling city centre with its array of arts and entertainments. Besides the numerous historic bars and cafés surrounding the marina, there are plenty of traditional taverns to be sampled in the Old Town, while also found here is the Street Life Museum, vividly depicting the history of the city.

Yachtsmen enter the marina via a tidal lock, operating HW±3, and should try to give 15 minutes' notice of arrival via VHF Ch 80. Hull is perfectly positioned for exploring the Trent, Ouse and the Yorkshire coast as well as across the North Sea to Holland or Belgium.

FACILITIES AT A GLANCE

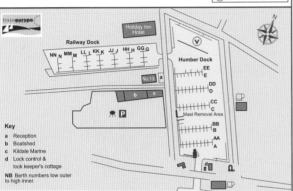

Key
a Reception
b Boatshed
c Kildale Marine
d Lock control & lock keeper's cottage
NB Berth numbers low outer to high inner.

BWML

Hull Marina
Yorkshire

Fully serviced pontoons

Visitors welcome

Fully serviced boatyard and workshops with 50 tonne hoist

Hull Marina is a proud member of the TransEurope Marinas group

01482 609960   bwml.co.uk   david.parkinson@bwml.co.uk

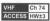

SOUTH FERRIBY MARINA

South Ferriby Marina
Red Lane, South Ferriby, Barton on Humber, Lincs, DN18 6JH
Tel: 01652 635620 (Lock 635219) Mobile: 07828 312071
Email: enquiries@southferribymarina.com

VHF	Ch 74
ACCESS	HW±3

Situated at the entrance to the non-tidal River Ancholme the existing marina has been established since 1966 and is well placed to provide easy access to the River Humber and North Sea. This is a family run business providing a range of services including a boatyard and chandlery. Access is by way of lock at HW±3.

The marina has excellent road and rail services within easy reach, while South Ferriby village has two pubs and a Post Office/Spar Shop just a short walk away.

The picturesque River Ancholme is navigable for about 17 miles; the maximum headroom under bridges is 4.42 metres (14ft 6ins).

FACILITIES AT A GLANCE

Key
a Chandlery
b Shipwrights workshop

WHITBY MARINA

Whitby Marina
Whitby Harbour Office, Endeavour Wharf
Whitby, North Yorkshire YO21 1DN
Harbour Office: 01947 602354 Marina: 01947 600165
Email: port.services@scarborough.gov.uk

VHF	Ch 11
ACCESS	HW±2

The only natural harbour between the Tees and the Humber, Whitby lies some 20 miles north of Scarborough on the River Esk. The historic town is said to date back as far as the Roman times, although it is better known for its abbey, which was founded over 1,300 years ago by King Oswy of Northumberland. Another place of interest is the Captain Cook Memorial Museum, a tribute to Whitby's greatest seaman.

A swing bridge divides the harbour into upper and lower sections, with the marina being in the Upper Harbour. The bridge opens on request (VHF Ch 11) each half hour for two hours either side of high water.

FACILITIES AT A GLANCE

Key
a Marina office
b Waste oil bin

HARTLEPOOL MARINA

Hartlepool Marina
Lock Office, Slake Terrace, Hartlepool, TS24 0RU
Tel: 01429 865744 www.hartlepool-marina.com
Email: enquiries@hartlepool-marina.com

VHF	Ch M, 80
ACCESS	

Hartlepool Marina is a modern boating facility on the NE coast now boasting an extensively refurbished North amenity block. Nestling on the Tees Valley the multi award winning marina promotes up to 500 pontoon berths alongside a variety of reputable services all surrounded by an exciting array of on water activities, a cosmopolitan mix of bistros, bars, restaurants, shopping, hotels and entertainment options.

Beautiful cruising waters and golden sands to the North and South of the marina approach which is channel dredged to CD and accessible via a lock: vessels wishing to enter should contact the Marina Lock Office on VHF Ch M/80 before arrival.

FACILITIES AT A GLANCE

Key
a Brittania House - amenity/cafe
b Neptune House - restaurant & bar
c Lock office and marina reception
d 220m complex with retail, restaurants and cafes
e Hartlepool Diving Club and HMS Abdiel sea cadet unit
f Fisherman's stores & landing area
g Office units
h Old West Quay Pub, restaurant and travel inn

SUNDERLAND MARINA

The Marine Activities Centre
Sunderland Marina, Sunderland, SR6 0PW
Tel: 0191 514 4721 Fax: 0191 514 1847
Email: mac.info@marineactivitiescentre.co.uk

VHF	Ch M
ACCESS	H24

Sunderland Marina sits on the the River Wear and is easily accessible through the outer breakwater at all states of tide. A short walk away from the city centre and beautiful beaches, facilities on site include the Snowgoose café and the Marina Vista Italian restaurant. Other pubs, restaurants, hotels and cafes are located nearby on the waterfront.

Sunderland Yacht Club is also located nearby and welcomes visiting yachtsman to its clubhouse.

FACILITIES AT A GLANCE

Key
a. Marina Reception
b. Aroma Essence - beautician
c. Snow Goose - Café
d. Hairdresser
e. Trattoria Due - Italian Restaurant
f. RNLI Lifeboat station
g. Hard stand compound
h. Refuse Compound

NORTH SHIELDS ROYAL QUAYS MARINA

North Shields Royal Quays Marina
Coble Dene Road, North Shields, NE29 6DU
Tel: 0191 272 8282 Fax: 0191 272 8288
www.quaymarinas.com
Email: royalquaysmarina@quaymarinas.com

VHF Ch 80
ACCESS H24

North Shields Royal Quays Marina enjoys close proximity to the entrance to the River Tyne, allowing easy access to and from the open sea as well as being ideally placed for cruising further up the Tyne. Just over an hour's motoring upstream brings you to the heart of the city of Newcastle, where you can tie up on a security controlled visitors' pontoon right outside the Pitcher and Piano Bar.

With a reputation for a high standard of service, the marina accommodates 300 pontoon berths, all of which are fully serviced. It is accessed via double sector lock gates which operate at all states of the tide and 24 hours a day.

FACILITIES AT A GLANCE

Key
a Marina office
   Toilets/showers
   Laundry
   Payphone
   Lock control
   Brokerage
b Refuse compound
c Chandlery & boat sales
d Access bridge & trolley park
e Boat sales and brokerage
f Bar/restaurant
g Waste oil disposal

ST PETERS MARINA

St Peters Marina, St Peters Basin
Newcastle upon Tyne, NE6 1HX
Tel: 0191 2654472 Fax: 0191 2762618
Email: info@stpetersmarina.co.uk
www.stpetersmarina.co.uk

VHF Ch 80
ACCESS HW±3

Nestling on the north bank of the River Tyne, some eight miles upstream of the river entrance, St Peters Marina is a fully serviced, 150-berth marina with the capacity to accommodate large vessels of up to 37m LOA. Situated on site is the Bascule Bar and Bistro, while a few minutes away is the centre of Newcastle. This city, along with its surrounding area, offers an array of interesting sites, among which are Hadrian's Wall, the award winning Gateshead Millennium Bridge and the Baltic Art Centre.

FACILITIES AT A GLANCE

ROYAL NORTHUMBERLAND YACHT CLUB

Royal Northumberland Yacht Club
South Harbour, Blyth, Northumberland, NE24 3PB
Tel: 01670 353636

VHF Ch 12
ACCESS H24

The Royal Northumberland Yacht Club is based at Blyth, a well-sheltered port that is accessible at all states of the tide and in all weathers except for when there is a combination of low water and strong south-easterly winds. The yacht club is a private club with some 75 pontoon berths and a further 20 fore and aft moorings.

Visitors usually berth on the north side of the most northerly pontoon and are welcome to use the clubship, HY *Tyne* – a wooden lightship built in 1880 which incorporates a bar, showers and toilet facilities. The club also controls its own boatyard, providing under cover and outside storage space plus a 20 ton boat hoist.

FACILITIES AT A GLANCE

AMBLE MARINA

Amble Marina Ltd
Amble, Northumberland, NE65 0YP
Tel: 01665 712168
Email: marina@amble.co.uk www.amble.co.uk

VHF Ch 80
ACCESS HW±4

Amble Marina is a small family run business offering peace, security and a countryside setting at the heart of the small town of Amble. It is located on the banks of the beautiful River Coquet and at the start of the Northumberland coast's area of outstanding natural beauty. Amble Marina has 250 fully serviced berths for residential and visiting yachts. Cafés, bars, restaurants and shops are all within a short walk.

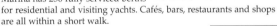

From your berth watch the sun rise at the harbour entrance and set behind Warkworth Castle or walk on wide, empty beaches. There is so much to do or if you prefer simply enjoy the peace, tranquillity and friendliness at Amble Marina.

FACILITIES AT A GLANCE

Key
a Marina office
b Toilets, showers, launderette, telephone and disabled facilities
c Reception pontoon
d Outboard engine sales and service
e Refuse bins and waste oil tank
f Security footgate 200m to town centre shops
g Trailer and cradle storage

SOUTH EAST SCOTLAND – Eyemouth to Rattray Head

Key to Marina Plans symbols

- Bottled gas
- Chandler
- Disabled facilities
- Electrical supply
- Electrical repairs
- Engine repairs
- First Aid
- Fresh Water
- Fuel - Diesel
- Fuel - Petrol
- Hardstanding/boatyard
- @ Internet Café
- Laundry facilities
- Lift-out facilities
- P Parking
- Pub/Restaurant
- Pump out
- Rigging service
- Sail repairs
- Shipwright
- Shop/Supermarket
- Showers
- Slipway
- WC Toilets
- Telephone
- Trolleys
- V Visitors berths
- Wi-Fi

Area 6 - South East Scotland

MARINAS
Telephone Numbers
VHF Channel
Access Times

Aberdeen
Stonehaven
Montrose
Arbroath Harbour
01241 872166
Ch 11, 16 HW±3
Arbroath
Tayport

Port Edgar Marina
0131 3313330
Ch 80 H24

Port Edgar
Granton Dunbar
Berwick-upon-Tweed

N

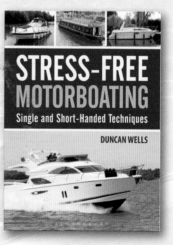

PORT EDGAR MARINA

Port Edgar Marina
Shore Road, South Queensferry
West Lothian, EH30 9SQ
Tel: 0131 331 3330 Fax: 0131 331 4878
Email: info@portedgar.co.uk

VHF	Ch 80
ACCESS	H24

Nestled between the iconic Forth Bridges, Edinburgh's 300 berth marina is the ideal base for exploring the Capital and the Forth coastline.

A short walk away is the historic High Street of Queensferry with a great selection of bars and restaurants. Situated 15 minutes away from Edinburgh Airport with easy road access, the secure site provides full boatyard facilities including a 25T slipway hoist, chandlery and café.

FACILITIES AT A GLANCE

Key
a Changing rooms and toilets
b Landing and trolleys
c Port Edgar Yacht Club
d Cafe
e Marina office
f Blue V
g Bosuns Locker

6

ARBROATH HARBOUR

Arbroath Harbour
Harbour Office, Arbroath, DD11 1PD
Tel: 01241 872166 Fax: 01241 878472
Email: harbourmaster@angus.gov.uk

VHF	Ch 11
ACCESS	HW±3

Arbroath harbour has 59 floating pontoon berths with security entrance which are serviced with electricity and fresh water to accommodate all types of leisure craft. Half height dock gates with walkway are located between the inner and outer harbours, which open and close at half tide, maintaining a minimum of 2.5m of water in the inner harbour.

The town of Arbroath offers a variety of social and sporting amenities to visiting crews and a number of quality pubs, restaurants, the famous twelfth century Abbey and Signal Tower Museum are located close to the harbour. Railway and bus stations are only 1km from the harbour with direct north and south connections.

FACILITIES AT A GLANCE

Key
a Signal Tower Museum
b Tourist Information
c RNLI
d Harbourmaster
e Harbour gates & walkway

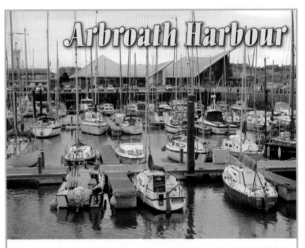

Arbroath Harbour

"Arbroath Harbour has 59 floating pontoon berths with security entrance which are serviced with electricity and fresh water to accommodate all types of leisure craft. Half height dock gates with a walkway are located between the inner and outer harbours, which open and close at half tide, maintaining a minimum of 2.5m of water in the inner harbour.

Other facilities in the harbour include free parking, toilets and showers, a crew room, fueling facilities, on site laundry facilities and boat builders' yard.

The town of Arbroath also offers a variety of social and sporting amenities to visiting crews and a number of quality pubs, restaurants, the famous twelfth century Abbey and Signal Tower Museum are located close to the harbour. The railway and bus stations are only 1km from the harbour with direct north and south connections."

Arbroath Harbour
Harbour Office . Arbroath . DD11 1PD

Harbour Master: Bruce Fleming
Tel: 01241 872166
Fax: 01241 878472
Email: harbourmaster@angus.gov.uk

Angus Council

NORTH EAST SCOTLAND – Peterhead to Cape Wrath & Orkney & Shetland Is

Key to Marina Plans symbols

Bottled gas		P	Parking
Chandler		✕	Pub/Restaurant
Disabled facilities			Pump out
Electrical supply			Rigging service
Electrical repairs			Sail repairs
Engine repairs			Shipwright
First Aid			Shop/Supermarket
Fresh Water			Showers
Fuel - Diesel			Slipway
Fuel - Petrol		WC	Toilets
Hardstanding/boatyard			Telephone
@ Internet Café			Trolleys
Laundry facilities		V	Visitors berths
Lift-out facilities			Wi-Fi

Area 7 - North East Scotland

MARINAS
Telephone Numbers
VHF Channel
Access Times

Kirkwall Marina
07810 465835
Ch 14 H24

Stromness Marina
07810 465825
Ch 14 H24

Orkney Islands

Shetland Islands

Scrabster

Wick Marina
01955 602030
Ch 14 H24

Wick

Helmsdale

Ullapool

Whitehills Marina
01261 861291
Ch 14 H4

Banff Harbour Marina
01261 815544
Ch 12 HW±4

Inverness Marina
07526 446348
Ch 12

Inverness

Buckie   Banff   Macduff

Findhorn

Peterhead

Peterhead Bay Marina
01779 477868
Ch 14 H24

Caley Marina
01463 236539
Ch 74 H24

Burghead

Lossiemouth 01343 813066
Ch 12 HW±4

Seaport Marina
01463 725500
Ch 74 HW±4

Nairn Marina
01667 456008
Ch 10 HW±2

Hopeman

Mallaig

Aberdeen

N

PETERHEAD BAY MARINA

Peterhead Port Authority
Harbour Office, West Pier, Peterhead, AB42 1DW
Tel: 01779 477868/483600
Email: marina@peterheadport.co.uk
www.peterheadport.co.uk

VHF	Ch 14
ACCESS	H24

Based in the south west corner of Peterhead Bay Harbour, the marina provides one of the finest marine leisure facilities in the east of Scotland. In addition to the services on site, there are plenty of nautical businesses in the vicinity, ranging from ship chandlers and electrical servicing to boat repairs and surveying.

Due to its easterly location, Peterhead affords an ideal stopover for those yachts heading to or from Scandinavia as well as for vessels making for the Caledonian Canal.

FACILITIES AT A GLANCE

BANFF HARBOUR MARINA

Banff Harbour Marina
Harbour Office, Quayside, Banff, Aberdeenshire, AB45 1HQ
Tel: 01261 815544 Fax: 01261 815544
Email: james.henderson@aberdeenshire.gov.uk

VHF	Ch 12
ACCESS	HW±4

A former fishing and cargo port now used as a recreational harbour. Banff offers excellent facilities to both regular and visiting users. The marina now provides 92 berths, of which 76 are serviced pontoon berths and 16 unserviced, traditional moorings, in one of the safest harbours on the NE coast of Scotland.

The outer basin offers adequate berthing for visitors and a tidal area for regulars.

The harbour is tidal with a sandy bottom. Movement during low water neaps is no problem for the shallow drafted boat.

FACILITIES AT A GLANCE

NAIRN MARINA

Nairn Marina
Nairn Harbour, Nairnshire, Scotland
Tel: 01667 456008 Fax: 01667 452877
Email: nairn.harbourmaster@virgin.net

VHF	Ch 10
ACCESS	HW±2

Nairn is a small town on the coast of the Moray Firth. Formerly renowned both as a fishing port and as a holiday resort dating back to Victorian times, it boasts miles of award-winning, sandy beaches, famous castles such as Cawdor, Brodie and Castle Stuart, and two championship golf courses. Other recreational activities include horse riding or walking through spectacular countryside.

The marina lies at the mouth of the River Nairn, entry to which should be avoided in strong N to NE winds. The approach is made from the NW at or around high water as the entrance is badly silted and dries out.

FACILITIES AT A GLANCE

WHITEHILLS MARINA

Whitehills Harbour Commissioners
Whitehills, Banffshire AB45 2NQ
Tel: 01261 861427
www.whitehillsharbour.co.uk
Email: harbourmaster@whitehillsharbour.co.uk

| VHF | Ch 14 |
| ACCESS | H24 |

Built in 1900, Whitehills is a Trust Harbour fully maintained and run by nine commissioners elected from the village. It was a thriving fishing port up until 1999, but due to changes in the fishing industry, was converted into a marina during 2000.

Photo by Colin Heggie

Three miles west of Banff Harbour the marina benefits from good tidal access – although there is just 1.5m at springs – comprising 38 serviced berths, with electricity, as well as eight non-serviced berths.

Whitehills village has a wide range of facilities including a convenience store, a cafe/fish & chip shop, two pubs, a fresh fish shop as well as two good restaurants. It is also a great base for families, with an excellent playpark at Blackpots, just a short walk from the harbour.

FACILITIES AT A GLANCE

Key
a   Harbour master
b   Fish market
c   Galley Restaurant

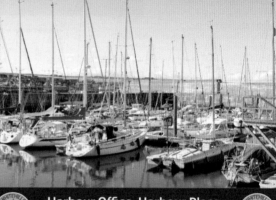
7

LOSSIEMOUTH MARINA

Marina Office
Lossiemouth, Moray, IV31 6PB
Tel: 01343 813066
Email: info@lossiemouthmarina.com

| VHF | Ch 12 |
| ACCESS | HW±4 |

Situated on the southern shore of the Moray Firth, Lossiemouth provides 95 serviced finger berths, 10 serviced dedicated visitor berths and 25 small boat berths. The Marina has full lift out facilities and a boat repair shed capable of handling 4 vessels at any one time with a marine engineer based on site.

The Marina is close to the town centre with a good range of shops and restaurants and also two championship golf courses. A regular bus service provides easy access to Elgin railway station (6 miles) and Inverness airport (35miles). Lossiemouth has miles of sandy beaches and is the ideal starting point for the Speyside Whisky trail.

FACILITIES AT A GLANCE

INVERNESS MARINA

Inverness Marina
Longman Drive, Inverness, IV1 1SU
Tel: 01463 220501
Email: info@invernessmarina.com
www.invernessmarina.com

VHF Ch 12
ACCESS H24

The marina is situated in the Inverness firth just one mile from the city centre and half a mile from the entrance to the Caledonian Canal. It has a minimum depth of 3m, 24hr access and 150 fully serviced berths. On site are a chandlery and services including rigging, engineering, electronics and boat repair.

Inverness has excellent transport networks to the rest of the UK and Europe and, as the gateway to the Highlands is a great location as a base for a touring golf courses, historic sites and the Whisky Trail. The marina is a perfect base for cruising Orkney, Shetland and Scandinavia.

FACILITIES AT A GLANCE

SEAPORT MARINA

Seaport Marina
Muirtown Wharf, Inverness, IV3 5LE
Tel: 01463 725500 Fax: 01463 710942
Email: enquiries@scottishcanals.co.uk
www.scottishcanals.co.uk

VHF Ch 74
ACCESS HW±4

Photo courtesy of D Edes

Seaport Marina is based at Muirtown Basin at the eastern entrance of the Caledonian Canal; a 60 mile coast-to-coast channel slicing through the majestic Great Glen. Only a 15 minute walk from the centre of Inverness, the Marina is an ideal base for visiting the Highlands.

There are shops and amenities nearby, as well as chandlers, boat repair services and a slipway. The marina also offers a variety of winter mooring packages and details of transit and short term licences, including the use of the Caledonian Canal can be found on the above website.

FACILITIES AT A GLANCE

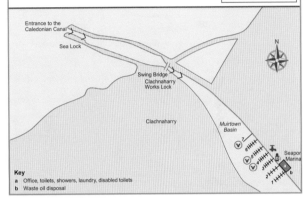

Key
a Office, toilets, showers, laundry, disabled toilets
b Waste oil disposal

CALEY MARINA

Caley Marina
Canal Road, Inverness, IV3 8NF
Tel: 01463 236539 Fax: 01463 238323
Email: info@caleymarina.com
www.caleymarina.com

VHF Ch 74
ACCESS H24

Caley Marina is a family run business based near Inverness. With the four flight Muirtown locks and the Kessock Bridge providing a dramatic backdrop, the marina runs alongside the Caledonian Canal which, opened in 1822, is regarded as one of the most spectacular waterways in Europe. Built as a short cut between the North Sea and the Atlantic Ocean, thus avoiding the potentially dangerous Pentland Firth on the north coast of Scotland, the canal is around 60 miles long and takes about three days to cruise from east to west. With the prevailing winds behind you, it takes slightly less time to cruise in the other direction.

FACILITIES AT A GLANCE

WICK MARINA

Wick Marina
Harbour Office, Wick, Caithness, KW1 5HA
Tel: 01955 602030 Fax: 01955 605936
Email: malcolm.bremner@wickharbour.co.uk

VHF Ch 14, 16
ACCESS H24

This is the most northerly marina on the British mainland and the last stop before the Orkney and Shetland Islands. Situated an easy five minutes walk from the town centre Wick Marina accommodates 70 fully serviced berths with all the support facilities expected in a modern marina including a boat lift.

This part of Scotland with its rugged coastline and rich history is easily accessible by air and a great starting point for cruising in the northern isles, Moray Firth, Caledonian Canal and Scandinavia, a comfortable 280-mile sail.

FACILITIES AT A GLANCE

KIRKWALL MARINA

Kirkwall Marina
Harbour Street, Kirkwall, Orkney, KW15
Tel: 07810 465835 Fax: 01856 871313
Email: info@orkneymarinas.co.uk www.orkneymarinas.co.uk

VHF	Ch 14
ACCESS	H24

The Orkney Isles, comprising 70 islands in total, provides some of the finest cruising grounds in Northern Europe. The Main Island, incorporating the ancient port of Kirkwall, is the largest, although 16 others have lively communities and are rich in archaeological sites as well as spectacular scenery and wildlife.

Kirkwall Marina, an all year facility, is located within the harbour and just yards from the visitor attractions of this ancient port. Local shops, hotels and restaurants are all within walking distance.

FACILITIES AT A GLANCE

STROMNESS MARINA

Stromness Marina
Stromness, Orkney, KW16
Tel: 07810 465825 Fax: 01856 871313
Email: info@orkneymarinas.co.uk
www.orkneymarinas.co.uk

VHF	Ch 14
ACCESS	H24

Stromness lies on the south-western tip of the Orkney Isles' Mainland. Sitting beneath the rocky ridge known as Brinkie's Brae, it is considered one of Orkney's major seaports, with sailors first attracted to the fine anchorage provided by the bay of Hamnavoe.

Stromness offers comprehensive facilities including a chandlery and repair services. Also on hand are an internet café, a fitness suite and swimming pool as well as car and bike hire.

FACILITIES AT A GLANCE

Key
a   Terminal building, Harbour Master's office
b   Cafe
c   Rope centre

NORTH WEST SCOTLAND – Cape Wrath to Crinan Canal

Key to Marina Plans symbols

	Bottled gas	**P**	Parking
	Chandler		Pub/Restaurant
	Disabled facilities		Pump out
	Electrical supply		Rigging service
	Electrical repairs		Sail repairs
	Engine repairs		Shipwright
+	First Aid		Shop/Supermarket
	Fresh Water		Showers
D	Fuel - Diesel		Slipway
P	Fuel - Petrol	**WC**	Toilets
	Hardstanding/boatyard		Telephone
@	Internet Café		Trolleys
	Laundry facilities	**V**	Visitors berths
	Lift-out facilities		Wi-Fi

Area 8 - North West Scotland

MARINAS
Telephone Numbers
VHF Channel
Access Times

N

Stornoway Marina
01851 702688
Ch 12 H24

Ullapool

Portree

Mallaig Marina
01687 462154
Ch 09/16 H24

Mallaig

Corpach

Tobermory
01688 302876
Ch 16/12 H24

Salen

Dunstaffnage Marina
01631 566555 Ch M H24

Oban Marina
01631 565333
Ch 80 H24

Craobh Haven Marina
01852 500222
Ch M, 80 H24

Melfort Pier
01852 200333

Ardfern Yacht Centre
01852 500247
Ch 80 H24

8

STORNOWAY MARINA

Stornoway Port Authority
Amity House, Esplanade Quay,
Stornoway, Isle of Lewis, HS1 2XS
Tel: 01851 702688 Fax: 01851 705714
Email: sypa@stornowayport.com

VHF Ch 12
ACCESS HW24

Stornoway Marina is sheltered and has easy access at all states of the tide and weather conditions. Vessels up to 24 metres in length and 3 metres draft can be accommodated.

The 80-berth marina provides a safe haven for island hoppers and days sailors. The marina is particularly popular as it is located right in the heart of the bustling town centre. Fresh water, electricity, wi-fi, toilet, shower and laundry facilities are available quayside for all visitors.

FACILITIES AT A GLANCE

MALLAIG MARINA

Mallaig Marina
East Bay, Mallaig, Inverness-shire, PH41 4QS
Tel: 07824 331031 Fax: 01687 462172
Email: info@mallaigharbourauthority.com

VHF Ch 09, 16
ACCESS H24

Mallaig Marina is truly the gateway to the Western Isles. Now in its seventh year of operation the 50-berth Marina – part funded by EC Sail West project – provides the ideal location for experiencing and exploring the magnificent sailing opportunities available on the West Coast of Scotland. Shower/toilet/laundrette facilities are housed in the Mallaig Marina Centre.

The village centre, only 300m from the Marina, offers plenty of options for the discerning diner, shopper or tourist. Fishing boats still operate from the busy harbour, ferries, large and small, sail to Skye/Small Isles/Inverie and there is the daily arrival of The Jacobite Steam Train.

FACILITIES AT A GLANCE

TOBERMORY

Tobermory Harbour Association
Taigh Solais, Tobermory, Isle of Mull, PA75 6NR
Mob: 07917 832497 Tel: 01688 302876
www.tobermoryharbour.co.uk
Email: jim.traynor@tobermoryharbour.co.uk

VHF Ch 16/12
ACCESS 0800–2000

Tobermory is the iconic Scottish west coast destination, a natural historic harbour and protected anchorage. The harbour pontoons are located on the west shore of Tobermory Bay with direct access to the town. There are also swinging moorings for hire – look for the blue moorings with white top.

Within easy walking distance, Tobermory offers an exceptional array of shops, bars and restaurants with fresh local produce. Mull Aquarium in the Harbour Building is Europe's first catch and release aquarium. Situated adjacent to the main car par, the pontoon has easy access to public transport to and from mainland ferry links or destination tours throughout the Island of Mull.

FACILITIES AT A GLANCE

DUNSTAFFNAGE MARINA

Dunstaffnage Marina Ltd
Dunbeg, by Oban, Argyll, PA37 1PX
Tel: 01631 566555 Fax: 01631 571044
Email: info@dunstaffnagemarina.com

VHF Ch M
ACCESS H24

Located just two to three miles north of Oban, Dunstaffnage Marina has been renovated to include an additional 36 fully serviced berths, a new breakwater providing shelter from NE'ly to E'ly winds and an increased amount of hard standing. Also on site is the Wide Mouthed Frog, offering a convivial bar, restaurant and accommodation with stunning views of the 13th century Dunstaffnage Castle.

The marina is perfectly placed to explore Scotland's west coast and Hebridean Islands. Only 10M NE up Loch Linnhe is Port Appin, while sailing 15M S, down the Firth of Lorne, brings you to Puldohran where you can walk to an ancient hostelry situated next to the C18 Bridge Over the Atlantic.

FACILITIES AT A GLANCE

OBAN MARINA

Oban Marina & Yacht Services Ltd
Isle of Kerrera, Oban, Argyll, PA34 4SX
Tel: 01631 565333
Email: info@obanmarina.com   www.obanmarina.com

VHF   Ch 80
ACCESS H24

Oban Marina is perfectly situated at the gateway to the Western Isles on the picturesque Isle of Kerrera. In sight of the town of Oban, it is a well serviced and popular marina offering access at all tides.

With 100 pontoons berths and 30 moorings, easily accessible diesel fuel berth, free wifi, shower block and laundry, this friendly, small marina offers visitors a warm welcome. A complimentary 2-hourly ferry service runs to and from Oban – must be pre-booked – where all the major facilities including restaurants, chandlery, banks and transport links are available.

FACILITIES AT A GLANCE

Key
a   Reception
b   Showers/toilets
c   Bar & grill
d   Shed

MELFORT PIER AND HARBOUR

Melfort Pier and Harbour
Kilmelford, by Oban, Argyll
Tel: 01852 200333
Email: melharbour@aol.com   www.mellowmelfort.com

VHF
ACCESS

Melfort Pier & Harbour is situated on the shores of Loch Melfort, one of the most peaceful lochs on the south west coast of Scotland. Overlooked by the Pass of Melfort and the Braes of Lorn, it lies approximately 18 miles north of Lochgilphead and 16 miles south of Oban. Its onsite facilities include showers, laundry, free Wi-Fi access and parking – pets welcome. Fuel, power and water are available at nearby Kilmelford Yacht Haven.

For those who want a few nights on dry land, Melfort Pier & Harbour offers lochside houses, each one equipped with a sauna, spa bath and balcony offering stunning views over the loch - available per night.

FACILITIES AT A GLANCE

CRAOBH MARINA

Craobh Marina
By Lochgilphead, Argyll, Scotland, PA31 8UA
Tel: 01852 500222 Fax: 01852 500252
Email: info@craobhmarina.co.uk
www.craobhmarina.co.uk

VHF   Ch M, 80
ACCESS H24

Craobh Marina is idyllically situated in the heart of Scotland's most sought after cruising grounds. Not only does Craobh offer ready access to a wonderful choice of scenic cruising throughout the western isles, the marina is conveniently close to Glasgow and its international transport hub.

Craobh Marina has been developed from a near perfect natural harbour, offering secure and sheltered berthing for up to 250 vessels to 40m LOA and with a draft of 4m. With an unusually deep and wide entrance Craobh Marina provides shelter and a warm welcome for all types of craft.

FACILITIES AT A GLANCE

Key
a   Holiday cottages
b   Village store
c   Bar
d   Gift shop
e   Waste oil
f   Boat shed
g   Marina office

ARDFERN YACHT CENTRE

Ardfern Yacht Centre
Ardfern, by Lochgilphead, Argyll, PA31 8QN
Tel: 01852 500247 Fax: 01852 500624
www.ardfernyacht.co.uk Email: office@ardfernyacht.co.uk

VHF   Ch 80
ACCESS H24

Developed around an old pier once frequented by steamers, Ardfern Yacht Centre lies at the head of Loch Craignish, one of Scotland's most sheltered and picturesque sea lochs. With several islands and protected anchorages nearby, Ardfern is an ideal place from which to cruise the west coast of Scotland and the Outer Hebrides.

The Yacht Centre comprises pontoon berths and swinging moorings as well as a workshop, boat storage and well-stocked chandlery, while a grocery store and eating places can be found in the village. Among the onshore activities available locally are horse riding, cycling, and walking.

FACILITIES AT A GLANCE

Key
a   Workshop
b   Showers, toilets and launderette
c   Chandlery and office

8

SOUTH WEST SCOTLAND – Crinan Canal to Mull of Galloway

Key to Marina Plans symbols

🛢	Bottled gas	🅿	Parking
	Chandler	✕	Pub/Restaurant
♿	Disabled facilities		Pump out
	Electrical supply		Rigging service
	Electrical repairs		Sail repairs
	Engine repairs	✗	Shipwright
✚	First Aid		Shop/Supermarket
	Fresh Water		Showers
D	Fuel - Diesel		Slipway
P	Fuel - Petrol	WC	Toilets
	Hardstanding/boatyard		Telephone
@	Internet Café		Trolleys
	Laundry facilities	Ⓥ	Visitors berths
	Lift-out facilities		Wi-Fi

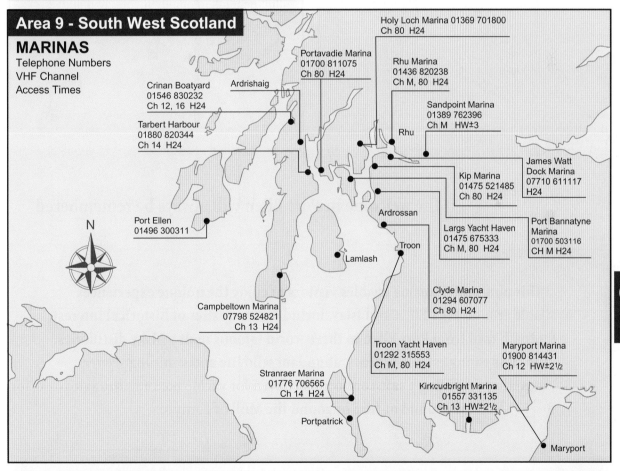

Area 9 - South West Scotland

MARINAS
Telephone Numbers
VHF Channel
Access Times

Holy Loch Marina 01369 701800
Ch 80 H24

Portavadie Marina
01700 811075
Ch 80 H24

Rhu Marina
01436 820238
Ch M, 80 H24

Crinan Boatyard
01546 830232
Ch 12, 16 H24

Ardrishaig

Sandpoint Marina
01389 762396
Ch M HW±3

Tarbert Harbour
01880 820344
Ch 14 H24

Rhu

James Watt
Dock Marina
07710 611117
H24

Kip Marina
01475 521485
Ch 80 H24

Port Ellen
01496 300311

Ardrossan

Port Bannatyne
Marina
01700 503116
CH M H24

Largs Yacht Haven
01475 675333
Ch M, 80 H24

Troon

Lamlash

Clyde Marina
01294 607077
Ch 80 H24

Campbeltown Marina
07798 524821
Ch 13 H24

Troon Yacht Haven
01292 315553
Ch M, 80 H24

Maryport Marina
01900 814431
Ch 12 HW±2½

Stranraer Marina
01776 706565
Ch 14 H24

Kirkcudbright Marina
01557 331135
Ch 13 HW±2½

Portpatrick

Maryport

N

PORT ELLEN MARINA

Port Ellen Marina
Port Ellen, Islay, Argyll, PA42 7DB
Tel: 07464 151200 www.portellenmarina.co.uk
Email: portellenmarina@outlook.com

VHF	
ACCESS	H24

A safe and relaxed marina for visitors to the *Malt Whisky Island*. There are seven classic distilleries and yet another still (private) to start production soon. If you are planning a cruise to the north then superb sailing will take you onward via Craighouse on Jura. Meeting guests or short term storage is trouble free with the excellent air and ferry services connecting to Glasgow. Once on Islay you will be tempted to extend your stay so be warned, check www.portellenmarina.com for the many reasons to visit, from golf to music.

FACILITIES AT A GLANCE

Key
a Bank
b Hotel

Local boats only

Dredged to 3m 2006

Stay inside green markers

CRINAN BOATYARD

Crinan Boatyard Ltd
Crinan, Lochgilphead, Argyll, PA31 8SW
Tel: 01546 830232 Fax: 01546 830281
Email: info@crinanboatyard.co.uk
www.crinanboatyard.co.uk

VHF	Ch 12, 16
ACCESS	H24

Situated at the westerly entrance of the scenic Crinan Canal, Crinan Boatyard offers swinging moorings nightly or longer term, a fuelling/loading berth, a well stocked Chandlery, heads, showers, laundry and an experienced work force for repair work all on site. A hotel and coffee shop, just a short walk away at the Canal basin, great walking and the historic Kilmartin Glen close by are some of the attractions on shore.

The nearby town of Lochgilphead 7 miles away offers shopping and good travel links to Glasgow (85 miles) and its International Airport.

FACILITIES AT A GLANCE

Eilean da Mhéin

Small craft moorings

R 15–17
R 14–11
G 5–11
R 18–21
R 22–24
R 25–27
R 1–10
Y 7–9
B 6–8
W 6–8

Crinan Boatyard

WC

Hotel

Lock

Crinan Canal

N

TARBERT HARBOUR

Tarbert Harbour Authority
Harbour Office, Garval Road, Tarbert, Argyll, PA29 6TR
Tel: 01880 820344
Email: info@tarbertharbour.co.uk

VHF	Ch 14
ACCESS	H24

East Loch Tarbert is situated on the western shores of Loch Fyne. The naturally sheltered harbour is accessible through an easily navigated narrow entrance, and is a prefect stopping point for those heading north to the Crinan Canal.

The pontoons can accommodate up to 100 visiting vessels of various sizes, with fresh water, electricity and wi-fi available FOC. Toilet, shower and laundry facilities are accessible 24/7, and the unique recreation area and community marquee are available to use - perfect for families, gatherings and musters. The marina pontoons are situated at the heart of the heritage village of Tarbert, which boasts a busy festival calendar and offers a wide range of amenities.

FACILITIES AT A GLANCE

PORT BANNATYNE MARINA

Port Bannatyne Marina
Marine Road, Port Bannatyne, PA20 0LT
Tel: 01700 503116 Mobile: 07711 319992
Email: portbannatynemarina@btconnect.com

VHF	Ch M
ACCESS	H24

Nestled in the bay at Port Bannatyne on the Isle of Bute, the marina is set in breathtakingly beautiful surroundings. The shore facilities include toilets and showers, lifting and winter storage and all boat repairs. Free wi-fi is available throughout the marina. Protected by a breakwater and accessible H24 the marina is dredged to –2.4m CD.

The village of Port Bannatyne offers a Post Office for essential groceries and three pubs. There are frequent bus services to both Rothesay and Ettrick Bay where a walk along a beautiful beach with amazing views can be completed with either a meal or tea and cake at the beach side restaurant.

FACILITIES AT A GLANCE

PORTAVADIE MARINA

Portavadie Marina
Portavadie, Loch Fyne, Argyll, PA21 2DA
Tel: 01700 811075 Fax: 01700 811074
Email: info@portavadiemarina.com

VHF	Ch 80
ACCESS	H24

Portavadie Marina offers deep and sheltered berthing to residential and visiting boats in an area renowned for its superb cruising waters. Situated on the east side of Loch Fyne in close proximity to several islands and the famous Kyles of Bute, Portavadie is within easy sailing distance of the Crinan Canal, giving access to the Inner and Outer Hebrides. The marina has 230 berths 60 of which are reserved for visitors, plus comprehensive on shore facilities, including a choice of restaurants, bars and self catering accommodation. There is also a shop and small chandlery overlooking the marina, a dedicated fuel berth for petrol and diesel and bike hire.

This unspoiled area of Argyll which is less than two hours by road from Glasgow offers an ideal base for boat owners looking for a safe and secure haven.

FACILITIES AT A GLANCE

Key
a Reception, offices, conference room, open deck viewing platform
b Bar & restaurant
c WC, Showers & laundry
d Luxury self-catering apartments
e Leisure complex
Berthing
A-H pontoons
Odd numbers on the north side
Even numbers on the south side
Numbers start at the inner end

Visitor S pontoon
Mostly alongside with just S46 to S60 at the access bridge remaining

Visitor N pontoon
Runs from N1 at the north end to N19 at the access bridge

CAMPBELTOWN MARINA

Campbeltown Marina Ltd
Dubh Artach, Roading, Campbeltown, PA28 6LU
Tel: 07798 524821
Email: campbeltownmarina@btinternet.com

VHF	Ch 13
ACCESS	H24

Campbeltown Marina is a brand new facility opened in June 2015 and is situated in the town centre at the head of the deep, sheltered waters of Campbeltown Loch on the SE aspect of the Kintyre Peninsula. It is within easy reach of the Antrim Coast, Ayrshire and the Upper Clyde. Diesel is available at the Old Quay and gas is across the road. Petrol can be bought a 5-minute walk away and a well stocked chandlery is situated in the town centre.

Campbeltown is the perfect getaway destination with plenty to offer the whole family. Golf, cycling and walking routes, modern swimming pool and horse riding are some of the activities on offer. Situated directly in the town centre there is a wide choice of shops, cafes, bars, restaurants and supermarkets within easy walking distance.

FACILITIES AT A GLANCE

9

HOLY LOCH MARINA

Holy Loch Marina
Rankin's Brae, Sandbank, Dunoon, PA23 8FE
Tel: 01369 701800
Email: info@holylochmarina.co.uk www.holylochmarina.co.uk

VHF	Ch 80
ACCESS	H24

Holy Loch Marina, the marine gateway to Loch Lomond and the Trossachs National Park, lies on the south shore of the loch, roughly half a mile west of Lazaretto Point. Holy Loch is among the Clyde's most beautiful natural harbours and, besides being a peaceful location, offers an abundance of wildlife, places of local historical interest as well as excellent walking and cycling through the Argyll Forest Park. The marina can be entered in all weather conditions and is within easy sailing distance of Loch Long and Upper Firth.

FACILITIES AT A GLANCE

Key
a Office/Harbourmaster
b Boat storage
c Holy Loch Sailing Club
d Pier

Sandbank Village

ARDFERN YACHT CENTRE

Located at the head of Loch Craignish, we offer fully serviced pontoon berths, swinging moorings, a comprehensively stocked chandlery and full workshop repair and maintenance facilities all within a traditional west coast village setting.

56° 10.95'N   5° 31.80'W
Admiralty Chart No. 2326 & Imray Chart No. C65

Tel:01852 500247
www.ardfernyacht.co.uk

RHU MARINA

Rhu Marina
Rhu, Dunbartonshire, G84 8LH
Tel: 01436 820238 Fax: 01436 821039
Email: rhumarina@quaymarinas.com

VHF	Ch M, 80
ACCESS	H24

Located on the north shore of the Clyde Estuary, Rhu Marina is accessible at all states of the tide and can accommodate yachts up to 24m in length. It also operates 40 swinging moorings in the bay adjacent to the marina, with a ferry service provided.

Within easy walking distance of the marina is Rhu village, a conservation village incorporating a few shops, a pub and the beautiful Glenarn Gardens as well as the Royal Northern & Clyde Yacht Club. A mile or two to the east lies the holiday town of Helensburgh, renowned for its attractive architecture and elegant parks and gardens, while Glasgow city is just 25 miles away and can be easily reached by train.

FACILITIES AT A GLANCE

SANDPOINT MARINA

Sandpoint Marina Ltd
Sandpoint, Woodyard Road, Dumbarton, G82 4BG
Tel: 01389 762396 Fax: 01389 732605
Email: sales@sandpoint-marina.co.uk
www.sandpoint-marina.co.uk

VHF	
ACCESS	HW±3

Lying on the north bank of the Clyde estuary on the opposite side of the River Leven from Dumbarton Castle, Sandpoint Marina provides easy access to some of the most stunning cruising grounds in the United Kingdom. It is an independently run marina, offering a professional yet personal service to every boat owner. Among the facilities to hand are an on site chandlery, storage areas, a 40 ton travel hoist and 20 individual workshop units.

Within a 20-minute drive of Glasgow city centre, the marina is situated close to the shores of Loch Lomond, the largest fresh water loch in Britain.

FACILITIES AT A GLANCE

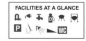

Key
a Marina office
b Workshops
c Undercover storage shed
d Chandler
e Undercover storage sheds

KIP MARINA

Kip Marina, The Yacht Harbour
Inverkip, Renfrewshire, Scotland, PA16 0AS
Tel: 01475 521485 Fax: 01475 568410
www.kipmarina.co.uk Email: info@kipmarina.co.uk

VHF | Ch 80
ACCESS | H24

Inverkip is a small village which lies on the south shores of the River Kip as it enters the Firth of Clyde. Once established for fishing, smuggling and, in the 17th century, witch-hunts, it became a seaside resort in the 1860s as a result of the installation of the railway. Today it is a yachting centre, boasting a state-of-the-art marina with over 600 berths and full boatyard facilities. With the capacity to accommodate yachts of up to 23m LOA, Kip Marina offers direct road and rail access to Glasgow and its international airport, therefore making it an ideal location for either a winter lay up or crew changeover.

FACILITIES AT A GLANCE

Key
a   Boat sales, chandlery and reception
b   Workshop and contractors
c   Chartroom bar and restaurant

JAMES WATT DOCK MARINA

James Watt Dock Marina
East Hamilton Street
Greenock, Renfrewshire, PA15 2TD
Tel: 01475 729838
www.jwdmarina.co.uk Email: info@jwdmarina.co.uk

VHF | 80
ACCESS | H24

Based in the historic James Watt Dock alongside the stunning Victorian Sugar Shed, this new marina opened in May 2011 and is the first step in establishing an exciting new River Clyde waterfront development only 23 miles from Glasgow and 15 miles from the airport. James Watt Dock will have all the usual amenities expected of a modern marina.

Within easy reach of Greenock's cinema, pool, ice rink, restaurants and shops, and with nearby transport connections, the marina will be a great location for both visitors and regular berthers.

FACILITIES AT A GLANCE

Key
a   Marina office

9

LARGS YACHT HAVEN

Largs Yacht Haven Ltd
Irvine Road, Largs, Ayrshire, KA30 8EZ
Tel: 01475 675333
Email: largs@yachthavens.com www.yachthavens.com

VHF | Ch M, 80
ACCESS | H24

Largs Yacht Haven offers a superb location among lochs and islands, with numerous fishing villages and harbours nearby. Sheltered cruising can be enjoyed in the inner Clyde, while the west coast and Ireland are only a day's sail away. With a stunning backdrop of the Scottish mountains, Largs incorporates 700 fully serviced berths and provides a range of on site facilities including chandlers, sailmakers, divers, engineers, shops, restaurants and club.

A 20-minute coastal walk brings you to the town of Largs, which has all the usual amenities as well as good road and rail connections to Glasgow.

FACILITIES AT A GLANCE

Key
a   Reception
b   Restaurant
c   Largs Sailing Club
d   Shops, offices, service companies
e   Sail loft
f   Boat repair shed
g   Boat sales

CLYDE MARINA

Clyde Marina Ltd
The Harbour, Ardrossan, Ayrshire, KA22 8DB
Tel: 01294 607077
www.clydemarina.com Email: info@clydemarina.com

VHF | Ch 80
ACCESS | H24

Situated on the Clyde Coast between Irvine and Largs, Clyde Marina is Scotland's third largest marina and boatyard. It is set in a landscaped environment boasting a 50T hoist and active boat sales. A deep draft marina berthing vessels up to 30m LOA, draft up to 5m. Peviously accommodated vessels include tall ships and Whitbread 60s plus a variety of sail and power craft. Fully serviced pontoons plus all the yard facilities you would expect from a leading marina including boatyard and boatshed for repairs or storage. Good road and rail connections and only 30 minutes from Glasgow and Prestwick airports.

FACILITIES AT A GLANCE

key
a   Winter storage shed
b   Secure winter hard standing area

Montgomerie Pier
Winton Pier
Ferry Basin
Cal-Mac Arran Ferry Terminal
Outer Basin
Ardrossan
Tower
Storm Gate
Marina Office
Berth Holders
Numbering starts from shoreside
For pontoons B–E from shoreside:
Even nos - starboard side of pontoon
Odd nos - port side of pontoon

TROON YACHT HAVEN

Troon Yacht Haven Ltd
The Harbour, Troon, Ayrshire, KA10 6DJ
Tel: 01292 315553
Email: troon@yachthavens.com
www.yachthavens.com

⚓⚓⚓

VHF	Ch 80
ACCESS	H24

Troon Yacht Haven, situated on the Southern Clyde Estuary, benefits from deep water at all states of the tide. Tucked away in the harbour of Troon, it is well sheltered and within easy access of the town centre.

There are plenty of cruising opportunities to be had from here, whether it be hopping across to the Isle of Arran, with its peaceful anchorages and mountain walks, sailing round the Mull or through the Crinan Canal to the Western Isles, or heading for the sheltered waters of the Clyde.

FACILITIES AT A GLANCE

Key
a   Main building
    Toilets
    Showers
    Baths
    Laundry
b   Marina office

STRANRAER MARINA

Stranraer Marina
Militia House, English Street, Dumfries, DG1 2HR
Tel: 01776 706565   Mob: 07734 073421
Email: dgfirst-harbouradministration@dumgal.gov.uk

VHF	Ch 14
ACCESS	H24

Stranraer marina is at the southern end of beautiful Loch Ryan with H24 access and modern facilities. The town centre with full facilities is only a short walk from the marina. A new 30T boat crane, boat transporter and hard standing proving very popular. The marina provides an excellent base for touring the picturesque Mull of Galloway.

It should be noted that the marina is exposed in strong N winds. Two ferry terminals are located on the E side of the loch approximately 6M N of the marina and extra care should be taken in this area.

FACILITIES AT A GLANCE

KIRKCUDBRIGHT MARINA

Kirkcudbright Marina
Militia House, English Street, Dumfries, DG1 2HR
Tel: 01557 331135   Mob: 07709 479663
Email: dgfirst-harbouradministration@dumgal.gov.uk

VHF	Ch 16, 73
ACCESS	HW±2.5

A very well sheltered picturesque marina accessed HW+/-2.5 hrs via a 3.5 mile long, narrow channel that is well marked and lit, contact should be made with Range Safety vessel 'Gallovidian' prior to approach. Limited visitors berths so vessels should contact the harbour master in advance.

The marina is only 250m from the centre of Kirkcudbright, an historic 'artist's' town where visitors may enjoy a wide range of facilities and tourist attractions including castle, museum, tollbooth, art galleries and traditional shops. There is a superb programme of summer festivities.

FACILITIES AT A GLANCE

MARYPORT MARINA

Maryport Development Ltd
Marine Road, Maryport, Cumbria, CA15 8AY
Tel: 01900 814431
www.maryportmarina.com
Email: enquires@maryportmarina.com

VHF	Ch 12,16
ACCESS	HW±2.5

Maryport Marina is located in the historic Senhouse Dock, which was originally built for sailing clippers in the late 19th century. The old stone harbour walls provide good shelter to the 190 berths from the prevailing south westerlies.

Maryport town centre and its shops, pubs and other amenities is within easy walking distance from the marina. Maryport a perfect location from which to explore the west coast of Scotland as well as the Isle of Man and the Galloway Coast. For those who wish to venture inland, then the Lake District is only seven miles away.

FACILITIES AT A GLANCE

Key
a   Marina Office
b   Boat repair facility
c   Coastguard building
d   Fish handling building
e   Wet fish shop
f   Aquarium, cafe
g   Play area
h   Amenity block

9

NW ENGLAND, ISLE OF MAN & N WALES – Mull of Galloway to Bardsey Is

Reeds PDF ebooks

In response to popular demand, all the Reeds Almanacs are now available as searchable, highlightable PDF ebooks. (All ebooks incorporate the Marina Guide.)

Visit www.reedsnauticalalmanac.co.uk for further information

Key to Marina Plans symbols

Bottled gas		Parking	
Chandler		Pub/Restaurant	
Disabled facilities		Pump out	
Electrical supply		Rigging service	
Electrical repairs		Sail repairs	
Engine repairs		Shipwright	
First Aid		Shop/Supermarket	
Fresh Water		Showers	
Fuel - Diesel		Slipway	
Fuel - Petrol		Toilets	
Hardstanding/boatyard		Telephone	
Internet Café		Trolleys	
Laundry facilities		Visitors berths	
Lift-out facilities		Wi-Fi	

Area 10 - North West England & Wales

MARINAS
Telephone Numbers
VHF Channel
Access Times

Workington

Whitehaven Marina
01946 692435
Ch 12 HW±4

Whitehaven

ENGLAND

Isle of Man

Ramsey

Peel Marina
01624 842338
Ch 12 HW±2

Peel

Douglas
01624 867543
Ch 12 HW±2

Glasson Basin Marina
01524 751491
Ch 69 HW-1 to HW

Walney Is

Ronaldsway

Port
St Mary

Glasson Dock

Fleetwood
Haven Marina
01253 879062
Ch 12 HW±1½

Fleetwood

Blackpool

N

Preston

Preston Marina
01772 733595
Ch 80 HW±2

Liverpool

Liverpool Marina
0151 707 6777
Ch M HW±2

Holyhead

Anglesey

Holyhead Marina
01407 764242
Ch M, M1 H24

Conwy

Deganwy Quays Marina
01492 576888
Ch 80 HW±2

Menai Strait

Conwy Marina
01492 593000
Ch 80 LW±3½

Pwllheli Marina
01758 701219
Ch 80 H24

Porthmadog

Pwllheli

WALES

Abersoch

Barmouth

WHITEHAVEN MARINA

Whitehaven Marina Ltd
Harbour Office, Bulwark Quay, Whitehaven, Cumbria, CA28 7HS
Tel: 01946 692435
Email: enquiries@whitehavenmarina.co.uk
www.whitehavenmarina.co.uk

VHF	Ch 12
ACCESS	HW±4

Whitehaven Marina can be found at the south-western entrance to the Solway Firth, providing a strategic departure point for those yachts heading for the Isle of Man, Ireland or Southern Scotland. The harbour is one of the more accessible ports of refuge in NW England, affording a safe entry in most weathers. The approach channel across the outer harbour is dredged to about 1.0m above chart datum, allowing entry into the inner harbour via a sea lock at around HW±4. Over 100 new walk ashore berths were installed in 2013.

Conveniently situated for visiting the Lake District, Whitehaven is an attractive Georgian town, renowned in the C18 for its rum and slave imports.

FACILITIES AT A GLANCE

BWML GLASSON BASIN MARINA

BWML, Glasson Basin Marina
School Lane, Glasson Dock, Lancaster, LA2 0AW
Tel: 01524 751491 Fax: 01524 752626
Email: barnaby.hayward@bwml.co.uk
www.bwml.co.uk

VHF	Ch 69
ACCESS	HW-1 to HW

Glasson Basin Marina lies on the River Lune, west of Sunderland Point. Access is via the outer dock which opens 45 minutes before HW. Liverpool and thence via BWB lock into the inner basin. It is recommended to leave Lune No. 1 Buoy approx 1.5 hrs before HW. Contact the dock on Channel 69. The Marina can only be contacted by telephone. All the necessary requirements can be found either on site or within easy reach of Glasson Dock, including boat, rigging and sail repair services as well as a launderette, ablution facilities, shops and restaurants.

FACILITIES AT A GLANCE

Key
a   Marina office
b   Glasson Sailing Club
c   Harbour House

BWML™

Glasson Basin Marina

Lancashire

Fully serviced pontoons

Visitors welcome

Comprehensive chandlery

Fully serviced boatyard and workshops with 50 tonne hoist

Professional workshop services including rigging and spray painting

We are a proud agent of Z Spars UK for yacht masts and rigging requirements

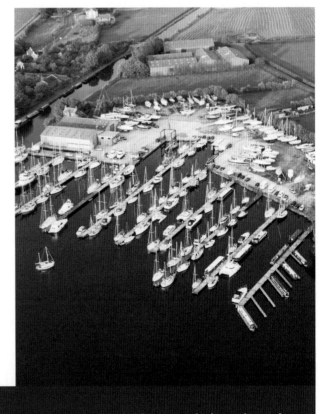

01524 751491   **bwml.co.uk**   **barnaby.hayward@bwml.co.uk**

DOUGLAS MARINA

Douglas Marina
Sea Terminal Building, Douglas, IM1 2RF
Tel: 01624 686627 Fax: 01624 686612
www.gov.im/harbours/
Email: enquiries.harboursdoi@gov.im

VHF	Ch 12, 16
ACCESS	HW±2

Douglas Marina is accessible HW±2 with 2.5m retained at LW. The depth of water inside the marina can vary so please advise draft. The maximum length accommodated on pontoons is 15m. Wall berths are also available. Douglas Marina Operations Centre requires clearance for entrance to the outer harbour due to commercial traffic. Please inform arrival on VHF Ch 12 10 minutes before port entry.

The marina has many facilities including electricity, fresh water, diesel, lift out, drying pad, gas, chandlery and showers/toilet facilities.

Douglas Marina is in the heart of the Isle of Man's capital so all local amenities and excellent transport links such as the Steam Railway are just a short walk away.

FACILITIES AT A GLANCE

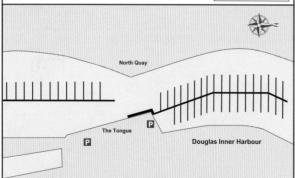

North Quay

The Tongue

Douglas Inner Harbour

PEEL MARINA

Peel Marina
The Harbour Office, East Quay, Peel, IM5 1AR
Tel: 01624 842338 Fax: 01624 843610
www.gov.im/harbours/
Email: harbours@gov.im

VHF	Ch 12
ACCESS	HW±2

The Inner harbour has provision on pontoons for visiting vessels up 15m with rafting also available on the harbour walls. Access is available HW±2hrs with a maximum draft of 2.5m retained at low water but this does vary so please advise vessel dimensions on approach via VHF Ch 12.

Fresh water and electricity are available on all pontoon and some wall berths. Diesel fuel is available at the quayside with petrol sourced from a local forecourt in Peel.

Peel is a lovely active fishing port with many local amenities and a beautiful castle overlooking the harbour.

FACILITIES AT A GLANCE

East Quay

FLEETWOOD HAVEN MARINA

Fleetwood Haven Marina
c/o ABP, Port & Marina Office, Fleetwood, FY7 8BP
Tel: 01253 879062 Fax: 01253 879063
Email: fleetwoodhaven@abports.co.uk

VHF	Ch 12
ACCESS	HW±1.5

Fleetwood Haven Marina provides a good location from which to cruise Morecambe Bay and the Irish Sea. To the north west is the Isle of Man, the north is the Solway Firth and the Clyde Estuary, while to the south west is Conwy, the Menai Straits and Holyhead.

Tucked away in a protected dock which dates to 1835, the marina has 266 full service berths and offers extensive facilities including a 75-tonne boat hoist, laundry and a first class shower/bathroom block.

Call Fleetwood Dock Radio on VHF Channel 12 (Tel 01253 872351) for permission to enter the dock channel.

FACILITIES AT A GLANCE

trans europe

Wyre Dock

See inset of marina extension above

Fish Dock

PRESTON MARINA

Preston Marine Services Ltd
The Boathouse, Navigation Way, Preston, PR2 2YP
Tel: 01772 733595 Fax: 01772 731881
Email: info@prestonmarina.co.uk www.prestonmarina.co.uk

VHF	Ch 80
ACCESS	HW±2

Preston Marina forms part of the comprehensive Riversway Docklands development, meeting all the demands of modern day boat owners. With the docks' history dating back over 100 years, today the marina comprises 40 acres of fully serviced pontoon berths sheltered behind the refurbished original lock gates.

Lying 15 miles up the River Ribble, which itself is an interesting cruising ground with an abundance of wildlife, Preston is well placed for sailing to parts of Scotland, Ireland or Wales. The Docklands development includes a wide choice of restaurants, shops and cinemas as well as being in easy reach of all the cultural and leisure facilities provided by a large town.

FACILITIES AT A GLANCE

Key
a Riverway control building
b Marina HQ
c Pub/restaurant

LIVERPOOL MARINA

Liverpool Marina
Coburg Wharf, Sefton Street, Liverpool, L3 4BP
Tel: 0151 707 6777 Fax: 0151 707 6770
Email: mail@liverpoolmarina.co.uk

VHF	Ch M
ACCESS	HW±2

Liverpool Marina is ideally situated for yachtsmen wishing to cruise the Irish Sea. Access is through a computerised lock that opens two and a half hours either side of high water between 0600 and 2200 daily. Once in the marina, you can enjoy the benefits of the facilities on offer, including a first class club bar and restaurant.

Liverpool is now a thriving cosmopolitan city, with attractions ranging from numerous bars and restaurants to museums, art galleries and the Beatles Story.

FACILITIES AT A GLANCE

Key
a Clubhouse bar, toilets and showers
b Fuel berth
c Hardstanding yard

CONWY MARINA

Conwy Marina
Conwy, LL32 8EP
Tel: 01492 593000
Email: jroberts@quaymarinas.com
www.quaymarinas.com

VHF	Ch 80
ACCESS	LW±3.5

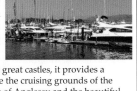

Situated in an area of outstanding natural beauty, with the Mountains of Snowdonia National Park providing a stunning backdrop, Conwy is the first purpose-built marina to be developed on the north coast of Wales. Enjoying a unique site next to the 13th century Conwy Castle, the third of Edward I's great castles, it provides a convenient base from which to explore the cruising grounds of the North Wales coast. The unspoilt coves of Anglesey and the beautiful Menai Straits prove a popular destination, while further afield are the Lleyn Peninsula and the Islands of Bardsey and Tudwells. The marina incorporates about 500 fully serviced berths which are accessible through a barrier gate between half tide and high water.

FACILITIES AT A GLANCE

Key
a Main services
    Marina office
    Network Yacht Brokers
    Seawake
b Toilets/showers
    Laundry store
    Network Chandlery
    The Mulberry Stores
    Rowlands Marine Electronics

DEGANWY MARINA

Deganwy Marina
Deganwy, Conwy, LL31 9DJ
Tel: 01492 576888 Fax: 01492 580066
Email: enquiries@deganwymarina.co.uk
www.deganwymarina.co.uk

VHF	Ch 80
ACCESS	HW±3

Deganwy Marina is located in the centre of the north Wales coastline on the estuary of the Conwy River and sits between the river and the small town of Deganwy with the beautiful backdrop of the Vardre hills. The views from the marina across the Conwy River are truly outstanding with the medieval walled town and Castle of Conwy outlined against the foothills of the Snowdonia National Park.

Deganwy Marina has 165 fully serviced berths, which are accessed via a tidal gate between half tide and high water.

FACILITIES AT A GLANCE

HOLYHEAD MARINA

Holyhead Marina Ltd
Newry Beach, Holyhead, Gwynedd, LL65 1YA
Tel: 01407 764242 Fax: 01407 769152
Email: info@holyheadmarina.co.uk

VHF	Ch M
ACCESS	H24

One of the few natural deep water harbours on the Welsh coast, Anglesey is conveniently placed as a first port of call if heading to North Wales from the North, South or West. Its marina at Holyhead, accessible at all states of the tide, is sheltered by Holyhead Mountain as well as an enormous harbour breakwater and extensive floating breakwaters, therefore offering good protection from all directions.

Anglesey boasts numerous picturesque anchorages and beaches in addition to striking views over Snowdonia, while only a tide or two away are the Isle of Man and Eire.

FACILITIES AT A GLANCE

Key
a Marina services
b Marina boatyard
c ILB
d Holyhead Sailing Club
e Lifeboat berth
f Fuel pontoon

Note:
DO NOT use visitors berths in north easterly winds

PWLLHELI MARINA

Pwllheli Marina
Glan Don, Pwllheli, North Wales, LL53 5YT
Tel: 01758 701219 Fax: 01758 701443
Email: hafanpwllheli@gwynedd.llwy.cymru

VHF	Ch 80
ACCESS	

Pwllheli is an old Welsh market town providing the gateway to the Llyn Peninsula, which stretches out as far as Bardsey Island to form an 'Area of Outstanding Natural Beauty'. Enjoying the spectacular backdrop of the Snowdonia Mountains, Pwllheli's numerous attractions include an open-air market every Wednesday, 'Neuadd Dwyfor', offering a mix of live theatre and latest films, and beautiful beaches.

Pwllheli Marina is situated on the south side of the Llyn Peninsula. One of Wales' finest marinas and sailing centres, it has over 400 pontoon berths and excellent onshore facilities.

FACILITIES AT A GLANCE

Key
a Marina offices
   Toilets
   Showers
   Baby change
   Launderette
b Domestic refuse point
c Short stay boat park
d Pwllheli sailing club
e Chandlery
f Events pontoons

SOUTH WALES & BRISTOL CHANNEL – Bardsey Island to Land's End

Reeds PDF ebooks

In response to popular demand, all the Reeds Almanacs are now available as searchable, highlightable PDF ebooks. (All ebooks incorporate the Marina Guide.)

Visit www.reedsnauticalalmanac.co.uk for further information

Key to Marina Plans symbols

Bottled gas		P	Parking
Chandler			Pub/Restaurant
Disabled facilities			Pump out
Electrical supply			Rigging service
Electrical repairs			Sail repairs
Engine repairs			Shipwright
First Aid			Shop/Supermarket
Fresh Water			Showers
Fuel - Diesel			Slipway
Fuel - Petrol		WC	Toilets
Hardstanding/boatyard			Telephone
@	Internet Café		Trolleys
Laundry facilities		V	Visitors berths
Lift-out facilities			Wi-Fi

Area 11 - South Wales & Bristol Channel

MARINAS
Telephone Numbers
VHF Channel
Access Times

Barmouth

Aberdovey

Aberystwyth
01970 611422
Ch 80 HW±2
Aberystwyth

WALES

Bristol Marina
0117 921 3198
Ch 80 HW-3 to HW

Sharpness Marina
01453 811476
Ch 13 HW-2 to HW

Fishguard

Milford Haven

Burry Port

Swansea

Penarth Quay Marina
02920 705021
Ch 80 H24

Milford Marina
01646 696312
Ch 14, M H24

Tenby

Swansea Marina
01792 470310
Ch 80 HW±4½

Cardiff

Barry

Bristol

Neyland Yacht Haven
01646 601601
Ch M, 80 H24

Bristol Channel

Cardiff Marina
02920 396078
Ch 27 H24

Portishead Quay Marina
01275 841941
Ch 80 HW±4

Ilfracombe

Watchet

Burnham-on-Sea

Appledore

N

Padstow Harbour
01841 532239
Ch 12 HW±2

Padstow

Land's End

Isles of Scilly   Round Is

ABERYSTWYTH MARINA

Aberystwyth Marina
Trefechan, Aberystwyth, Ceredigion, SY23 1AS
Tel: 01970 611422 Fax: 01970 624122
Email: aber@themarinegroup.co.uk www.bayscape.co.uk

VHF	Ch 80
ACCESS	HW±2

The location of Aberystwyth Marina, in a historic university town, ensures there are a range of cultural, active and educational activities close to the marina for berth holders to enjoy. The marina offers 165 first class berths providing safe, secure and sheltered moorings for motor boats and yachts within the historic harbour.

The town itself has a range of cafes, seaside fish and chip shops, restaurants and bars, many a short walk from the marina. The seafront, Promenade and pier is a great location for a walk and to look out over the Irish Sea. Facilities include a slipway, chandlery, brokerage and 10t boat hoist.

FACILITIES AT A GLANCE

Key
a Offices
b Offices
c Marina office
d Apartments
e Aberystwyth BC

MILFORD MARINA

Milford Marina
Milford Docks, Milford Haven, Pembrokeshire, SA73 3AF
Tel: 01646 696312 Fax: 01646 696314
Email: enquiries@milfordmarina.com www.milfordmarina.com

VHF	Ch 14
ACCESS	H24

Set within one of the deepest natural harbours in the world, Milford Marina is situated in a non-tidal basin within the UK's only coastal National Park, the ideal base for discovering the fabulous coastline in

Pembrokeshire, Wales and Ireland. Continued investment has meant that the marina provides safe, secure and sheltered boat berths with a full range of shoreside facilities in the heart of SW Wales.

Accessed via an entrance lock (with waiting pontoons both inside and outside the lock), the marina is perfect for exploring the picturesque upper reaches of the River Cleddau or cruising out beyond St Ann's Head to the unspoilt islands of Skomer, Skokholm and Grassholm.

FACILITIES AT A GLANCE

Key
a Neil Hart Joinery
b Mustang Marine
c Neyland Marine Services
d Fish Processing
e Fish Markets
f Galley Café
g MPSC
h Servitec
i MITEC Building
j Seal Hospital
k Sail loft
l Charles Bar
m Norrad Electrics
n All Pets Vet Care
o Locks on Line
p Museum
q Marina Control
Martha's Vineyard
Dyfed Electronics
r Phoenix Bowl
s Windjammer Marine

NEYLAND YACHT HAVEN

Neyland Yacht Haven Ltd
Brunel Quay, Neyland, Pembrokeshire, SA73 1PY
Tel: 01646 601601
Email: neyland@yachthavens.com www.yachthavens.com

VHF	Ch M, 80
ACCESS	H24

Approximately 10 miles from the entrance to Milford Haven lies Neyland Yacht Haven. Tucked away in a well protected inlet just before the Cleddau Bridge, this marina has 420 berths and can accommodate yachts up to 25m LOA with draughts of up to 2.5m.
The marina is divided into two basins, with the lower one enjoying full tidal access, while entry to the upper one is restricted by a tidal sill. Visitor and annual berthing enquiries welcome.

Offering a comprehensive range of services, Neyland Yacht Haven is within a five minute walk of the town centre where the various shops and takeaways cater for most everyday needs; bicycle hire is also available. The Yacht Haven is a member of the TransEurope Group.

FACILITIES AT A GLANCE

Key
a Marine services building
   Harbour Master's office
   Laundry
   Chandlery and café
   Restaurant and bar
   Showers and toilets
b Storage compound - refuse disposal
c Upper Basin - showers and toilets
d Refuse, recycling, battery disposal
e Holding berth
f Dale Sailing Co Ltd
   Disabled persons toilets
g Tidal sill with depth gauge
h Yacht club and slipway
i Waste oil and used battery collection point
j Glamping pods
   yacht repair yard
NB Berth numbering flows from low outer

■ Weather information collection point

Visitors welcome

Neyland Yacht Haven
Full tidal access

– Pembrokeshire's Picturesque Marina
– Full tidal access within a well-protected creek
– TransEurope Member – visitor discounts
– Café, Bar/Restaurant & Chandlery
– FREE Wi-Fi for berth holders & visitors
– Full marina services
– Free Wi-Fi
– Bike Hire

Call **01646 601601** or **VHF Ch 37 & 80**
or visit **yachthavens.com**

Neyland
Yacht Haven

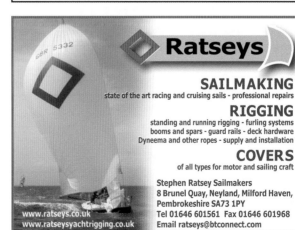
11

SWANSEA MARINA

Swansea Marina
Lockside, Maritime Quarter, Swansea, SA1 1WG
Tel: 01792 470310 Fax: 01792 463948
www.swansea.gov.uk/swanseamarina
Email: swanmar@swansea.gov.uk

VHF	Ch 80
ACCESS	HW±4.5

At the hub of the city's redeveloped and award winning Maritime Quarter, Swansea Marina can be accessed HW±4½ hrs via a lock. Surrounded by a plethora of shops, restaurants and marine businesses to cater for most yachtsmen's needs, the marina is in close proximity to the picturesque Gower coast, where

there is no shortage of quiet sandy beaches off which to anchor. It also provides the perfect starting point for cruising to Ilfracombe, Lundy Island, the North Cornish coast or West Wales.

Within easy walking distance of the marina is the city centre, boasting a covered shopping centre and market. For those who prefer walking or cycling, take the long promenade to the Mumbles fishing village from where there are plenty of coastal walks.

FACILITIES AT A GLANCE

Key
a Leisure Centre
b Maritime Museum
c Pumphouse Restaurant
d Yacht Club
e Repair shed
f Mariott Hotel

PENARTH QUAYS MARINA

Penarth Quays Marina
Penarth, Vale of Glamorgan, CF64 1TQ
Tel: 02920 705021
Email: sjones@quaymarinas.com
www.quaymarinas.com

VHF	Ch 80
ACCESS	H24

Penarth Quays Marina has been established in the historic basins of Penarth Docks for over 20 years and is the premier boating facility in the region. The marina is Cardiff Bay's only 5 Gold Anchor marina and provides an ideal base for those using the Bay and the Bristol Channel. With 24hr access there is always water available for boating. Penarth and Cardiff boast an extensive range of leisure facilities, shops and restaurants making this marina an ideal base or destination. The marina has a blue flag and is a member of the TransEurope Group.

FACILITIES AT A GLANCE

Key
a Marina office
b Inner basin services building
c Boat shed
d Refuse compound/recycling
e Boat sales/Café
f Restaurant

CARDIFF MARINA

Cardiff Marina
Watkiss Way, Cardiff, CF11 0SY
Tel: 02920 396078 Fax: 02920 345116
Email: info@themarinegroup.co.uk
www.themarinegroup.co.uk

VHF	Ch M
ACCESS	H24

The location of Cardiff Marina, in theWelsh capital city, within close proximity to the marina to provide a dynamic location to berth your boat. New landside facilities opened in summer 2018 include a marina office, showers/toilets and a coffee shop. A sheltered haven on the River Ely,

offering 350 fully serviced berths, the marina is perfectly situated for yachts and motorboats alike with the barrage offering easy access to the Bristol Channel. Facilities include a 50t Sealift, platform crane for mast work and brokerage. In addition, there is a drystack service, comprehensive boatyard and refit and repair centre at Cardiff Marine Village with undercover workshops and boat lifting facilities.

FACILITIES AT A GLANCE

Key
a Marina Office
b Showers, toilets
c Workshop

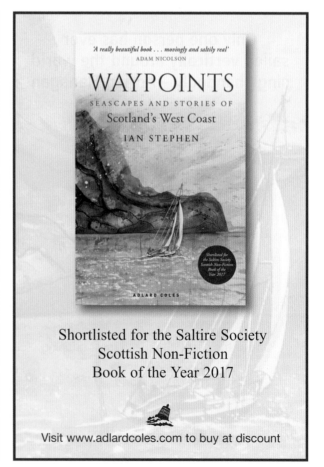

BRISTOL MARINA

Bristol Marina Ltd
Hanover Place, Bristol, BS1 6UH
Tel: 0117 921 3198 Fax: 0117 929 7672
Email: info@bristolmarina.co.uk

VHF Ch 80
ACCESS HW-3 to HW

Situated in the heart of the city, Bristol is a fully serviced marina providing over 100 pontoon berths for vessels up to 20m LOA. Among the facilities are a new fuelling berth and pump out station as well as an on site chandler and sailmaker. It is situated on the south side of the Floating Harbour, about eight miles from the mouth of the River Avon. Accessible from seaward via the Cumberland Basin, passing through both Entrance Lock and Junction Lock, it can be reached approximately three hours before HW.

  Shops, restaurants, theatres and cinemas are all within easy reach of the marina, while local attractions include the SS *Great Britain*, designed by Isambard Kingdom Brunel, and the famous Clifton Suspension Bridge, which has an excellent visitors' centre depicting its fascinating story.

FACILITIES AT A GLANCE

Key
a Albion Boatyard
b Marina office

PORTISHEAD QUAYS MARINA

Portishead Quays Marina
Newfoundland Way, Portishead, North Somerset, BS20 7DF
Tel: 01275 841941
Email: portisheadmarina@quaymarinas.com
www.quaymarinas.com

VHF Ch 80
ACCESS HW±3.5

Portishead Marina is a popular destination for cruising in the Bristol Channel. Providing an excellent link between the inland waterways at Bristol and Sharpness and offering access to the open water and marinas down channel. The entrance to the Marina is via a lock, with a minimum access of HW+/- 3.5hrs. Contact the Marina on VHF Ch 80 ahead of time for next available lock. The Marina provides 320 fully serviced berths and can accommodate vessels up to 40m LOA, draft up to 5.5m. The marina has a 35 tonnes boat hoist and the boatyard offers all the facilities you would expect from a Quay Marinas site.

FACILITIES AT A GLANCE

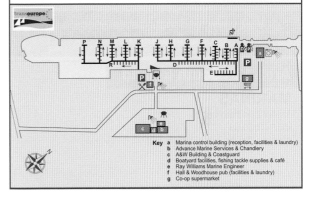

Key a Marina control building (reception, facilities & laundry)
     b Advance Marine Services & Chandlery
     c A&W Building & Coastguard
     d Boatyard facilities, fishing tackle supplies & café
     e Ray Williams Marine Engineer
     f Hall & Woodhouse pub (facilities & laundry)
     g Co-op supermarket

PADSTOW HARBOUR

Padstow Harbour Commissioners
The Harbour Office, Padstow, Cornwall, PL28 8AQ
Tel: 01841 532239 Fax: 01841 533346
Email: padstowharbour@btconnect.com
www.padstow-harbour.co.uk

VHF Ch 12, 16
ACCESS HW±2

Padstow is a small commercial port with a rich history situated 1.5 miles from the sea within the estuary of the River Camel. The inner harbour is serviced by a tidal gate – part of the 1988–1990 flood defence scheme, which is open approximately two hours either side of high water. A minimum of 3m of water is maintained in the inner harbour at all times. Onshore facilities are excellent, please enquire at the Harbour Office.

  This is a thriving fishing port, so perhaps it wasn't surprising that celebrity chefs like Rick Stein and Jamie Oliver would set up shop in the town. This is a great resting point for everything Cornish from surf and coastal walks to fish and chips and cream teas.

FACILITIES AT A GLANCE

Key a Residents' pontoons
     b Harbour office
     * Electricity and water points
     1-20 around harbour denote ladder numbers

11

SOUTH IRELAND – Malahide, clockwise to Liscannor Bay

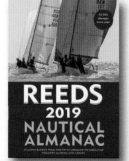
Key to Marina Plans symbols

Bottled gas		P	Parking
Chandler			Pub/Restaurant
Disabled facilities			Pump out
Electrical supply			Rigging service
Electrical repairs			Sail repairs
Engine repairs			Shipwright
First Aid			Shop/Supermarket
Fresh Water			Showers
Fuel - Diesel			Slipway
Fuel - Petrol		WC	Toilets
Hardstanding/boatyard			Telephone
@ Internet Café			Trolleys
Laundry facilities		V	Visitors berths
Lift-out facilities			Wi-Fi

Area 12 - South Ireland

MARINAS
Telephone Numbers
VHF Channel
Access Times

REPUBLIC OF IRELAND

Malahide
01 845 4129
Ch M, 80 HW±4

Howth YC Marina
01 839 2777
Ch M, 80 H24

Dun Laoghaire Marina
01202 0040
Ch M, 16 H24

Arklow Marina
0402 39901 H24

Kilrush
065 9052072
Ch 80 H24

Dingle Marina
066 9151629
Ch M H24

Fenit Marina 066 713 6231 Ch M H24

Cahersiveen Marina
066 947 2777
Ch M H24

Waterford City Marina
051 849503
H24

Kilmore Quay
053 91 29955
Ch 09, 16 H24

Lawrence Cove
027 75044
Ch 16 H24

Cork Harbour Marina 087 366 9009 H24
Crosshaven BY Marina 021 483 1161 Ch M H24
East Ferry Marina 086 735 7785 H24
Royal Cork YC Marina 021 483 1023 Ch M H24
Salve Marine 021 483 1145 Ch M H24

Kinsale YC Marina
021 477 2196 Ch M H24
Castlepark Marina
021 477 4959 Ch 06 H24

Galway
Malahide
DUBLIN
Howth
Dun Laoghaire
Wicklow
Arklow
Kilrush
Limerick
R.Shannon
Fenit Harbour
Dingle
Cahersiveen
Kenmare
Bantry
Schull
Baltimore
Castlehaven
Crookhaven
Crosshaven
Kinsale
Cork
Youghal
Dunmore East
Waterford
Wexford

N

MALAHIDE MARINA

Malahide Marina
Malahide, Co. Dublin
Tel: +353 1 845 4129 Fax: +353 1 845 4255
Email: info@malahidemarina.net
www.malahidemarina.net

VHF	Ch M, 80
ACCESS	HW±4

Malahide Marina, situated just 10 minutes from Dublin Airport and 20 minutes north of Dublin's city centre, is a fully serviced marina accommodating up to 350 yachts. Capable of taking vessels of up to 75m in length, its first class facilities include a boatyard with hard standing for approximately 170 boats and a 30-ton mobile hoist. Its on site restaurant provides a large seating area in convivial surroundings. The village of Malahide has plenty to offer the visiting yachtsmen, with a wide variety of eating places, nearby golf courses and tennis courts as well as a historic castle and botanical gardens.

FACILITIES AT A GLANCE

Key
a Boat handling & storage area
b Refuelling bay
c Marina centre
d Boatyard
e Marina access bridge
f Restaurant
g Wash area

HOWTH MARINA

Howth Marina
Howth Marina, Harbour Road, Howth, Co. Dublin
Tel: +353 1 8392777 Fax: +353 1 8392430
Email: marina@hyc.ie
www.hyc.ie

VHF	Ch M, 80
ACCESS	H24

Based on the north coast of the rugged peninsula that forms the northern side of Dublin Bay, Howth Marina is ideally situated for north or south-bound traffic in the Irish Sea. Well sheltered in all winds, it can be entered at any state of the tide. Overlooking the marina is Howth Yacht Club, which has in recent years been expanded and is now said to be the largest yacht club in Ireland. With good road and rail links, Howth is in easy reach of Dublin's airport and ferry terminal, making it an obvious choice for crew changeovers.

FACILITIES AT A GLANCE

Key
a Harbour office
b RNLI boathouse
c Clubhouse
d Drying pad
e Waiting pontoons (A&B)

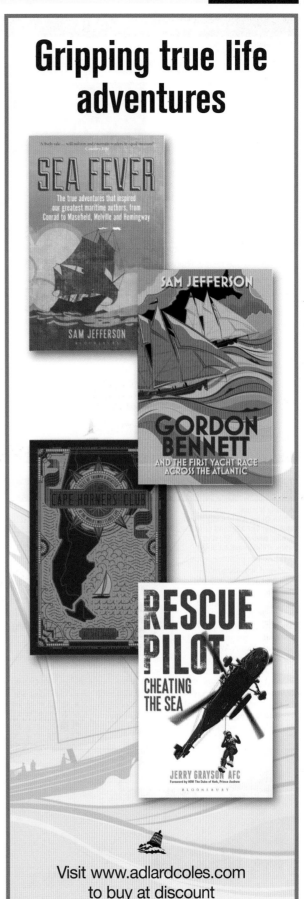

DUN LAOGHAIRE MARINA

Dun Laoghaire Marina
Harbour Road, Dun Laoghaire, Co Dublin, Eire
Tel: +353 1 202 0040 Fax: +353 1 202 0043
Email: info@dlmarina.com   www.dlmarina.com

VHF Ch M, 16
ACCESS H24

Dun Laoghaire Marina – Gateway to Dublin and the first marina in the Republic of Ireland to be awarded five Gold anchors by THYA and also achieved the ICOMIA 'Clean Marina' accreditation – is the largest marina in Ireland. 24 hour access in all weather conditions. The town centre is located within 400m. Serviced berthing for 820 boats from 6m to 23m with visitors mainly on the hammerheads.

Larger vessels up to 30m and 80 tonne displacement can be accommodated alongside breakwater pontoons. Minimum draft is 3.6m LWS. With adjacent ferry terminal and rail station, Dublin 12kms and airport 35kms, the marina is an ideal location for crew change etc. Easy access to Dublin Bay, home to the biennial Dun Laoghaire Regatta.

FACILITIES AT A GLANCE

Key
a Royal Irish Yacht Club
b Marina office
c WC
d Royal St George Yacht Club
Berth numbering - odds to port, evens to starboard, increase inwards

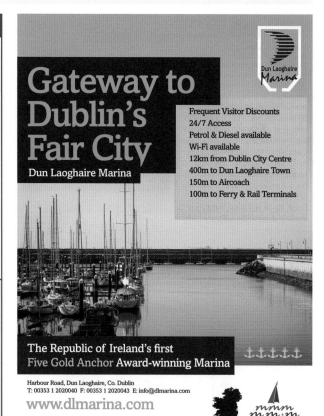

Gateway to Dublin's Fair City

Dun Laoghaire Marina

Frequent Visitor Discounts
24/7 Access
Petrol & Diesel available
Wi-Fi available
12km from Dublin City Centre
400m to Dun Laoghaire Town
150m to Aircoach
100m to Ferry & Rail Terminals

The Republic of Ireland's first
Five Gold Anchor Award-winning Marina

Harbour Road, Dun Laoghaire, Co. Dublin
T: 00353 1 2020040 F: 00353 1 2020043 E: info@dlmarina.com

www.dlmarina.com

ARKLOW MARINA

Arklow Marina
North Quay, Arklow, Co. Wicklow, Eire
Mobiles: 087 2375189 or 087 2588078
Email: personnel@asl.ie
www.arklowmarina.com

VHF
ACCESS H24

Arklow is a popular fishing port and seaside town situated at the mouth of the River Avoca, 16 miles south of Wicklow and 11 miles north east of Gorey. The town is ideally placed for visiting the many beauty spots of County Wicklow including Glenmalure, Glendalough and Clara Lara, Avoca (Ballykissangel).

Arklow Marina is on the north bank of the river (dredged 2014) just upstream of the commercial quays, with 42 berths in an inner harbour and 30 berths on pontoons outside the marina entrance. Vessels over 14m LOA should moor on the river pontoons.

FACILITIES AT A GLANCE

KILMORE QUAY

Kilmore Quay
Wexford, Ireland
Tel: +353 53 9129955 Fax: +353 53 9129955 www.wexford.ie
Email: assistant.marineofficer@wexfordcoco.ie

VHF Ch 09, 16
ACCESS H24

Located in the SE corner of Ireland, Kilmore Quay is a small rural fishing village situated approximately 14 miles from the town of Wexford and 12 miles from Rosslare ferry port.

Its 55-berthed marina, offering shelter from the elements as well as various on shore facilities, including diesel available 24/7, has become a regular port of call for many cruising yachtsmen. With several nearby areas of either historical or natural significance accessible using local bike hire, Kilmore is renowned for its 'green' approach to the environment.

FACILITIES AT A GLANCE

Key
a Harbour master's office - onshore facilities
b Lifeboat station
c Information board
d Stella Maris - community centre

WATERFORD CITY MARINA

Waterford City Marina
Waterford, Ireland
Tel: +353 87 238 4944
Email: jcodd@waterfordcouncil.ie

VHF
ACCESS H24

Famous for its connections with Waterford Crystal, manufactured in the city centre, Waterford is the capital of the SE region of Ireland. As a major city, it benefits from good rail links with Dublin, and Limerick, a regional airport with daily flights to Britain and an extensive bus service to surrounding towns and villages. The marina is found on the banks of the River Suir, in the heart of this historic Viking city dating back to the ninth century. Yachtsmen can make the most of Waterford's wide range of shops, restaurants and bars without having to walk too far from their boats. With 100 fully serviced berths and first rate security, Waterford City Marina now provides shower, toilet and laundry facilities in its new reception building.

FACILITIES AT A GLANCE

CROSSHAVEN BOATYARD MARINA

Crosshaven Boatyard Marina
Crosshaven, Co Cork, Ireland
Tel: +353 214 831161 Fax: +353 214 831603
Email: info@crosshavenboatyard.com

VHF Ch M
ACCESS H24

One of three marinas at Crosshaven, Crosshaven Boatyard was founded in 1950 and originally made its name from the construction of some of the most world-renowned yachts, including *Gypsy Moth* and Denis Doyle's *Moonduster*. Nowadays, however, the yard has diversified to provide a wide range of services to both the marine leisure and professional industries. Situated on a safe and sheltered river only 12 miles from Cork City Centre, the marina boasts 100 fully-serviced berths along with the capacity to accommodate yachts up to 35m LOA with a 4m draught. In addition, it is ideally situated for cruising the stunning south west coast of Ireland.

FACILITIES AT A GLANCE

SALVE MARINE

Salve Marine
Crosshaven, Co Cork, Ireland
Tel: +353 21 483 1145 Fax: +353 21 483 1747
Email: salvemarine@eircom.net

VHF Ch M
ACCESS H24

Crosshaven is a picturesque seaside resort providing a gateway to Ireland's south and south west coasts. Offering a variety of activities to suit all types, its rocky coves and quiet sandy beaches stretch from Graball to Church Bay and from Fennell's Bay to nearby Myrtleville. Besides a selection of craft shops selling locally produced arts and crafts, there are plenty of pubs, restaurants and takeaways to suit even the most discerning of tastes. Lying within a few hundred metres of the village centre is Salve Marine, accommodating yachts up to 43m LOA with draughts of up to 4m. Its comprehensive services range from engineering and welding facilities to hull and rigging repairs.

FACILITIES AT A GLANCE

CORK HARBOUR MARINA

Cork Harbour Marina
Monkstown, Co Cork, Ireland
Tel: +353 87 366 9009
Email: info@corkharbourmarina.ie www.corkharbourmarina.ie

VHF
ACCESS H24

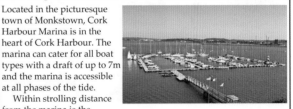

Located in the picturesque town of Monkstown, Cork Harbour Marina is in the heart of Cork Harbour. The marina can cater for all boat types with a draft of up to 7m and the marina is accessible at all phases of the tide.

Within strolling distance from the marina is the 'Bosun' restaurant and 'Napoli', an Italian delicatessen. There is also a sailing club, tennis club and golf club located nearby. Monkstown is just a short riverside walk from Passage West, with all the amenities one might require.

There is a frequent bus service from the marina gates to Cork City. Cork Harbour Marina is 15km from Cork International Airport.

FACILITIES AT A GLANCE

ROYAL CORK YACHT CLUB

Royal Cork Yacht Club Marina
Crosshaven, Co Cork, Ireland
Tel: +353 21 483 1023 Fax: +353 21 483 2657
Email: mark@royalcork.com   www.royalcork.com

VHF	Ch M
ACCESS	H24

Founded in 1720, the Royal Cork Yacht Club is the oldest and one of the most prominent yacht clubs in the world. Organising, among many other events, the prestigious biennial Volvo Cork Week, it boasts a number of World, European and national sailors among its membership.

The Yacht Club's marina is situated at Crosshaven, on the hillside at the mouth of the Owenabue River, just inside the entrance to Cork Harbour. The harbour is popular with yachtsmen as it is accessible and well sheltered in all weather conditions. It also benefits from the Gulf Stream producing a temperate climate practically all year round.

FACILITIES AT A GLANCE

Blue Flag
ᘔ An Taisce

KINSALE YACHT CLUB MARINA

Kinsale Yacht Club Marina
Kinsale, Co Cork, Ireland
Tel: +353 21 4772196 Fax: +353 21 4774455
Email: kyc@iol.ie

VHF	Ch M
ACCESS	H24

Kinsale is a natural, virtually land-locked harbour on the estuary of the Bandon River, approximately 12 miles south west of Cork harbour entrance. Home to a thriving fishing fleet as well as frequented by commercial shipping, it boasts two fully serviced marinas, with the Kinsale Yacht Club & Marina being the closest to the town. Visitors to this marina automatically become temporary members of the club and are therefore entitled to make full use of the facilities, which include a fully licensed bar and restaurant serving evening meals on Wednesdays, Thursdays and Saturdays. Fuel, water and repair services are also available.

FACILITIES AT A GLANCE

CASTLEPARK MARINA

Castlepark Marina Centre
Kinsale, Co Cork, Ireland
Tel: +353 21 4774959
Email: info@castleparkmarina.com

VHF	Ch 16, 14
ACCESS	H24

Situated on the south side of Kinsale Harbour, Castlepark is a small marina with deep water pontoon berths that are accessible at all states of the tide. Surrounded by rolling hills, it boasts its own beach as well as being in close proximity to the parklands of James Fort and a traditional Irish pub. The attractive town of Kinsale, with its narrow streets and slate-clad houses, lies just 1.5 miles away by road or five minutes away by ferry. Known as Ireland's 'fine food centre', it incorporates a number of gourmet food shops and high quality restaurants as well as a wine museum.

FACILITIES AT A GLANCE

trans-europe

LAWRENCE COVE MARINA

Lawrence Cove Marina
Lawrence Cove, Bere Island, Co Cork, Ireland
Tel: +353 27 75044 mob: +353 879 125930
Email: rachelsherig@gmail.com
www.lawrencecovemarina.ie

VHF	Ch 16
ACCESS	H24

Lawrence Cove enjoys a peaceful location on an island at the entrance to Bantry Bay. Privately owned and run, it offers sheltered and secluded waters as well as excellent facilities and fully serviced pontoon berths. A few hundred yards from the marina you will find a shop, pub and restaurant, while the mainland, with its various attractions, can be easily reached by ferry. Lawrence Cove lies at the heart of the wonderful cruising grounds of Ireland's south west coast and, just two hours from Cork airport, is an ideal place to leave your boat for long or short periods.

FACILITIES AT A GLANCE

CAHERSIVEEN MARINA

Cahersiveen Marina
The Pier, Cahersiveen, Co. Kerry, Ireland
Tel: +353 66 9472777 Fax: +353 66 9472993
Email: acard@eircom.net
www.cahersiveenmarina.ie

VHF | Ch M
ACCESS | H24

Situated two miles up Valentia River from Valentia Harbour, Cahersiveen Marina is well protected in all wind directions and is convenient for sailing to Valentia Island and Dingle Bay as well as for visiting some of the spectacular uninhabited islands in the surrounding area. Boasting a host of sheltered sandy beaches, the region is renowned for salt and fresh water fishing as well as being good for scuba diving.

Within easy walking distance of the marina lies the historic town of Cahersiveen, incorporating an array of convivial pubs and restaurants.

FACILITIES AT A GLANCE

DINGLE MARINA

Dingle Marina
c/o Dingle Fishery Harbour Centre, Strand Street, Dingle, Co Kerry, Ireland
Tel: +353 (0)87 925 4115 Fax: +353 (0)69 5152546
Email:dingleharbour@agriculture.gov.ie
www.dinglemarina.ie

VHF | Ch 14
ACCESS | H24

Dingle is Ireland's most westerly marina, lying at the heart of the sheltered Dingle Harbour, and is easily reached both day and night via a well buoyed approach channel. The surrounding area is an interesting and unfrequented cruising ground, with several islands, bays and beaches for the yachtsman to explore.

The marina lies in the heart of the old market town, renowned for its hospitality and traditional Irish pub music. Besides enjoying the excellent seafood restaurants and 52 pubs, other recreational pastimes include horse riding, golf, climbing and diving.

FACILITIES AT A GLANCE

Key
a Marina centre building - cafe, dive centre, sailing and rowing centre, chandlery and showers
b Sea Life Centre
c Commercial berths - FVs & ferries
d Marina office

FENIT HARBOUR MARINA

Fenit Harbour & Marina
Fenit, Tralee, Co. Kerry, Republic of Ireland
Tel: +353 66 7136231 Fax: +353 66 7136473
Email: info@fenitharbour.com www.fenitharbour.com

VHF | Ch M
ACCESS | H24

Fenit Harbour Marina is tucked away in Tralee Bay, not far south of the Shannon Estuary. Besides offering a superb cruising ground, being within a day's sail of Dingle and Kilrush, the marina also provides a convenient base from which to visit inland attractions such as the picturesque tourist towns of Tralee and Killarney. This 120-berth marina accommodates boats up to 15m LOA and benefits from deep water at all states of the tide.

The small village of Fenit incorporates a grocery shop as well a several pubs and restaurants, while among the local activities are horse riding, swimming from one of the nearby sandy beaches and golfing.

FACILITIES AT A GLANCE

Key
a Warehouse
b Marina services, harbour office, lifeboat station

KILRUSH MARINA

Kilrush Marina Ltd
Kilrush, Co. Clare, Ireland
Tel: +353 65 9052072 Mobile: +353 86 2313870
Email: info@kilrushmarina.ie

VHF | Ch 80
ACCESS | H24

Kilrush Marina and boatyard is well placed for exploring the unspoilt west coast of Ireland, including Galway Bay, Dingle, W Cork and Kerry. It also provides a gateway to over 150 miles of cruising on Lough Derg, the R Shannon and the Irish canal system. Accessed via lock gates, the marina lies at one end of the main street in Kilrush, the marina centre provides all the facilities for the visiting sailor. Kilrush is a vibrant market town with a long maritime history. A 15-minute ferry ride from the marina takes you to Scattery Is, once a 6th century monastic settlement but now only inhabited by wildlife. The Shannon Estuary is reputed for being the country's first marine Special Area of Conservation (SAC) and is home to Ireland's only known resident group of bottlenose dolphins.

FACILITIES AT A GLANCE

Set Sail for Carlingford Marina

Tel: +353 (O) 42 93 73 072
Email: info@carlingfordmarina.ie
Web: www.carlingfordmarina.ie

About the Marina

Carlingford Marina is located in the picturesque coastal inlet of Carlingford Lough, with the Cooley Mountains o one side, and the Mountains of Mourne on the other.

A day's sail from Dublin, Belfast, The Isle of Man, the West Coast of England and North Wales, Carlingford is an ideal location from which to explore the Irish Sea.

Carlingford Lough is a vibrant sailing ground that supports 3 clubs. This makes it more than a cruising destination, but also an ideal place for families, beginner and racing enthusiasts to settle permanently.

There are 170 Berths in the Marina, with an additional 5 Dry Berths in the Boat Yard. Electricity and fresh water is available throughout, and the Yard is serviced by a 50 tonne travel hoist.

About the Location

Carlingford is one of the best preserved medieval village in Ireland with a number of important pre-historic and medieval sites.

The village has a deserved reputation for hospitality, wit some of the finest restaurants and friendliest pubs in Ireland. Known as Ireland's best kept secret, the area has been recognized as a European Destination of Excellenc and an area of outstanding natural beauty.

Carlingford is an hour's away from both Dublin and Be fast, and the busy international airports of both cities.

Berthage Rates

Annual Berthage:	€278 per metre
Summer 4 Months:	€142 per metre
Winter 6 Months:	€126 per metre
Visitor Nightly Rate:	€2.45 per metre

Contact

+353 (O) 42 93 73072 / info@carlingfordmarina.ie

NORTH IRELAND – Liscannor Bay, clockwise to Lambay Island

Reeds PDF ebooks

In response to popular demand, all the Reeds Almanacs are now available as searchable, highlightable PDF ebooks. (All ebooks incorporate the Marina Guide.)

Visit www.reedsnauticalalmanac.co.uk
for further information

Key to Marina Plans symbols

	Bottled gas	P	Parking
	Chandler		Pub/Restaurant
	Disabled facilities		Pump out
	Electrical supply		Rigging service
	Electrical repairs		Sail repairs
	Engine repairs		Shipwright
	First Aid		Shop/Supermarket
	Fresh Water		Showers
	Fuel - Diesel		Slipway
	Fuel - Petrol	WC	Toilets
	Hardstanding/boatyard		Telephone
@	Internet Café		Trolleys
	Laundry facilities	V	Visitors berths
	Lift-out facilities		Wi-Fi

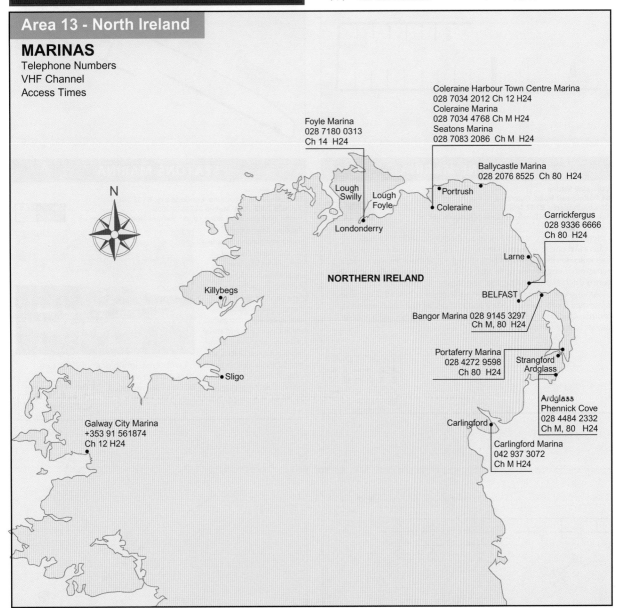

Area 13 - North Ireland

MARINAS
Telephone Numbers
VHF Channel
Access Times

N

NORTHERN IRELAND

Coleraine Harbour Town Centre Marina
028 7034 2012 Ch 12 H24
Coleraine Marina
028 7034 4768 Ch M H24
Seatons Marina
028 7083 2086 Ch M H24

Ballycastle Marina
028 2076 8525 Ch 80 H24

Foyle Marina
028 7180 0313
Ch 14 H24

Lough Swilly

Lough Foyle

Portrush

Coleraine

Londonderry

Carrickfergus
028 9336 6666
Ch 80 H24

Larne

BELFAST

Killybegs

Bangor Marina 028 9145 3297
Ch M, 80 H24

Portaferry Marina
028 4272 9598
Ch 80 H24

Strangford
Ardglass

Sligo

Ardglass
Phennick Cove
028 4484 2332
Ch M, 80 H24

Carlingford

Galway City Marina
+353 91 561874
Ch 12 H24

Carlingford Marina
042 937 3072
Ch M H24

GALWAY CITY MARINA

Galway City Marina
Galway Harbour Co, Harbour Office, Galway, Ireland
Tel: +353 91 561874 Fax: +353 91 563738
Email: info@theportofgalway.com

VHF	Ch 12
ACCESS	HW-2 to HW

The Galway harbour Company operates a small marina in the confines of Galway Harbour with an additional 60m of pontoon-walkway. Freshwater and electrical power is available at the pontoons. Power cars can be purchased from the harbour office during the day. A number of visitors pontoons are available for hire during the summer and for winter layup. Sailors intending to call to Galway Harbour should first make contact with the Harbour office to determine if a berth is available — advisable as demand is high in this quiet and beautiful part of Ireland.

FACILITIES AT A GLANCE

FOYLE MARINA

Foyle Marina
Londonderry Port, Lisahally, L'Derry, BT47 6FL
Tel: 02871 860555 Fax: 02871 861656
www.londonderryport.com/leisure
Email: info@londonderryport.com

VHF	Ch 14
ACCESS	H24

Foyle Marina lies in the heart of the city, 17M from the mouth of Lough Foyle, is accessible at any state of the tide and is sheltered from all directions of wind. Approach is via well-marked navigation channel with a maintained depth of 8m.

The marina has recently undergone extensive improvements with over 680m of secure pontoon mooring now available. Foyle Marina now offers full facilities to visiting vessels. Toilets and showers on site, water and electricity at each berth. Vessels up to 130m LOA can be accommodated. Craft can berth either side of the pontoons in depths of 5–7m at LW.

The pontoons are within easy walking distance of the city centre where you will find restaurants, bars, cinemas, shopping and a host of tourist attractions.

FACILITIES AT A GLANCE

Key a Council offices
b Appartments
c Doctor's surgery

COLERAINE MARINA

Coleraine Marina
64 Portstewart Road, Coleraine,
Co Londonderry, BT52 1RR
Tel: 028 7034 4768 Email: rickiemac@talktalk.net

VHF	Ch M
ACCESS	H24

Coleraine Marina complex enjoys a superb location in sheltered waters just one mile north of the town of Coleraine and four and a half miles south of the River Bann Estuary and the open sea. Besides accommodating vessels up to 18m LOA, this modern marina with 78 berths offers hard standing, fuel and shower facilities.

Among one of the oldest known settlements in Ireland, Coleraine is renowned for its linen, whiskey and salmon. Its thriving commercial centre includes numerous shops, a four-screen cinema and a state-of-the-art leisure complex.

FACILITIES AT A GLANCE

SEATONS MARINA

Seatons Marina
Drumslade Rd, Coleraine, Londonderry, BT52 1SE
Tel: 028 7083 2086 Mobile 07718 883099
Email: jill@seatonsmarina.co.uk www.seatonsmarina.co.uk

VHF	Ch M
ACCESS	H24

Seatons Marina is a privately owned business on the north coast of Ireland, which was established by Eric Seaton in 1962. It lies on the east bank of the River Bann, approximately two miles downstream from Coleraine and three miles from the sea. Long term pontoon berths are available for yachts up to 11.5 with a maximum draft of 2.4m; fore and aft moorings are available for larger vessels. Lift out and mast stepping facilities are provided by a 12 tonne trailer hoist.

FACILITIES AT A GLANCE

COLERAINE HARBOUR MARINA

Coleraine Harbour Town Centre Marina
Coleraine Harbour Office, 4 Riversdale Road, Coleraine, BT52 1XA
Tel: 028 7034 2012 Fax: 028 7035 2000
Email: info@coleraineharbour.com
www.coleraineharbour.com

| VHF | Ch 12 |
| ACCESS | H24 |

The Marina lies upstream about five miles from the sea ideally situated in the centre of the town, just a few minutes stroll from a selection of shops, restaurants and bars.

In addition to the pontoon berths there is a 40 tonne Roodberg slipway launch/recovery trailer. Hard standing and covered storage are available.

Coleraine is an ideal base for exploring the many nearby attractions including the Old Bushmills Distillery and the Giants Causeway.

FACILITIES AT A GLANCE

Coleraine Harbour Town Centre Marina

The ideal place to berth a yacht when visiting the River Bann.
Pontoon berths for visitors.
Situated in the centre of town.
Excellent facilities including free showers and all your marina needs.

**Access via the lifting bridge –
Telephone the Harbour Manager on
028 70 34 2012 or Channel 12 VHF**

BALLYCASTLE MARINA

Ballycastle Marina
Bayview Road, Ballycastle, Northern Ireland
Tel: 028 2076 8525/07803 505084 Fax: 028 2076 6215
Email: info@moyle-council.org

| VHF | Ch 80 |
| ACCESS | H24 |

Ballycastle is a traditional seaside town situated on Northern Ireland's North Antrim coast. The 74-berthed, sheltered marina provides a perfect base from which to explore the well known local attractions such as the Giant's Causeway world heritage site, the spectacular Nine Glens of Antrim, and Rathlin, the only inhabited island in Northern Ireland. The most northern coastal marina in Ireland, Ballycastle is accessible at all states of the tide, although yachts are required to contact the marina on VHF Ch 80 before entering the harbour. Along the seafront are a selection of restaurants, bars and shops, while the town centre is only about a five minute walk away.

FACILITIES AT A GLANCE

CARRICKFERGUS MARINA

Carrickferus Marina
3 Quayside, Carrickfergus, Co. Antrim, BT38 8BJ
Tel: 028 9336 6666 Fax: 028 9335 0505
Email: marina.reception@midandeastantrim.gov.uk
www.carrickfergus.org

| VHF | Ch 80 |
| ACCESS | H24 |

Located on the north shore of Belfast Lough, Carrickfergus Marina and harbour incorporates two sheltered areas suitable for leisure craft. The harbour is dominated by a magnificent 12th century Norman Castle which, recently renovated, includes a film theatre, banqueting room and outdoor models depicting the castle's chequered history.

With a wide range of services available to the visitor, the marina is located 250m west of the harbour and has become increasingly popular since its opening in 1985. An interesting variety of shops and restaurants along the waterfront caters for most yachtsmen's needs.

FACILITIES AT A GLANCE

Key
a Apartments
b Hotel/bar/restaurant
c Marina office
d Cinema/café/restaurant
e Retail superstore

BANGOR MARINA

Quay Marinas Limited
Bangor Marina, Bangor, Co. Down, BT20 5ED
Tel: 028 9145 3297 Fax: 028 9145 3450
Email: kbaird@quaymarinas.com
www.quaymarinas.com

VHF Ch 11, 80
ACCESS H24

Situated on the south shore of Belfast Lough, Bangor is located close to the Irish Sea cruising routes. The marina is right at the town's centre, within walking distance of shops, restaurants, hotels and bars. The Tourist information centre is across the road from marina reception and there are numerous visitors' attractions in the Borough. The Royal Ulster Yacht Club and the Ballyholme Yacht Club are both nearby and welcome visitors.

FACILITIES AT A GLANCE

Key
a Boat hoist - BJ Marine
b Boat yard - BJ Marine
c Bregenz House
d Chandlery/brokerage BJ Marine
e Dinghy berths
f Access bridge
g Lifeboat slipway
h Domestic waste facilities
i Waste oil tank
j Disabled berthing
NB Berth numbers low outer to high inner, odd numbers on right, even left

CARLINGFORD MARINA

Carlingford Marina
Co. Louth, Ireland
Tel: +353 (0)42 937 3072 Fax: +353 (0)42 937 3075
Email: info@carlingfordmarina.ie
www.carlingfordmarina.ie

VHF Ch M
ACCESS H24

Carlingford Lough is an eight-mile sheltered haven between the Cooley Mountains to the south and the Mourne Mountains to the north. The marina is situated on the southern shore, about four miles from Haulbowline Lighthouse, and can be easily reached via a deep water shipping channel. Among the most attractive destinations in the Irish Sea, Carlingford is only 60 miles from the Isle of Man and within a day's sail from Strangford Lough and Ardglass. Full facilities in the marina include a first class bar and restaurant offering superb views across the water.

FACILITIES AT A GLANCE

Key
a Bar and restaurant
b Toilets, showers and laundry
c Refuse
d Office
e Chandlery
f Marina office
g Waiting pontoon

ARDGLASS MARINA

Ardglass Marina
19 Quay Street, Ardglass, BT30 7SA
Tel: 028 4484 2332
Email: infoardglassmarina@gmail.com
www.ardglassmarina.co.uk

VHF Ch M, 80
ACCESS H24

Situated just south of Strangford, Ardglass has the capacity to accommodate up to 22 yachts as well as space for small craft. Despite being relatively small in size, the marina boasts an extensive array of facilities, either on site or close at hand. Recent access improvements have been made for wheelchair users in the shower/WC and reception. Grocery stores, a post office, chemist and off-licence, are all within a five-minute walk from the marina. Among the local onshore activities are golf, mountain climbing in Newcastle, which is 18 miles south, as well as scenic walks at Ardglass and Delamont Park.

FACILITIES AT A GLANCE

Key
a Administration building
b Boat storage

Additional Facilities
Reception car park - 60 vehicles
Waste oil tanks
Local charts for Strangford Lough
Heavy duty battery charging
High pressure water washing
Internet and email access
Barbeque facilities
Car hire
Weather fax

PORTAFERRY MARINA

Portaferry Marina
1 Mill View, Portaferry, BT22 1LQ
Mobile: 07703 209780 Fax: 028 4272 9784
Email: info@portaferrymarina.co.uk

VHF Ch 80
ACCESS H24

Portaferry Marina lies on the east shore of the Narrows, the gateway to Strangford Lough on the north east coast of Ireland. A marine nature reserve of outstanding natural beauty, the Lough offers plenty of recreational activities. The marina, which caters for draughts of up to 2.5m, is fairly small, accommodating around 30 yachts. The office is situated about 200m from the marina itself, where you will find ablution facilities along with a launderette.

Portaferry incorporates several pubs and restaurants as well as a few convenience stores, while one of its prime attractions is the Exploris Aquarium. Places of historic interest in the vicinity include Castleward, an 18th century mansion in Strangford, and Mount Stewart House & Garden in Newtownards.

FACILITIES AT A GLANCE

CHANNEL ISLANDS – Guernsey & Jersey

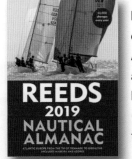
Key to Marina Plans symbols

Symbol		Symbol	
🛢	Bottled gas	P	Parking
	Chandler	✕	Pub/Restaurant
♿	Disabled facilities		Pump out
	Electrical supply		Rigging service
	Electrical repairs		Sail repairs
	Engine repairs		Shipwright
✚	First Aid		Shop/Supermarket
	Fresh Water		Showers
D	Fuel - Diesel		Slipway
P	Fuel - Petrol	WC	Toilets
	Hardstanding/boatyard		Telephone
@	Internet Café		Trolleys
▣	Laundry facilities	V	Visitors berths
	Lift-out facilities		Wi-Fi

Area 14 - Channel Islands

MARINAS

Telephone Numbers
VHF Channel
Access Times

ALDERNEY

Beaucette Marina
01481 245000
Ch 80 HW±3

GUERNSEY

HERM

SARK

St Peter Port
Victoria Marina
01481 725987
Ch 12, Ch 80 HW±2½

Maître Ile

N

JERSEY

St Helier Marina
01534 447730
Ch 14 HW±3

BEAUCETTE MARINA

Beaucette Marina
Vale, Guernsey, GY3 5BQ
Tel: 01481 245000 Fax: 01481 247071
Mobile: 07781 102302
Email: info@beaucettemarina.com

VHF	Ch 80
ACCESS	HW±3

Situated on the north east tip of Guernsey, Beaucette enjoys a peaceful, rural setting in contrast to the more vibrant atmosphere of Victoria Marina. Now owned by a private individual and offering a high standard of service, the site was originally formed from an old quarry.

There is a general store close by, while the bustling town of St Peter Port is only 20 minutes away by bus.

FACILITIES AT A GLANCE

Key
a Harbour office
b Restaurant
c Showers/toilets
d Laundry & telephone
e Manager's cabin
f Boatyard

Beaucette
Celebrating 50 years in 2019

- Blasted out from a quarry in 1969
- Peaceful and serene
- Referred to as 'the Gem of the Channel Islands'
- Transeurope member – visitor discounts
- Boatyard services
- Bar and restaurant
- Bike hire
- Full marina services

Beaucette Marina Tel: **01481 245000**
Email: **info@beaucettemarina.com**   VHF: **Channel 80**

ST PETER PORT

Guernsey Harbours
PO Box 631, St Julian's Emplacement, St Peter Port
Tel: 01481 720229 Fax: 01481 714177
Email: guernsey.harbour@gov.gg

VHF	Ch 12, 80
ACCESS	HW±2.5

The harbour of St Peter Port comprises the Queen Elizabeth II Marina to the N and Victoria and Albert Marinas to the S, with visiting yachtsmen usually accommodated in Victoria Marina.

St Peter Port is the capital of Guernsey. Its regency architecture and picturesque cobbled streets filled with restaurants and boutiques help to make it one of the most attractive harbours in Europe. Among the places of interest are Hauteville House, home of the writer Victor Hugo, and Castle Cornet. There are regular bus services to all parts of the island for visitors to explore a rich heritage.

FACILITIES AT A GLANCE

Key
a Customs shed
b Tourist Information
c Royal Channel Islands Yacht Club
d Toilets, showers, launderette, shops, pub and restaurant
e Guernsey Yacht Club
f Ferry terminal

ST PETER PORT VICTORIA MARINA

Guernsey Harbours
PO Box 631, St Julian's Emplacement, St Peter Port
Tel: 01481 720229 Fax: 01481 714177
Email: guernsey.harbour@gov.gg

VHF	Ch 80
ACCESS	HW±2.5

Victoria Marina in St Peter Port accommodates some 300 visiting yachts. In the height of the season it gets extremely busy, but when full visitors can berth on 5 other pontoons in the Pool or pre-arrange a berth in the QE II or Albert marinas. There are no visitor moorings in the Pool. Depending on draught, the marina is accessible approximately two and a half hours either side of HW, with yachts crossing over a sill drying to 4.2m. The marina dory will direct you to a berth on arrival or else will instruct you to moor on one of the waiting pontoons just outside.

Guernsey is well placed for exploring the rest of the Channel Islands and nearby French ports.

FACILITIES AT A GLANCE

Key
a Toilets, showers, launderette and shops
b Royal Channel Islands Yacht Club
c Refuse skip
d Marina control, port office
e Dinghy/tender landing pontoon
f Pub/restaurant
g Tourist information

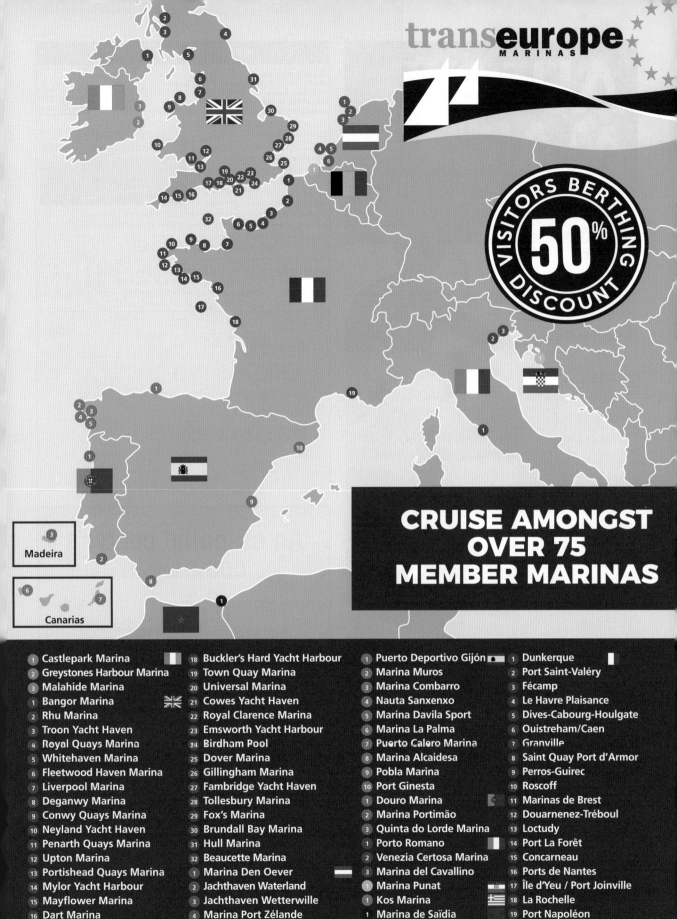

transeurope
MARINAS

VISITORS BERTHING 50% DISCOUNT

CRUISE AMONGST OVER 75 MEMBER MARINAS

1	Castlepark Marina
2	Greystones Harbour Marina
3	Malahide Marina
1	Bangor Marina
2	Rhu Marina
3	Troon Yacht Haven
4	Royal Quays Marina
5	Whitehaven Marina
6	Fleetwood Haven Marina
7	Liverpool Marina
8	Deganwy Marina
9	Conwy Quays Marina
10	Neyland Yacht Haven
11	Penarth Quays Marina
12	Upton Marina
13	Portishead Quays Marina
14	Mylor Yacht Harbour
15	Mayflower Marina
16	Dart Marina
17	Poole Quay Boathaven

18	Buckler's Hard Yacht Harbour
19	Town Quay Marina
20	Universal Marina
21	Cowes Yacht Haven
22	Royal Clarence Marina
23	Emsworth Yacht Harbour
24	Birdham Pool
25	Dover Marina
26	Gillingham Marina
27	Fambridge Yacht Haven
28	Tollesbury Marina
29	Fox's Marina
30	Brundall Bay Marina
31	Hull Marina
32	Beaucette Marina
1	Marina Den Oever
2	Jachthaven Waterland
3	Jachthaven Wetterwille
4	Marina Port Zélande
5	Jachthaven Biesbosch
6	Delta Marina

1	Puerto Deportivo Gijón
2	Marina Muros
3	Marina Combarro
4	Nauta Sanxenxo
5	Marina Davila Sport
6	Marina La Palma
7	Puerto Calero Marina
8	Marina Alcaidesa
9	Pobla Marina
10	Port Ginesta
1	Douro Marina
2	Marina Portimão
3	Quinta do Lorde Marina
1	Porto Romano
2	Venezia Certosa Marina
3	Marina del Cavallino
4	Marina Punat
5	Kos Marina
1	Marina de Saïdia
1	VVW Nieuwpoort

1	Dunkerque
2	Port Saint-Valéry
3	Fécamp
4	Le Havre Plaisance
5	Dives-Cabourg-Houlgate
6	Ouistreham/Caen
7	Granville
8	Saint Quay Port d'Armor
9	Perros-Guirec
10	Roscoff
11	Marinas de Brest
12	Douarnenez-Tréboul
13	Loctudy
14	Port La Forêt
15	Concarneau
16	Ports de Nantes
17	Île d'Yeu / Port Joinville
18	La Rochelle
19	Port Napoléon

Madeira

Canarias

Annual berth-holders based in TransEurope Marinas can benefit from a 50% visitor's berthing discount for up to five days per year in each member marina using their TransEurope membership card. For a current list of members and further information, please visit **www.transeuropemarinas.com**

ST HELIER HARBOUR

St Helier Harbour
Maritime House, La Route du Port Elizabeth
St Helier, Jersey, JE1 1HB
Tel: 01534 447708
www.portofjersey.je Email: marinas@ports.je

VHF Ch 14
ACCESS HW±3

Set in the Norman Breton Gulf, Jersey is the most southerly of the Channel Islands, offering over 200 visitor berths on a flexible daily, weekly or monthly basis. With its close proximity to the adjacent French coast and with sheltered bays and anchorages there are plenty of opportunities to explore new cruising areas, making Jersey an ideal base. Jersey airport is only 15 minutes away from St Helier Marina by bus or car.

Visiting craft are directed into St Helier Marina which is located in the town with access is HW±3. Alternatively, there is a holding pontoon just outside of the marina entrance providing full services and walk ashore access. Visiting vessels of up to 20m may be directed into Elizabeth Marina by prior arrangement.

FACILITIES AT A GLANCE

Key
a Marina office
b Water/toilets/ public phone
c Tourism
d Harbour office and Customs
e Maritime house
f Waiting pontoon
g Passenger Terminal
h Trailer park
i Port control
j Marina shop
k Cafe
l Self-service fuel

SECTION 2
MARINE SUPPLIES AND SERVICES GUIDE

ADHESIVES

Casco Adhesives
Darwen   07710 546899

CC Marine Services Ltd
West Mersea   07751 734510

Industrial Self Adhesives Ltd
Nottingham   0115 9681895

Sika Ltd Garden City   01707 394444

Technix Rubber & Plastics Ltd
Southampton   01489 789944

Tiflex Liskeard   01579 320808

Trade Grade Products Ltd
Poole   01202 820177

UK Epoxy Resins
Burscough   01704 892364

Wessex Resins & Adhesives Ltd
Romsey   01794 521111

3M United Kingdom plc
Bracknell   01344 858315

ASSOCIATIONS/ AGENCIES

Cruising Association
London   020 7537 2828

Fishermans Mutual Association (Eyemouth) Ltd
Eyemouth   01890 750373

Maritime and Coastguard Agency
Southampton   0870 6006505

Royal Institute of Navigation
London   020 7591 3130

Royal National Lifeboat Institution
Poole   01202 663000

Royal Yachting Association (RYA) Southampton   0845 345 0400

BERTHS & MOORINGS

ABC Powermarine
Beaumaris   01248 811413

Aqua Bell Ltd Norwich   01603 713013

Ardfern Yacht Centre
Lochgilphead   01852 500247/500636

Ardmair Boat Centre
Ullapool   01854 612054

Arisaig Marine Ltd
Inverness-shire   01687 450224

Bristol Boat Ltd Bristol   01225 872032

British Waterways
Argyll   01546 603210

Burgh Castle Marine
Norfolk   01493 780331

Cambrian Marine Services Ltd
Cardiff   029 2034 3459

Chelsea Harbour Ltd
London   020 7225 9108

Clapson & Son (Shipbuilders) Ltd
Barton-on-Humber   01652 635620

Crinan Boatyard, Crinan 01546 830232

Dartside Quay Brixham 01803 845445

Douglas Marine
Preston   01772 812462

Dublin City Moorings
Dublin   +353 1 8183300

Emsworth Yacht Harbour
Emsworth   01243 377727

Exeter Ship Canal   01392 274306

HAFAN PWLLHELI
Glan Don, Pwllheli, Gwynedd LL53 5YT
Tel: (01758) 701219
Fax: (01758) 701443 VHF Ch80
Hafan Pwllheli has over 400 pontoon berths and offers access at virtually all states of the tide. Ashore, its modern purpose-built facilities include luxury toilets, showers, launderette, a secure boat park for winter storage, 40-ton travel hoist, mobile crane and plenty of space for car parking. Open 24-hours a day, 7 days a week.

Highway Marine
Sandwich   01304 613925

Iron Wharf Boatyard
Faversham   01795 537122

Jalsea Marine Services Ltd
Northwich   01606 77870

Jersey Harbours
St Helier   01534 447788

Jones (Boatbuilders), David
Chester   01244 390363

Lawrenny Yacht Station
Kilgetty   01646 651212

MacFarlane & Son
Glasgow   01360 870214

NEPTUNE MARINA LTD
Neptune Quay, Ipswich, Suffolk IP4 1AX
Tel: (01473) 215204
Fax: (01473) 215206
e-mail:
enquiries@neptune-marina.com
www.neptune-marina.com
The quay to the heart of Ipswich! Call Ipswich lock gates on Channel 68 and Neptune Marina on Channel 80. Bring your crew to the wonderful Ipswich waterfront, with plenty of watering holes and town centre activities. You won't want to leave!

Orkney Marinas Ltd
Kirkwall   07810 465835

V Marine
Shoreham-by-Sea   01273 461491

Sutton Harbour Marina
Plymouth   01752 204186

WicorMarine Fareham   01329 237112

Winters Marine Ltd
Salcombe   01548 843580

Yarmouth Marine Service
Yarmouth   01983 760521

Youngboats
Faversham   01795 536176

BOAT BUILDERS & REPAIRS

ABC Hayling Island   023 9246 1968

ABC Powermarine
Beaumaris   01248 811413

Advance Yacht Systems
Southampton   023 8033 7722

Aqua-Star Ltd
St Sampsons   01481 244550

Ardoran Marine
Oban   01631 566123

Baumbach Bros Boatbuilders
Hayle   01736 753228

Beacon Boatyard
Rochester   01634 841320

Bedwell & Co
Walton on the Naze   01255 675873

Blackwell, Craig
Co Meath   +353 87 677 9605

Boyd Boat Building
Falmouth   07885 436722

Boatcraft
Ardrossan   01294 603047

B+ St Peter Port   01481 726071

Brennan, John
Dun Laoghaire   +353 1 280 5308

Burghead Boat Centre
Findhorn   01309 690099

Carrick Marine Projects
Co Antrim   02893 355884

Chapman & Hewitt Boatbuilders
Wadebridge   01208 813487

Chicks Marine Ltd
Guernsey   01481 723716

Clarence Boatyard
East Cowes   01983 294243

Cooks Maritime Craftsmen - Poliglow
Lymington   01590 675521

Creekside Boatyard (Old Mill Creek)
Dartmouth   01803 832649

CTC Marine & Leisure
Middlesbrough   01642 372600

Davies Marine Services
Ramsgate   01843 586172

Dickie International
Bangor   01248 363400

Dickie International
Pwllheli   01758 701828

East Llanion Marine Ltd
Pembroke Dock   01646 686866

Emblem Enterprises
East Cowes   01983 294243

Fairlie Quay
Fairlie   01475 568267

Fairweather Marine
Fareham   01329 283500

Farrow & Chambers Yacht Builders
Humberston
            www.farrowandchambers.co.uk

Fast Tack Plymouth   01752 255171

Fergulsea Engineering
Ayr 01292 262978

Ferrypoint Boat Co
Youghal +353 24 94232

Floetree Ltd (Loch Lomond Marina)
Balloch 01389 752069

Freshwater Boatyard
Truro 01326 270443

Frogmore Boatyard
Kingsbridge 01548 531257

Furniss Boat Building
Falmouth 01326 311766

Gallichan Marine Ltd
Jersey 01534 746387

Garvel Clyde
Greenock 01475 725372

Goodchild Marine Services
Great Yarmouth 01493 782301

Gosport Boatyard
Gosport 023 9252 6534

Gweek Quay Boatyard
Helston 01326 221657

Halls
Walton on the Naze 01255 675596

Harris Pye Marine
Barry 01446 720066

Haven Boatyard
Lymington 01590 677073

Hayling Yacht Company
Hayling Island 023 9246 3592

Hoare Ltd, Bob
Poole 01202 736704

Holyhead Boatyard
Holyhead 01407 760111

Jackson Marine
Lowestoft 01502 539772

Jackson Yacht Services
Jersey 01534 743819

JEP Marine
Canterbury 01227 710102

JWS Marine Services
Southsea 023 9275 5155

Kimelford Yacht Haven
Oban 01852 200248

Kingfisher Marine
Weymouth 01305 766595

Kingfisher Ultraclean UK Ltd
Tarporley 0800 085 7039

King's Boatyard
Pin Mill 01473 780258

Kinsale Boatyard
Kinsale +353 21477 4774

Kippford Slipway Ltd
Dalbeattie 01556 620249

Lavis & Son, CH
Exmouth 01395 263095

Lawrenny Yacht Station
Lawrenny 01646 651212

Lencraft Boats Ltd
Dungarvan +353 58 682220

Mackay Boatbuilders
Arbroath 01241 872879

Marine Services
Norwich 01692 582239

Mashford Brothers
Torpoint 01752 822232

Mayor & Co Ltd, J
Preston 01772 812250

Mears, HJ Axmouth 01297 23344

Mill, Dan, Galway +353 86 337 9304

Miller Marine
Tyne & Wear 01207 542149

Morrison, A
Killyleagh 028 44828215

Moss (Boatbuilders), David
Thornton-Cleveleys 01253 893830

Multi Marine Composites Ltd
Torpoint 01752 823513

Newing, Roy E
Canterbury 01227 860345

Noble and Sons, Alexander
Girvan 01465 712223

Northney Marine Services
Hayling Island 023 9246 9246

Northshore Sport & Leisure
King's Lynn 01485 210236

O'Sullivans Marine Ltd
Tralee +353 66 7124957

Pachol, Terry
Brighton 01273 620192

Partington Marine Ltd, William
Pwllheli 01758 612808

Pasco's Boatyard
Truro 01326 270269

Penrhos Marine
Aberdovey 01654 767478

Penzance Marine Services
Penzance 01736 361081

PJ Bespoke Boat Fitters Ltd
Crewe 01270 812244

Preston Marine Services Ltd
Preston 01772 733595

Red Bay Boats Ltd
Cushendall 028 2177 1331

Reliance Marine
Wirral 0151 625 5219

Retreat Boatyard Ltd
Exeter 01392 874720/875934

Richardson Boatbuilders, Ian
Stromness 01856 850321

Richardson Yacht Services Ltd
Newport 01983 821095

Cordell Grove
Middlesbrough 01642 226226

Roberts Marine Ltd, S
Liverpool 0151 707 8300

Rothman Pantall & Co
Fareham 01329 280221

Rustler Yachts
Falmouth 01326 310210

Salterns Boatyard
Poole 01202 707391

Sea & Shore Ship Chandler
Dundee 01382 450666

SEAFIT MARINE SERVICES LTD
Falmouth Marina, North Parade,
Falmouth, Cornwall TR11 2TD
Tel: (01326) 313713
Fax: (01326) 313713
Mob: 07971 196175
Email: mary.townsend@homecall.
co.uk
For installation maintenance and repair work - electrical, plumbing, hulls, rigs etc.

Seamark-Nunn & Co
Felixstowe 01394 275327

Seapower
Woolverstone 01473 780090

Slipway Cooperative Ltd
Bristol 0117 907 9938

Smith, GB, & Sons
Rock 01208 862815

Spicer Boatbuilder, Nick
Weymouth Marina 01305 767118

Storrar Marine Store
Newcastle upon Tyne 0191 266 1037

TT Marine Ashwell 01462 742449

Waterfront Marine
Bangor 01248 352513

Way, A&R, Boat Building
Tarbert, Loch Fyne 01546 606657

WestCoast Marine
Troon 01292 318121

Western Marine
Dublin +353 1 280 0321

Wigmore Wright Marine Services
Penarth 029 2070 9983

Williams, Peter
Fowey 01726 870987

WQI Ltd
Bournemouth 01202 771292

Yarmouth Marine Service
01983 760521

Youngboats
Faversham 01795 536176

BOATYARD SERVICES & SUPPLIES

ABC Marine
Hayling Island 023 9246 1968

Abersoch Boatyard Services Ltd
Abersoch 01758 713900

Amble Boat Co Ltd
Amble   01665 710267

Amsbrisbeg Ltd
Port Bannatyne   01700 831215

Ardmair Boat Centre
Ullapool   01854 612054

Ardmaleish Boat Building Co Rothesay
01700 502007

www.ardoran.co.uk
West coast Scotland. All marine
facilities.

Ardrishaig Boatyard
Lochgilphead   01546 603280

Arklow Slipway
Arklow   +353 402 33233

Baltic Wharf Boatyard
Totnes   01803 867922

Baltimore Boatyard
Baltimore   +353 28 20444

Bedwell and Co
Walton-on-the-Naze   01255 675873

Berthon Boat Co
Lymington   01590 673312

Birdham Shipyard
Chichester   01243 512310

BJ Marine Ltd Bangor   028 91271434

Blagdon, A
Plymouth   01752 561830

Boatcraft Ardrossan   01294 603047

Boatworks + Ltd
St Peter Port   01481 726071

Brennan, John
Dun Laoghaire   +353 1 280 5308

Brighton Marina Boatyard
Brighton   01273 819919

Bristol Marina (Yard)
Bristol   0117 921 3198

Buckie Shipyard Ltd
Buckie   01542 831245

Bucklers Hard Boat Builders Ltd
Brockenhurst   01590 616214

C & J Marine Services
Newcastle Upon Tyne   0191 295 0072

Caley Marina Inverness   01463 236539

Cambrian Boat Centre
Swansea   01792 467263

Cambrian Marine Services Ltd
Cardiff   029 2034 3459

Cantell and Son Ltd
Newhaven   01273 514118

Canvey Yacht Builders Ltd
Canvey Island   01268 696094

Carroll's Ballyhack Boatyard
New Ross   +353 51 389164

Castlepoint Boatyard
Crosshaven   +353 21 4832154

Chabot, Gary
Newhaven   07702 006767

Chapman & Hewitt Boatbuilders
Wadebridge   01208 813487

Chippendale Craft Rye   01797 227707

Clapson & Son (Shipbuilders) Ltd
Barton on Humber   01652 635620

Clarence Boatyard
East Cowes   01983 294243

Coastal Marine Boatbuilders
(Berwick upon Tweed)
Eyemouth   01890 750328

Coastcraft Ltd
Cockenzie   01875 812150

Coates Marine Ltd
Whitby   01947 604486

Connor, Richard
Coleraine   07712 115751

Coombes, AA
Bembridge   01983 872296

Corpach Boatbuilding Company
Fort William   01397 772861

Craobh Marina
By Lochgilphead   01852 500222

Creekside Boatyard (Old Mill Creek)
Dartmouth   01803 832649

Crinan Boatyard
By Lochgilphead   01546 830232

Crosshaven Boatyard Co Ltd
Crosshaven   +353 21 831161

Dale Sailing Co Ltd
Neyland   01646 603110

Darthaven Marina
Kingswear   01803 752242

Dartside Quay Brixham   01803 845445

Dauntless Boatyard Ltd
Canvey Island   01268 793782

Davis's Boatyard Poole   01202 674349

Dinas Boat Yard Ltd
Y Felinheli   01248 671642

Dorset Yachts
Poole   01202 674531

Douglas Boatyard
Preston   01772 812462

Dover Yacht Co Dover   01304 201073

Dun Laoghaire Marina
Dun Laoghaire   +353 1 2020040

Elephant Boatyard
Southampton   023 8040 3268

Elton Boatbuilding Ltd
Kirkcudbright   01557 330177

Felixstowe Ferry Boatyard
Felixstowe   01394 282173

Ferguson Engineering
Wexford   +353 6568 66822133

Ferry Marine South
Queensferry   0131 331 1233

Findhorn Boatyard
Findhorn   01309 690099

Firmhelm Ltd Pwllheli   01758 612251

Fleming Engineering, J
Stornoway   01851 703488

Fowey Boatyard
Fowey   01726 832194

Fox's Marina Ipswich   01473 689111

Frank Halls & Son
Walton on the Naze   01255 675596

Freeport Marine
Jersey   01534 888100

Furniss Boat Building
Falmouth   01326 311766

Garval Clyde
Greenock   01475 725372

Goodchild Marine Services
Great Yarmouth   01493 782301

Gosport Boatyard
Gosport   023 9252 6534

Gweek Quay Boatyard
Helston   01326 221657

Haines Boatyard
Chichester   01243 512228

Harbour Marine
Plymouth   01752 204691

Harbour Marine Services Ltd
Southwold   01502 724721

Harris Pye Marine
Barry   01446 720066

Hartlepool Marine Engineering
Hartlepool   01429 867883

Hayles, Harold
Yarmouth, IoW   01983 760373

Henderson, J Shiskine   01770 860259

Heron Marine
Whitstable   01227 361255

Hewitt, George
Binham   01328 830078

Holyhead Marina & Trinity Marine Ltd
Holyhead   01407 764242

Instow Marine Services
Bideford   01271 861081

Ipswich Haven Marina
Ipswich   01473 236644

Iron Wharf Boatyard
Faversham   01795 537122

Island Boat Services
Port of St Mary   01624 832073

Isle of Skye Yachts
Ardvasar   01471 844216

Jalsea Marine Services Ltd Weaver
Shipyard, Northwich   01606 77870

JBS Group
Peterhead   01779 475395

J B Timber Ltd
North Ferriby   01482 631765

Jersey Harbours Dept
St Helier   01534 885588

Kilnsale Boatyard
Kinsale   +353 21 4774774

Kingfisher Ultraclean UK Ltd
Tarporley   01928 787878

Kilrush Marina Boatyard
Kilrush   +35 87 7990091

Kinsale Boatyard +353 21477 4774

KPB Beaucette 07781 152581

Lake Yard Poole 01202 674531

Lallow, C Isle of Wight 01983 292112

Latham's Boatyard
Poole 01202 748029

Laxey Towing
Douglas, Isle of Man 07624 493592

Leonard Marine, Peter
Newhaven 01273 515987

Lincombe Marine
Salcombe 01548 843580

Lomax Boatbuilders
Cliffony +353 71 66124

Lymington Yt Haven 01590 677071

MacDougalls Marine Services
Isle of Mull 01681 700294

Macduff Shipyard Ltd
Macduff 01261 832234

Madog Boatyard
Porthmadog 01766 514205/513435

Mainbrayce Marine
Alderney 01481 822772

Malakoff and Moore
Lerwick 01595 695544

Mallaig Boat Building and Engineering
Mallaig 01687 462304

Maramarine
Helensburgh 01436 810971

Marindus Engineering
Kilmore Quay +353 53 29794

Mariners Farm Boatyard
Gillingham 01634 233179

McGruar and Co Ltd
Helensburgh 01436 831313

Mevagh Boatyard
Mulroy Bay +353 74 915 4470

Mill, Dan, Galway +353 86 337 9304

Mitchell's Boatyard
Poole 01202 747857

Mooney Boats
Killybegs +353 73 31152/31388

Moore & Son, J
St Austell 01726 842964

Morrison, A Killyleagh 028 44828215

Moss (Boatbuilders), David
Thornton-Cleveleys 01253 893830

Mustang Marine
Milford Haven 01646 696320

New Horizons Rhu 01436 821555

Noble and Sons, Alexander
Girvan 01465 712223

North Pier (Oban)
Oban 01631 562892

North Wales Boat Centre
Conwy 01492 580740

Northam Marine
Brightlingsea 01206 302003

Northshore Yacht Yard
Chichester 01243 512611

Oban Yachts and Marine Services
By Oban 01631 565333

Pearn and Co, Norman
Looe 01503 262244

Penrhos Marine
Aberdovey 01654 767478

Penzance Dry Dock and Engineering Co Ltd Penzance 01736 363838

Philip & Son Dartmouth 01803 833351

Phillips, HJ Rye 01797 223234

Ponsharden Boatyard
Penryn 01326 372215

Powersail and Island Chandlers Ltd
East Cowes Marina 01983 299800

Priors Boatyard
Burnham-on-Crouch 01621 782160

R K Marine Ltd
Swanwick 01489 583572

Rat Island Sailboat Company (Yard) St Mary's 01720 423399

Rennison, Russell
Gosport 07734 688819

Retreat Boatyard Ltd
Exeter 01392 874720/875934

Rice and Cole Ltd
Burnham-on-Crouch 01621 782063

Richardson Boatbuilders, Ian Stromness 01856 850321

Richardsons Boatbuilders
Binfield 01983 821095

Riverside Yard
Shoreham Beach 01273 592456

River Yar Boatyard
Yarmouth, IoW 01983 761000

Robertsons Boatyard
Woodbridge 01394 382305

Rossbrin Boatyard
Schull +353 28 37352

Rossiter Yachts Ltd
Christchurch 01202 483250

Rossreagh Boatyard
Rathmullan +353 74 9150182

Rudders Boatyard & Moorings
Milford Haven 01646 600288

Ryan & Roberts Marine Services
Askeaton +353 61 392198

Rye Harbour Marina Rye 01797 227667

Rynn Engineering, Pat
Galway +353 91 562568

Salterns Boatyard
Poole 01202 707391

Sandbanks Yacht Company
Poole 01202 611262

Scarborough Marine Engineering Ltd
Scarborough 01723 375199

Severn Valley Cruisers Ltd (Boatyard)
Stourport-on-Severn 01299 871165

Shepards Wharf Boatyard Ltd
Cowes 01983 297821

Shipshape
King's Lynn 01553 764058

Shotley Marina Ltd
Ipswich 01473 788982

Shotley Marine Services Ltd
Ipswich 01473 788913

Silvers Marina Ltd
Helensburgh 01436 831222

Skinners Boat Yard
Baltimore +353 28 20114

Smith, GB, & Sons
Rock 01208 862815

Smith & Gibbs
Eastbourne 07802 582009

Sparkes Boatyard
Hayling Island 023 92463572

Spencer Sailing Services, Jim
Brightlingsea 01206 302911

Standard House Boatyard
Wells-next-the-Sea 01328 710593

Storrar Marine Store
Newcastle upon Tyne 0191 266 1037

Strand Shipyard Rye 01797 222070

Surry Boatyard
Shoreham-by-Sea 01273 461491

The Shipyard
Littlehampton 01903 713327

Titchmarsh Marina
Walton-on-the-Naze 01255 672185

Tollesbury Marina
Tollesbury 01621 869202

T J Rigging Conwy 07780 972411

Toms and Son Ltd, C
Fowey 01726 870232

Tony's Marine Service
Coleraine 028 7035 6422

Torquay Marina
Torquay 01803 200210

Trinity Marine & Holyhead Marina
Holyhead 01407 763855

Trouts Boatyard (River Exe)
Topsham 01392 873044

Upson and Co, RF
Aldeburgh 01728 453047

Versatility Workboats
Rye 01797 224422

Weir Quay Boatyard
Bere Alston 01822 840474

West Solent Boatbuilders
Lymington 01590 642080

WicorMarine Fareham 01329 237112

Woodrolfe Boatyard
Maldon 01621 869202

Yarmouth Marine Services
Yarmouth, IoW 01983 760521

BOAT DELIVERIES & STORAGE

ABC Marine
Hayling Island 023 9246 1968

Abersoch Boatyard Services Ltd
Pwllheli 01758 713900

Ambrisbeg Ltd
Port Bannatyne 01700 502719

Arisaig Marine
Inverness-shire   01687 450224

Bedwell and Co
Walton-on-the-Naze   01255 675873

Berthon Boat Company
Lymington   01590 673312

Boat Shifters
                 07733 344018/01326 210548

C & J Marine Services
Newcastle upon Tyne   0191 295 0072

Caley Marine
Inverness   01463 233437

Carrick Marine Projects
Co Antrim   02893 355884

Challenger Marine
Penryn   01326 377222

Coates Marine Ltd
Whitby   01947 604486

Convoi Exceptionnel Ltd
Hamble   023 8045 3045

Creekside Boatyard (Old Mill Creek) Dartmouth   01803 832649

Crinan Boatyard Ltd
Crinan   01546 830232

Dale Sailing Co Ltd
Neyland   01646 603110

Dart Marina Ltd
Dartmouth   01803 833351

Dartside Quay
Brixham   01803 845445

Dauntless Boatyard Ltd
Canvey Island   01268 793782

Debbage Yachting
Ipswich   01473 601169

Douglas Marine Preston   01772 812462

East & Co, Robin
Kingsbridge   01548 531257

East Coast Offshore Yachting
                         01480 861381

Emsworth Yacht Harbour
Emsworth   01243 377727

Exeter Ship Canal   01392 274306

Exmouth Marina   01395 269314

Firmhelm Ltd Pwllheli 01758 612244

Forrest Marine Ltd
Exeter   08452 308335

Fowey Boatyard
Fowey   01726 832194

Freshwater Boatyard
Truro   01326 270443

Hafan Pwllheli Pwllheli 01758 701219

Houghton Boat Transport
Tewkesbury   07831 486710

Gweek Quay Boatyard
Helston   01326 221657

Iron Wharf Boatyard
Faversham   01795 537122

Jalsea Marine Services Ltd
Northwich   01606 77870

KG McColl
Oban   01852 200248

Latham's Boatyard
Poole   01202 748029

Lavis & Son, CH
Exmouth   01395 263095

Lincombe Boat Yard
Salcombe   01548 843580

Marine Blast
Holy Loch   01369 705394

Marine Resource Centre Ltd
Oban   01631 720291

Marine & General Engineers
Guernsey   01481 245808

Milford Marina
Milford Haven   01646 696312/3

Moonfleet Sailing
Poole   01202 682269

Southerly Chichester   01243 512611

Pasco's Boatyard
Truro   01326 270269

Pearn and Co, Norman
Looe   01503 262244

Performance Yachting
Plymouth   01752 565023

Peters & May Ltd
Southampton   023 8048 0480

Ponsharden Boatyard
Penryn   01326 372215

Portsmouth Marine Engineering
Fareham   01329 232854

Priors Boatyard
Burnham-on-Crouch   01621 782160

Reeder School of Seamanship, Mike
Lymington   01590 674560

Rossiter Yachts
Christchurch   01202 483250

Sealand Boat Deliveries Ltd
Liverpool   01254 705225

Shearwater Sailing
Southampton   01962 775213

Shepards Wharf Boatyard Cowes Harbour Commission
Cowes   01983 297821

Silvers Marina Ltd
Helensburgh   01436 831222

Southcoasting Navigators
Devon   01626 335626

Waterfront Marine
Bangor   01248 352513

West Country Boat Transport
                         01566 785651

WicorMarine
Fareham   01329 237112

Winters Marine Ltd
Salcombe   01548 843580

Wolff, David   07659 550131 **Yacht Solutions Ltd**
Portsmouth   023 9275 5155

Yarmouth Marine Service
Yarmouth, IoW   01983 760521

Youngboats
Faversham   01795 536176

BOOKS, CHARTS & PUBLISHERS

Adlard Coles Nautical
London   020 7631 5600

Brown Son & Ferguson Ltd
Glasgow   0141 429 1234

Cooke & Son Ltd, B Hull 01482 223454

Dubois Phillips & McCallum Ltd
Liverpool   0151 236 2776

Imray, Laurie, Norie & Wilson
Huntingdon   01480 462114

Kelvin Hughes
Southampton   023 8063 4911

Lilley & Gillie Ltd, John 0191 257 2217

Marine Chart Services
Wellingborough   01933 441629

Price & Co Ltd, WF
Bristol   0117 929 2229

QPC
Fareham   01329 287880

Stanford Charts
Bristol   0117 929 9966

Stanford Charts
London   020 7836 1321

Stanford Charts   0845 880 3730
Manchester   0870 890 3730

Wiley Nautical
Chichester   01243 779777

BOW THRUSTERS

ARS Anglian Diesels Ltd
Wakefield   01924 332492

Buckler's Hard Boat Builders Ltd
Beaulieu   01590 616214

JS Mouldings International
Bursledon   023 8063 4400

BREAKDOWN

BJ Marine Ltd
Bangor, Ireland   028 9127 1434

Seafit Marine Services
Falmouth   01326 313713

CHANDLERS

ABC Powermarine
Beaumaris   01248 811413

Admiral Marine Supplies
Bootle   01469 575909

Allgadgets.co.uk
Exmouth   01395 227727

Alpine Room & Yacht Equipment
Chelmsford   01245 223563

Aquatogs Cowes   01983 295071

Arbroath Fishermen's Association
Arbroath   01241 873132

Ardfern Yacht Centre Ltd
Argyll   01852 500247

Ardoran Marine
Oban   01631 566123

Arthurs Chandlery
Gosport 023 9252 6522

Arun Canvas and Rigging Ltd
Littlehampton 01903 732561

Aruncraft Chandlers
Littlehampton 01903 713327

ASAP Supplies – Equipment & Spares
Worldwide
Beccles 0845 1300870

Auto Marine
Southsea 02392 825601

Bayside Marine
Brixham 01803 856771

Bedwell and Co
Walton on the Naze 01255 675873

BJ Marine Ltd Bangor 028 9127 1434

Bluecastle Chandlers
Portland 01305 822298

Blue Water Marine Ltd
Pwllheli 01758 614600

Boatacs
Westcliffe on Sea 01702 475057

Boathouse, The
Penryn 01326 374177

Boston Marina 01205 364420

Bosun's Locker, The
Falmouth 01326 312212

Bosun's Locker, The
Ramsgate 01843 597158

Bosuns Locker, The
South Queensferry 0131 331 3875/4496

B+ St Peter Port 01481 726071

Bridger Marine, John
Exeter 01392 250970

Bristol Boat Ltd Bristol 01225 872032

Brixham Yacht Supplies Ltd
Brixham 01803 882290

Brunel Chandlery Ltd
Neyland 01646 601667

Buccaneer Ltd
Macduff 01261 835199

Bucklers Hard Boat Builders
Beaulieu 01590 616214

Burghead Boat Centre
Findhorn 01309 690099

Bussell & Co, WL
Weymouth 01305 785633

Buzzard Marine
Yarmouth 01983 760707

C & M Marine
Bridlington 01262 672212

Cabin Yacht Stores
Rochester 01634 718020

Caley Marina Inverness 01463 236539

Cambrian Boat Centre
Swansea 01792 655925

Cantell & Son Ltd
Newhaven 01273 514118

Carne (Sales) Ltd, David
Penryn 01326 374177

Carrickcraft
Malahide +353 1 845 5438

Caters Carrick Ltd
Carrickfergus 028 93351919

CH Marine (Cork) +353 21 4315700

CH Marine Skibbereen +353 28 23190

Charity & Taylor Ltd
Lowestoft 01502 581529

Chertsey Marine Ltd
Penton Hook Marina 01932 565195

Chicks Marine Ltd
Guernsey 01481 740771

Christchurch Boat Shop
Christchurch 01202 482751

Clancy Hardware
Kilrush +35 65 905 1085

Clapson & Son (Shipbuilders) Ltd South
Ferriby Marina 01652 635620

Clarke, Albert, Marine
Newtownards 028 9187 2325

Clyde Chandlers
Ardrossan 01294 607077

CMC Campbeltown 01586 551441

Coastal Marine Boatbuilders Ltd
(Dunbar) Eyemouth 01890 750328

Coates Marine Ltd
Whitby 01947 604486

Collins Marine St Helier 01534 732415

Compass Marine
Lancing 01903 761773

Cosalt International Ltd
Aberdeen 01224 588327

Cosalt International Ltd
Southampton 023 8063 2824

Cotter, Kieran
Baltimore +353 28 20106

Cox Yacht Charter Ltd, Nick
Lymington 01590 673489

C Q Chandlers Ltd
Poole 01202 682095

Crinan Boats Ltd
Lochgilphead 01546 830232

CTC Marine & Leisure
Middlesbrough 01642 372600

Dale Sailing Co Ltd
Milford Haven 01646 603110

Danson Marine
Sidcup 0208 304 5678

Dartmouth Chandlery
Dartmouth 01803 839292

Dartside Quay
Brixham 01803 845445

Dauntless Boatyard Ltd
Canvey Island 01268 793782

Davis's Yacht Chandler
Littlehampton 01903 722778

Denney & Son, EL
Redcar 01642 483507

Deva Marine Conwy 01492 572777

Dickie & Sons Ltd, AM
Bangor 01248 363400

Dickie & Sons Ltd, AM
Pwllheli 01758 701828

Dinghy Supplies Ltd/Sutton Marine Ltd
Sutton +353 1 832 2312

Diverse Yacht Services
Hamble 023 80453399

Dixon Chandlery, Peter
Exmouth 01395 273248

Doling & Son, GW
Barrow In Furness 01229 823708

Dovey Marine
Aberdovey 01654 767581

Down Marine Co Ltd
Belfast 028 9048 0247

Douglas Marine Preston 01772 812462

Dubois Phillips & McCallum Ltd
Liverpool 0151 236 2776

Duncan Ltd, JS Wick 01955 602689

Duncan Yacht Chandlers
Ely 01353 663095

East Anglian Sea School
Ipswich 01473 659992

Eccles Marine Co
Middlesbrough 01642 372600

Ely Boat Chandlers
Hayling Island 023 9246 1968

Emsworth Chandlery
Emsworth 01243 375500

Force 4 Chandlery
Stroud 0845 1300710

Exe Leisure Exeter 01392 879055

Express Marine Services
Chichester 01243 773788

Fairways Chandlery
Burnham-on-Crouch 01621 782659

Fairweather Marine
Fareham 01329 283500

Fal Chandlers
Falmouth Marina 01326 212411

Ferrypoint Boat Co
Youghal +353 24 94232

Findhorn Marina & Boatyard
Findhorn 01309 690099

Firmhelm Ltd P
wllheli 01758 612244

Fisherman's Mutual Asssociation
(Eyemouth) Ltd
Eyemouth 01890 750373

Floetree Ltd (Loch Lomond Marina)
Balloch 01389 752069

Force 4 (Deacons)
Bursledon 023 8040 2182

Force 4 Chichester 01243 773788

Force 4 Chandlery
Mail order 0845 1300710

Force 4 Chandlery
Plymouth 01752 252489

Force 4 (Hamble Point)
Southampton 023 80455 058

Force 4 (Mercury)
Southampton 023 8045 4849

Force 4 (Port Hamble) Southampton	023 8045 4858
Force 4 (Shamrock) Southampton	023 8063 2725
Force 4 (Swanwick) Swanwick	01489 881825
Freeport Marine Jersey	01534 888100
French Marine Motors Ltd Brightlingsea	01206 302133
Furneaux Riddall & Co Ltd Portsmouth	023 9266 8621
Gael Force Glasgow	0141 941 1211
Gael Force Stornoway	01851 705540
Gallichan Marine Ltd Jersey	01534 746387
Galway Marine Chandlers Ltd Galway	+353 91 566568
GB Attfield & Company Dursley	01453 547185
Gibbons Ship Chandlers Ltd Sunderland	0191 567 2101
Goodwick Marine Fishguard	01348 873955
Gorleston Marine Ltd Great Yarmouth	01493 661883
GP Barnes Ltd Shoreham	01273 591705/596680
Great Outdoors Clarenbridge, Galway	+353 87 2793821
Green Marine, Jimmy Fore St Beer	01297 20744
Grimsby Rigging Services Ltd Grimsby	01472 362758
Gunn Navigation Services, Thomas Aberdeen	01224 595045
Hale Marine, Ron Portsmouth	023 92732985
Harbour Marine Services Ltd (HMS) Southwold	01502 724721
Hardware & Marine Supplies Wexford	+353 53 29791
Hartlepool Marine Supplies Hartlepool	01429 862932
Harwoods Yarmouth	01983 760258
Hawkins Marine Shipstores, John Rochester	01634 840812
Hayles, Harold Yarmouth	01983 760373
Herm Seaway Marine Ltd St Peter Port	01481 726829
Highway Marine Sandwich	01304 613925
Hoare Ltd, Bob, Poole	01202 736704
Hodges, T Coleraine	028 7035 6422
Hornsey (Chandlery) Ltd, Chris Southsea	023 9273 4728
Hunter & Combes Cowes	01983 299599

Iron Stores Marine St Helier	01534 877755
Isles of Scilly Steamship Co St Mary's	01720 422710
Jackson Yacht Services Jersey	01534 743819
Jamison and Green Ltd Belfast	028 9032 2444
Jeckells and Son Ltd Lowestoft	01502 565007
JF Marine Chandlery Rhu	01436 820584
JNW Services Aberdeen	01224 594050
JNW Services Peterhead	01779 477346
JSB Ltd Tarbert, Loch Fyne	01880 820180
Johnston Brothers Mallaig	01687 462215
Johnstons Marine Stores Lamlash	01770 600333
Kearon Ltd, George Arklow	+353 402 32319
Kelvin Hughes Ltd Southampton	023 80634911
Kildale Marine Hull	01482 227464
Kingfisher Marine Weymouth	01305 766595
Kings Lock Chandlery Middlewich	01606 737564
Kip Chandlery Inverkip Greenock	01475 521485
Kirkcudbright Scallop Gear Ltd Kirkcudbright	01557 330399
Kyle Chandlers Troon	01292 311880
Landon Marine, Reg Truro	01872 272668
Largs Chandlers Largs	01475 686026
Lencraft Boats Ltd Dungarvan	+353 58 68220
Lincoln Marina Lincoln	01522 526896
Looe Chandlery West Looe	01503 264355
Lynch Ltd, PA Morpeth	01670 512291
Mackay Boatbuilders (Arbroath) Ltd Aberdeen	01241 872879
Mackay Marine Services Aberdeen	01224 575772
Mailspeed Marine Crawley	01273837823
Mailspeed Marine Essex Marina	01342 710618
Mailspeed Marine Warrington	01342 710618
Mainbrayce Chandlers Braye, Alderney	01481 822772
Manx Marine Ltd Douglas	01624 674842
Marine & Leisure Europe Ltd Plymouth	01752 268826

Marine MegaStore Hamble	023 8045 4400
Marine MegaStore Morpeth	01670 516151
Marine Parts Direct Swords, Co Dublin	+353 1 807 5144
Marine Scene Bridgend	01656 671822
Marine Scene Cardiff	029 2070 5780
Marine Services Jersey	01534 626930
Marine Store Wyatts West Mersea	01206 384745
Marine Store Maldon	01621 854380
Marine Store Titchmarsh Marina	01255 679028
Marine Store Walton on the Naze	01255 679028
Marine Superstore Port Solent Chandlery Portsmouth	023 9221 9843
MarineCo Torpoint	01752 816005
Maryport Harbour and Marina Maryport	01900 814431
Matthews Ltd, D Cork	+353 214 277633
McClean Greenock	01475 728234
McCready Sailboats Ltd Holywood	028 9042 1821
Moore, Kevin Cowes	01983 289699
Moore & Son, J Mevagissey	01726 842964
Morgan & Sons Marine, LH Brightlingsea	01206 302003
Mount Batten Boathouse Plymouth	01752 482666
Murphy, Nicholas Dunmore East	+353 51 383259
Mylor Chandlery & Rigging Falmouth	01326 375482
Nautical World Bangor	028 91460330
New World Yacht Care Helensburgh	01436 820586
Newhaven Chandlery Newhaven	01273 612612
Nifpo Ardglass	028 4484 2144
Norfolk Marine Great Yarmouth	01692 670272
Norfolk Marine Chandlery Shop Norwich	01603 783150
Ocean Leisure Ltd London	020 7930 5050
One Stop Chandlery Maldon	01621 853558
O'Sullivans Marine Ltd Tralee	+353 66 7129635
Partington Marine Ltd, William Pwllheli	01758 612808

Pascall Atkey & Sons Ltd
Isle of Wight   01983 292381

Pennine Marine Ltd
Skipton   01756 792335

Penrhos Marine
Aberdovey   01654 767478

Penzance Marine Services
Penzance   01736 361081

Perry Marine, Rob
Axminster   01297 631314

Pepe Boatyard
Hayling Island   023 9246 1968

Performance Yachting & Chandlery
Plymouth   01752 565023

Peters PLC Chichester   01243 511033

Pinnell & Bax
Northampton   01604 592808

Piplers of Poole Poole   01202 673056

Pirate's Cave, The
Rochester   01634 295233

Powersail Island Chandlers Ltd
East Cowes Marina   01983 299800

Preston Marine Services Ltd
Preston   01772 733595

Price & Co Ltd, WF
Bristol   0117 929 2229

PSM Ltd Alderney   07781 106635

Purcell Marine
Clarenbridge   +353 87 279 3821

Purple Sails & Marine
Walsall   08456 435510

Quay West Marine
Poole   01202 732445

Quayside Marine
Salcombe   01548 844300

R&A Fabrication
Kirkcudbright   01557 330399

Racecourse Yacht Basin (Windsor) Ltd
Windsor   01753 851501

Rat Rigs Water Sports
Cardiff   029 2062 1309

Reliance Marine Wirral 0151 625 5219

Rigmarine Padstow   01841 532657

Riversway Marine
Preston   0844 879 4901

RHP Marine Cowes   01983 290421

RNS Marine Northam   01237 474167

Sail Loft Bideford   01271 860001

Sailaway
St Anthony   01326 231357

Salcombe Boatstore
Salcombe   01548 843708

Salterns Chandlery
Poole   01202 701556

Shipmate Salcombe   01548 844555

Sandrock Marine Rye   01797 222679

Schull Watersports Centre
Schull   +353 28 28554

Sea & Shore Ship Chandler
Dundee   01382 450666

Sea Cruisers of Rye Rye 01797 222070

Sea Span Edinburgh   0131 552 2224

Sea Teach Ltd Emsworth 01243 375774

Seafare Tobermory   01688 302277

Seahog Boats Preston   01772 633016

Seamark-Nunn & Co
Felixstowe   01394 451000

Seaquest Marine Ltd
St Peter Port   01481 721773

Seaware Ltd Penryn   01326 377948

Seaway Marine Macduff 01261 832877

Sharp & Enright Dover   01304 206295

Shearwater Engineering Services Ltd
Dunoon   01369 706666

Shipshape Marine
King's Lynn   01553 764058

Ship Shape Ramsgate   01843 597000

Shorewater Sports
Chichester   01243 672315

Simpson Marine Ltd
Newhaven   01273 612612

Simpson Marine Ltd, WA
Dundee   01382 566670

Sketrick Marine Centre
Killinchy   028 9754 1400

Smith AM (Marine) Ltd
London   020 8529 6988

Solent Marine Chandlery Ltd
Gosport   023 9258 4622

South Coast Marine
Christchurch   01202 482695

South Pier Shipyard
St Helier   01534 711000

Southampton Yacht Services Ltd
Southampton   023 803 35266

Sparkes Chandlery
Hayling Island   02392 463572

S Roberts Marine Ltd
Liverpool   0151 707 8300

SSL Marine
Eastbourne   01323 47900

Standard House Chandlery
Wells-next-the-Sea   01328 710593

Stornoway Fishermen's Co-op
Stornoway   01851 702563

Sunset Marine & Watersports
Sligo   +353 71 9162792

Sussex Marine
St Leonards on Sea   01424 425882

Sussex Yachts Lyd
Shoreham   01273 605482

Sussex Marine Centre
Shoreham   01273 454737

Sutton Marine (Dublin)
Sutton   +353 1 832 2312

SW Nets Newlyn   01736 360254

Tarbert Ltd, JSB
Tarbert   01880 820180

TCS Chandlery
Essex Marina   01702 258094

TCS Chandlery Grays   01375 374702

TCS Chandlery
Southend   01702 444423

Thulecraft Ltd Lerwick   01595 693192

Tony's Marine Services
Coleraine   07866 690436

Torbay Boating Centre
Paignton   01803 558760

Torquay Chandlers
Torquay   01803 211854

Trafalgar Yacht Services
Fareham   01329 822445

Trident UK
N Shields   0191 490 1736

Union Chandlery
Cork   +353 21 4554334

Uphill Boat Services
Weston-Super-Mare   01934 418617

Upper Deck Marine and Outriggers
Fowey   01726 832287

V Ships (Isle of Man)
Douglas   01624 688886

V F Marine Rhu   01436 820584

Viking Marine Ltd
Dun Laoghaire   +353 1 280 6654

Waterfront Marine
Bangor   01248 352513

Watersport and Leisure
Kings Lynn   01485 210236

Wayne Maddox Marine
Margate   01843 297157

Western Marine
Dalkey   +353 1280 0321

Wetworks, The
Burnham-on-Crouch   01621 786413

Whitstable Marine
Whitstable   01227 274168

Williams Ltd, TJ Cardiff 029 20 487676

Windjammer Marine
Milford Marina   01646 699070

Yacht & Boat Chandlery
Faversham   01795 531777

Yacht Chandlers Conwy 01492 572777

Yacht Equipment
Chelmsford   01245 223563

Yachtmail Ltd
Lymington   01590 672784

Yachtshop Holyhead   01407 760031

You Boat Chandlery
Gosport   02392 522226

CHART AGENTS

Brown Son & Ferguson Ltd
Glasgow   0141 429 1234

Chattan Security Ltd
Edinburgh   0131 554 7527

Cooke & Son Ltd, B
Hull 01482 223454

Dubois Phillips & McCallum Ltd
Liverpool 0151 236 2776

Imray Laurie Norie and Wilson Ltd
Huntingdon 01480 462114

Kelvin Hughes
Southampton 023 8063 4911

Lilley & Gillie Ltd, John
North Shields 0191 257 2217

MARINE CHART SERVICES
Maritime House, 32 Denington Rd,
Wellingborough NN8 2QH
Tel: 01933 441629
Fax: 01933 442662
www.chartsales.co.uk
Access to many thousands of
Navigation Charts & publications in
different format.

Price & Co, WF
Bristol 0117 929 2229

Sea Chest Nautical Bookshop
Plymouth 01752 222012

Seath Instruments (1992) Ltd
Lowestoft 01502 573811

Small Craft Deliveries
Woodbridge 01394 382655

Smith (Marine) Ltd, AM
London 020 8529 6988

South Bank Marine Charts Ltd Grimsby
01472 361137

Stanford Charts Bristol 0117 929 9966

Stanford Charts
London 020 7836 1321

Todd Chart Agency Ltd
County Down 028 9146 6640

UK Hydrographics Office
Taunton 01823 337900

Warsash Nautical Bookshop
Warsash 01489 572384

CLOTHING

Absolute
Gorleston on Sea 01493 442259

Aquatogs Cowes 01983 245892

Crew Clothing
London 020 8875 2300

Crewsaver
Gosport 01329 820000

Douglas Gill
Nottingham 0115 9460844

Fat Face fatface.com

Gul International Ltd
Bodmin 01208 262400

Guy Cotten UK Ltd
Liskeard 01579 347115

Harwoods Yarmouth 01983 760258

Helly Hansen
Nottingham 0115 979 5997

Henri Lloyd
Manchester 0161 799 1212

Joules 0845 6066871

Mad Cowes Clothing Co
Cowes 0845 456 5158

Matthews Ltd, D
Cork +353 214 277633

Mountain & Marine
Poynton 01625 859863

Musto Ltd Laindon 01268 491555

Purple Sails & Marine
Walsall 0845 6435510

Quba Sails
Lymington 01590 689362

Quba Sails
Salcombe 01548 844599

Yacht Parts Plymouth 01752 252489

CODE OF PRACTICE EXAMINERS

Booth Marine Surveys, Graham
Birchington-on-Sea 01843 843793

Cannell & Associates, David M
Wivenhoe 01206 823337

COMPUTERS & SOFTWARE

Dolphin Maritime Software
White Cross 01524 841946

Forum Software Ltd
Nr Haverfordwest 01646 636363

Kelvin Hughes Ltd
Southampton 023 8063 4911

Memory-Map
Aldermaston 0844 8110950

PC Maritime Plymouth 01752 254205

DECK EQUIPMENT

Aries Van Gear Spares
Penryn 01326 377467

Ronstan
Gosport 023 9252 5377

Harken UK Lymington 01590 689122

IMP Royston 01763 241300

Kearon Ltd George +353 402 32319

Pro-Boat Ltd
Burnham-on-Crouch 01621 785455

Ryland, Kenneth
Stanton 01386 584270

Smith, EC & Son Ltd
Luton 01582 729721

Timage & Co Ltd
Braintree 01376 343087

DIESEL MARINE/ FUEL ADDITIVES

Corralls Poole 01202 674551

Cotters Marine & General Supplies
Baltimore +353 28 20106

Expresslube
Henfield 01444 254115

Gorey Marine Fuel Supplies
Gorey 07797 742384

Hammond Motorboats
Dover 01304 206809

Iron Wharf Boatyard
Faversham 01795 536296

Lallow, Clare Cowes 01983 760707

Marine Support & Towage
Cowes 01983 200716/07860 297633

Quayside Fuel
Weymouth 07747 182181

Rossiter Yachts
Christchurch 01202 483250

Sleeman & Hawken
Shaldon 01626 778266

DIVERS

Abco Divers Belfast 028 90610492

Andark Diving
Burseldon 01489 581755

Argonaut Marine
Aberdeen 01224 706526

**Baltimore Diving and Watersports
Centre** West Cork +353 28 20300

C & C Marine Services
Largs 01475 687180

Cardiff Commercial Boat Operators Ltd
Cardiff 029 2037 7872

Clyde Diving Centre
Inverkip 01475 521281

Divetech UK King's Lynn 01485 572323

Diving & Marine Engineering
Barry 01446 721553

Donnelly, R
South Shields 07973 119455

DV Diving 028 9146 4671

Falmouth Divers Ltd
Penryn 01326 374736

Fathoms Ltd Wick 01955 605956

Felixarc Marine Ltd
Lowestoft 01502 509215

Grampian Diving Services
New Deer 01771 644206

Higgins, Noel +353 872027650

Hudson, Dave
Trearddur Bay 01407 860628

Hunt, Kevin Tralee +353 6671 25979

Kaymac Diving Services
Swansea 08431 165523

Keller, Hilary Buncrana +353 77 62146

Kilkee Diving Centre
Kilkee +353 6590 56707

Leask Marine
Kirkwall 01856 874725

Looe Divers Hannafore 01503 262727

MacDonald, D Nairn 01667 455661

Medway Diving Contractors Ltd
Gillingham   01634 851902

MMC Diving Services
Lake, Isle of Wight   07966 579965

Mojo Maritime
Penzance   01736 762771

Murray, Alex
Stornoway   01851 704978

New Dawn Dive Centre
Lymington   01590 675656

Northern Divers (Engineering) Ltd
Hull   01482 227276

Offshore Marine Services Ltd
Bembridge   01983 873125

Parkinson (Sinbad Marine Services), J
Killybegs   +353 73 31417

Port of London Authority
Gravesend   01474 560311

Purcell, D – Crouch Sailing School
Burnham   01621 784140/0585 33

Salvesen UK Ltd
Liverpool   0151 933 6038

Sea-Lift Diving Dover   01304 829956

Southern Cylinder Services
Fareham   01329 221125

Sub Aqua Services
North Ormesby   01642 230209

Teign Diving Centre
Teignmouth   01626 773965

Tuskar Rock Marine
Rosslare   +353 53 33376

Underwater Services
Dyffryn Arbwy   01341 247702

Wilson Alan c/o Portrush Yacht Club
Portrush   028 2076 2225

Woolford, William
Bridlington   01262 671710

ELECTRICAL AND ELECTRONIC ENGINEERS

AAS Marine
Aberystwyth   01970 631090

Allworth Riverside Services, Adrian
Chelsea Harbour Marina
                          07831 574774

ASL Auto Services
Boston   01205 761560

Auto Marine Electrics
Holy Loch   01369 701555

Baker, Keith Brentford 07792 937790

Belson Design Ltd, Nick
Southampton   077 6835 1330

Biggs, John Weymouth Marina,
Weymouth   01305 778445

BJ Marine Ltd Bangor   028 9127 1434

BM Electrical
Kirkcudbright   07584 657192

Boat Electrics Troon   01292 315355

Buccaneer Ltd
Macduff   01261 835199

Calibra Marine
Dartmouth   01803 833094

Campbell & McHardy Lossiemouth
Marina, Lossiemouth   01343 812137

CES Sandown Sparkes Marina,
Hayling Island   023 9246 6005

Colin Coady Marine
Malahide   +353 87 265 6496

Contact Electrical
Arbroath   01241 874528

DDZ Marine Ardossan   01294 607077

EC Leisure Craft
Essex Marina   01702 568482

Energy Solutions
Rochester   01634 290772

Enterprise Marine Electronic & Technical Services Ltd
Aberdeen   01224 593281

Eurotek Marine
Eastbourne   01323 479144

Evans, Lyndon
Brentford   07795 218704

Floetree Ltd (Loch Lomond Marina)
Balloch   01389 752069

Hamble Marine
Hamble   02380 001088

HNP Engineers (Lerwick) Ltd
Lerwick   01595 692493

Jackson Yacht Services
Jersey   01534 743819

Jedynak, A Salcombe   01548 843321

Kippford Slipway Ltd
Dalbeattie   01556 620249

Lynch Ltd, PA Morpeth 01670 512291

Lynch, John Tralee   +353 87 992 3102

Mackay Boatbuilders (Arbroath) Ltd
Aberdeen   01241 872879

Marine, AW Gosport   023 9250 1207

Marine Electrical Repair Service
London   020 7228 1336

Maxfield Electrical
Doncaster   07976 825349

MB Marine Troon   01292 311944

McMillan, Peter
Kilrush   +35 86 8388617

MES Falmouth Marina,
Falmouth   01326 378497

Mount Batten Boathouse
Plymouth   01752 482666

New World Yacht Care
Rhu   01436 820586

Neyland Marine Services Ltd
Milford Haven   01646 600358

Powell, Martin Shamrock Quay,
Southampton   023 8033 2123

R & J Marine Electricians Suffolk Yacht
Harbour Ltd, Ipswich   01473 659737

Radio & Electronic Services Beaucette Marina,
Guernsey   01481 728837

RHP Marine Cowes   01983 290421

Rothwell, Chris
Torquay Marina   01803 850960

Ruddy Marine
Galway   +353 87 742 7439

Rutherford, Jeff Largs 01475 568026

SM International
Plymouth   01752 662129

Sussex Fishing Services
Rye   01797 223895

Tony's Marine Services
Coleraine   07866 690436

Ultra Marine Systems
Mayflower International Marina,
Plymouth   07989 941020

Upham, Roger
Chichester   01243 514511

Volspec Ipswich   01473 780144

Weyland Marine Services
Milford Haven   01646 600358

ELECTRONIC DEVICES AND EQUIPMENT

Anchorwatch UK
Edinburgh   0131 447 5057

Aquascan International Ltd
Newport   01633 841117

Atlantis Marine Power Ltd
Plymouth   01752 208810

Autosound Marine
Bradford   01274 688990

B&G Romsey   01794 518448

Brookes & Gatehouse
Romsey   01794 518448

Boat Electrics & Electronics Ltd
Troon   01292 315355

Cactus Navigation & Communication
London   020 7833 3435

CDL Aberdeen   01224 706655

Charity & Taylor Ltd
Lowestoft   01502 581529

Diverse Yacht Services
Hamble   023 8045 3399

Dyfed Electronics Ltd
Milford Haven   01646 694572

Echopilot Marine Electronics Ltd
Ringwood   01425 476211

Enterprise Marine
Aberdeen   01224 593281

Euronav Ltd
Portsmouth   023 9237 3855

Exposure Lights
Pulborough 01798 83930

Furuno UK
Fraserburgh 01346 518300
Havant 023 9244 1000

Garmin (Europe) Ltd
Romsey 0870 850 1242

Golden Arrow Marine Ltd
Southampton 023 8071 0371

Greenham Regis Marine Electronics
Lymington 01590 671144

Greenham Regis Marine Electronics
Poole 01202 676363

Greenham Regis Marine Electronics
Southampton 023 8063 6555

ICS Electronics
Arundel 01903 731101

JG Technologies Ltd
Weymouth 0845 458 9616

KM Electronics
Lowestoft 01502 569079

Kongsberg Simrad Ltd
Aberdeen 01224 226500

Kongsberg Simrad Ltd
Wick 01955 603606

Landau UK Ltd Hamble 02380 454040

Enterprise Marine
Aberdeen 01224 593281

Marathon Leisure
Hayling Island 023 9263 7711

Marine Instruments
Falmouth 01326 375483

MB Marine Troon 01292 311944

Microcustom Ltd Ipswich 01473 215777

Nasa Marine Instruments
Stevenage 01438 354033

Navionics UK Plymouth 01752 204735

Ocean Leisure Ltd
London 020 7930 5050

Plymouth Marine Electronics
Plymouth 01752 227711

Radio & Electronic Services Ltd
St Peter Port 01481 728837

Raymarine Ltd
Portsmouth 02392 714700

Redfish Car Company
Stockton-on-Tees 01642 633638

Robertson, MK Oban 01631 563836

Satcom Distribution Ltd
Salisbury 01722 410800

Seaquest Marine Ltd
Guernsey 01481 721773

Seatronics Aberdeen 01224 853100

Selex Communications
Aberdeen 01224 890316

Selex Communications
Bristol 0117 931 3550

Selex Communications
Brixham 01803 882716

Selex Communications
Fraserburgh 01346 518187

Selex Communications
Glasgow 0141 882 6909

Selex Communications
Hull 01482 326144

Selex Communications
Kilkeel 028 4176 9009

Selex Communications
Liverpool 01268 823400

Selex Communications
Lowestoft 01502 572365

Selex Communications
Newcastle upon Tyne 0191 265 0374

Selex Communications
Newlyn 01736 361320

Selex Communications
Penryn 01326 378031

Selex Communications
Plymouth 01752 222878

Selex Communications
Rosyth 01383 419606

Selex Communications
Southampton 023 8051 1868

Silva Ltd Livingston 01506 419555

SM International
Plymouth 01752 662129

Sperry Marine Ltd
Peterhead 01779 473475

Stenmar Ltd Aberdeen 01224 827288

Transas Nautic
Portsmouth 023 9267 4016

Veripos Precise Navigation
Aberdeen 01224 965800

Wema (UK) Honiton 01404 881810

Wilson & Co Ltd, DB
Glasgow 0141 647 0161

Woodsons of Aberdeen Ltd
Aberdeen 01224 722884

ENGINES AND ACCESSORIES

Airylea Motors
Aberdeen 01224 872891

Amble Boat Co Ltd
Amble 01665 710267

Anchor Marine Products
Benfleet 01268 566666

Aquafac Ltd Luton 01582 568700

Barrus Ltd, EP Bicester 01869 363636

British Polar Engines Ltd
Glasgow 0141 445 2455

Bukh Diesel UK Ltd
Poole 01202 668840

CJ Marine Mechanical
Troon 01292 313400

Cleghorn Waring Ltd
Letchworth 01462 480380

Cook's Diesel Service Ltd
Faversham 01795 538553

Southern Shipwright (SSL)
Brighton 01273 601779

Southern Shipwright (SSL)
Eastbourne 01323 479000

Fender-Fix
Maidstone 01622 751518

Fettes & Rankine Engineering
Aberdeen 01224 573343

Fleetwood & Sons Ltd, Henry
Lossiemouth 01343 813015

Gorleston Marine Ltd
Great Yarmouth 01493 661883

Halyard Salisbury 01722 710922

Interseals (Guernsey) Ltd
Guernsey 01481 246364

Kelpie Boats
Pembroke Dock 01646 683661

Keypart Watford 01923 330570

Lancing Marine
Brighton 01273 410025

Lencraft Boats Ltd
Dungarvan +353 58 68220

Lewmar Ltd Havant 023 9247 1841

Liverpool Power Boats
Bootle 0151 944 1163

Lynch Ltd, PA
Morpeth 01670 512291

MacDonald & Co Ltd, JN
Glasgow 0141 810 3400

Mariners Weigh
Shaldon 01626 873698

MMS Ardrossan 01294 604831

Mooring Mate Ltd
Bournemouth 01202 421199

Newens Marine, Chas
Putney 020 8788 4587

Ocean Safety
Southampton 023 8072 0800

RK Marine Ltd
Hamble 01489 583585
Swanwick 01489 583572

Sillette Sonic Ltd
Sutton 020 8337 7543

Smith & Son Ltd, EC
Luton 01582 729721

Sowester Simpson-Lawrence Ltd
Poole 01202 667700

Timage & Co Ltd
Braintree 01376 343087

Thorne Boat Services
Thorne 01405 814197

Vetus Den Ouden Ltd
Totton 023 8045 4507

Western Marine
Dublin   +353 1 280 0321

Whitstable Marine
Whitstable   01227 262525

Yates Marine, Martin
Galgate   01524 751750

Ynys Marine
Cardigan   01239 613179

FOUL-WEATHER GEAR

Aquatogs Cowes   01983 295071
Crew Clothing London   020 8875 2300
Century
Finchampstead   0118 9731616
Crewsaver Gosport   01329 820000
Douglas Gill
Nottingham   0115 946 0844
FBI Leeds   0113 270 7000
Gul International Ltd
Bodmin   01208 262400
Helly Hansen
Nottingham   0115 979 5997
Henri Lloyd
Manchester   0161 799 1212
Musto Ltd Laindon   01268 491555
Pro Rainer Windsor   07752 903882

GENERAL MARINE EQUIPMENT & SPARES

Ampair
Ringwood   01425 480780
Aries Vane Gear Spares
Penryn   01326 377467
Arthurs Chandlery, R
Gosport   023 9252 6522
Atlantis Marine Power Ltd
Plymouth   01752 208810
Barden UK Ltd Fareham 01489 570770
Calibra Marine International Ltd
Southampton   08702 400358
CH Marine (Cork)   +353 21 4315700
Chris Hornsey (Chandlery) Ltd
Southsea   023 9273 4728
Compass Marine
(Dartmouth) Dartmouth 01803 835915
Cox Yacht Charter Ltd, Nick
Lymington   01590 673489
CTC Marine & Leisure
Middlesbrough   01642 372600
Exposure Lights
Pulborough   01798 83930
Frederiksen Boat Fittings (UK) Ltd
Gosport   023 9252 5377
Furneaux Riddall & Co Ltd
Portsmouth   023 9266 8621
Hardware & Marine Supplies
Co Wexford   +353 (53) 29791
Index Marine
Bournemouth   01202 470149

Kearon Ltd, George
Arklow   +353 402 32319

Marathon Leisure
Hayling Island   023 9263 7711

Pro-Boat Ltd
Burnham-on-Crouch   01621 785455

Pump International Ltd
Cornwall   01209 831937

Quay West Marine
Poole   01202 732445

Rogers, Angie Bristol   0117 973 8276

Ryland, Kenneth
Stanton   01386 584270

Tiflex
Liskeard   01579 320808

Vetus Boating Equipment
Southampton   02380 454507

Whitstable Marine
Whitstable   01227 262525

Yacht Parts
Plymouth   01752 252489

HARBOUR MASTERS

Aberaeron   01545 571645
Aberdeen   01224 597000
Aberdovey   01654 767626
Aberystwyth   01970 611433
Alderney & Burhou   01481 822620
Amble   01665 710306
Anstruther   01333 310836
Appledore   01237 474569
Arbroath   01241 872166
Ardglass   028 4484 1291
Ardrossan Control Tower
                           01294 463972
Arinagour Piermaster   01879 230347
Arklow   +353 402 32466
Baltimore   +353 28 22145
Banff   01261 815544
Bantry Bay   +353 27 53277
Barmouth   01341 280671
Barry   01446 732665
Beaucette   01481 245000
Beaulieu River   01590 616200
Belfast Lough   028 90 553012
Belfast River Manager   028 90 328507
Bembridge   01983 872828
Berwick-upon-Tweed   01289 307404
Bideford   01237 346131
Blyth   01670 352678
Boston   01205 362328
Bridlington   01262 670148/9

Bridport   01308 423222
Brighton   01273 819919
Bristol   0117 926 4797
Brixham   01803 853321
Buckie   01542 831700
                           07842 532360
Bude   01288 353111
Burghead   01343 835337
Burnham-on-Crouch   01621 783602
Burnham-on-Sea   01278 782180
Burtonport   +353 075 42155
Caernarfon   01286 672118
Caernarfon   07786 730865
Camber Berthing Offices – Portsmouth
                           023 92297395
Campbeltown   01586 552552
                           07825 732862
Caledonian Canal Off.
(Inverness)   01463 725500
Cardiff   029 20400500
Carnlough Harbour   07703 606763
Castletown Bay   01624 823549
Charlestown   01726 67526
Chichester Harbour   01243 512301
Clovelly   01273 431549
                           07975 501380
Conwy   01492 596253
Cork   +353 21 4273125
Corpach Canal Sea Lock
                           01397 772249
Courtmacsherry   +353 8673 94299
                      +353 23 46311/46600
Coverack   01326 380679
Cowes   01983 293952
Crail   01333 450820
Craobh Haven   01852 502222
Crinan Canal Office   01546 603210
Cromarty Firth   01381 600479
Cromarty Harbour   01381 600493
Crookhaven   +353 28 35319
Cullen   01542 831700
Dingle   +353 66 9151629
Douglas   01624 686628
Dover   01304 240400 Ext 4520
Dublin   +353 1 874871
Dun Laoghaire   +353 1 280 1130/8074
Dunbar   07958 754858
Dundee   01382 224121
East Loch Tarbert   01859 502444

Eastbourne	01323 470099	Lerwick	01595 692991	Porthmadog	01766 512927
Eigg Harbour	01687 482428	Littlehampton	01903 721215	Portknockie	01542 840833
Elie	01333 330051	Liverpool	0151 949 6134/5	Portland	01305 824044
Estuary Control - Dumbarton	01389 726211	Loch Gairloch	01445 712140	Portpatrick	01776 810355
Exe	01392 274306	Loch Inver	01571 844267 07958 734610	Portree	01478 612926
Exeter	01392 265791	Looe	01503 262839 07918 728955	Portrush	028 70822307
Eyemouth	01890 750223 07885 742505			Portsmouth Harbour Commercial Docks	023 92297395
Felixstowe	07803 476621	Lossiemouth (Marina)	07969 213513 07969 213521	Portsmouth Harbour Control	023 92723694
Findochty	07842 532360	Lough Foyle	028 7186 0555	Portsmouth Harbour	023 92723124
Fisherrow	0131 665 5900	Lowestoft	01502 572286	Preston	01772 726711
Fishguard (Lower Harbour)	01348 874726	Lyme Regis	01297 442137	Pwllheli	01758 701219
		Lymington	01590 672014	Queenborough	01795 662051
Fishguard	01348 404425	Lyness	01856 791387	Queens Gareloch/Rhu	01436 674321
Fleetwood	01253 872323	Macduff	01261 832236	Ramsey	01624 812245
Flotta	01856 701411	Maryport	01900 814431	Ramsgate	01843 572100
Folkestone	01303 715354	Menai Strait	01248 712312	River Bann & Coleraine	028 7034 2012
Fowey	01726 832471/2.	Methil	01333 462725	River Blackwater	01621 856487
Fraserburgh	01346 515858	Mevagissey	01726 843305	River Colne (Brightlingsea)	01206 302200
Galway Bay	+353 91 561874	Milford Haven	01646 696100		
Garlieston	01988 600274	Minehead (Mon-Fri)	01643 702566	River Dart	01803 832337
Glasson Dock	07910 315606	Montrose	01674 672302	River Deben	01473 736257
Gorey Port Control	01534 447788	Mousehole	01736 731511	River Exe Dockmaster	01392 274306
Gourdon	01569 762741	Mullion Cove	01326 240222	River Humber	01482 327171
Great Yarmouth	01493 335501	Nairn Harbour Office	01667 452453	River Medway	01795 596593
Grimsby Dockmaster	01472 359181	Newhaven Harbour Admin	01273 612872/612926	River Orwell	01473 231010
Groomsport Bay	028 91 278040			River Roach	01621 783602
Hamble River	01489 576387	Newlyn	01736 731897	River Stour	01255 243000
Hayle	07500 993867	Newquay	07737 387217	River Tyne/North Shields	0191 257 2080
Helford River	01326 732544	Newport Harbour Office	01983 525994		
Helmsdale	01431 821692	North Berwick	00776 467373	River Yealm	01752 872533
Holy Island	01289 389217	Oban	01631 562892	Rivers Alde & Ore	07528 092635
Holyhead	01407 763071	Padstow	01841 532239	Rosslare Europort	+353 53 915 7921
Hopeman	01343 835337	Peel	01624 842338	Rothesay	01700 503842 07799 724225
Howth	+353 1 832 2252	Penrhyn Bangor	01248 352525		
Ilfracombe	01271 862108	Penzance	01736 366113	Ryde	01983 613879
Inverness	01463 715715	Peterhead	01779 483630	Salcombe	01548 843791
Ipswich	01473 211771	Pierowall	01857 677216	Sark	01481 832323
Irvine	01294 487286	Pittenweem	01333 312591	Scalloway	01595 880574
Johnshaven	01561 362262	Plockton	01599 534589	Schull	+353 27 28136
Kettletoft Bay	01857 600227	Polperro	01503 272809	Scarborough	01723 373530
Killybegs	+353 73 31032	Poole	01202 440233	Scrabster	01847 892779
Kilmore Quay	+353 53 912 9955	Port Ellen Harbour Association	01496 302458	Seaham	07786 565205
Kinlochbervie	01971 521235 07901 514350			Sharpness, Gloucester Harbour Trustees	01453 811913
Kinsale	+353 21 4772503	Port Isaac	01208 880321 07855 429422	Shoreham	01273 598100
Kirkcudbright	01557 331135	Port St Mary	01624 833205	Silloth	016973 31358
Kirkwall	01856 872292	Porth Dinllaen	01758 720276	Sligo	+353 91 53819
Langstone Harbour	023 9246 3419	Porthleven	01326 574207		
Larne	02828 872100				

Southampton	023 8033 9733
Southend-on-Sea	01702 611889
Southwold	01502 724712
St Helier	01534 447788
St Ives	07793 515460
St Margaret's Hope	01856 831454
St Mary's	01720 422768
St Michael's Mount	07870 400282
St Monans (part-time)	07930 869538
St Peter Port	01481 720229
Stonehaven	01569 762741
Stornoway	01851 702688
Strangford Lough	028 44 881637
Stranraer	07734 073421
Stromness	07810 465825
Stronsay	01857 616317
Suilom Voe	01806 242551
Sunderland	0191 567 2626
Swale	01795 561234
Swansea	01792 653787
Tayport Hbr Trust	01382 553799
Tees & Hartlepool Port Authority	01429 277205
Teignmouth	01626 773165
Tenby	01834 842717
Thames Estuary	01474 562200
Tobermory Moorings Officer	07917 832497
Torquay	01803 292429
Troon	01292 281687
Truro	01872 272130
Ullapool	01854 612091
Waldringfield	01394 736291
Walton-on-the-Naze	01255 851899
Watchet	01643 703704
Waterford	+353 51 899801
Wells-next-the-Sea	01328 711646
West Bay (Bridport)	01308 423222
	07870 240636
Wexford	+353 53 912 2039
Weymouth	01305 206423
Whitby	01947 602354
Whitehaven	01946 692435
Whitehills	01261 861291
Whitstable	01227 274086
Wick	01955 602030
Wicklow	+353 404 67455
Workington	01900 602301
Yarmouth	01983 760321
Youghal	+353 24 92626

HARBOURS

Bristol Harbour	0117 903 1484
Clyde Marina – Ardrossan	01294 607077
Jersey Harbours St Helier	01534 885588
Maryport Harbour and Marina Maryport	01900 818447/4431
Peterhead Bay Authority Peterhead	01779 474020
Sark Moorings – Channel Islands	01481 832260

INSURANCE/FINANCE

Admiral Marine Ltd Salisbury	01722 416106
Bishop Skinner Boat Insurance London	0800 7838057
Bluefin London	0800 074 5200
Castlemain Ltd St Peter Port	01481 721319
Clark Insurance, Graham Tyneside	0191 455 8089
Craven Hodgson Associates Leeds	0113 243 8443
Giles Insurance Brokers Irvine	01294 315481
GJW Direct Liverpool	0151 473 8000
Haven Knox-Johnston West Malling	01732 223600
Lombard Southampton	023 8024 2171
Mercia Marine Malvern	01684 564457
Nautical Insurance Services Ltd Leigh-on-Sea	01702 470811
Navigators & General Brighton	01273 863400
Pantaenius UK Ltd Plymouth	01752 223656
Porthcawl Insurance Consultants Porthcawl	01656 784866
Saga Boat Insurance Folkestone	01303 771135
St Margarets Insurances London	020 8778 6161
Towergate Insurance Shrewsbury	0344 892 1987

LIFERAFTS & INFLATABLES

Adec Marine Ltd Croydon	020 8686 9717
Avon Inflatables Llanelli	01554 882000
Cosalt International Ltd Aberdeen	01224 826662
Glaslyn Marine Supplies Ltd Porthmadog	01766 513545
Hale Marine, Ron Portsmouth	023 9273 2985
Guernsey Yacht Club St Peter Port	01481 722838
IBS Boats South Woodham Ferrers	01245 323211/425551
KTS Seasafety Kilkeel	028 918 28405
Nationwide Marine Hire Warrington	01925 245788
Norwest Marine Ltd Liverpool	0151 207 2860
Ocean Safety Southampton	023 8072 0800
Polymarine Ltd Conwy	01492 583322
Premium Liferaft Services Burnham-on-Crouch	0800 243673
Ribeye Dartmouth	01803 832060
South Eastern Marine Services Ltd Basildon	01268 534427
Suffolk Marine Safety Ipswich	01473 833010
Whitstable Marine Whitstable	01227 262525

MARINAS

Aberystwyth Marina	01970 611422
Amble Marina	01665 712168
Arbroath Harbour	01241 872166
Ardfern Yacht Centre Ltd	01852 500247
Ardglass Marina	028 44842332
Arklow Marina	+353 87 258 8078
Ballycastle Marina	028 2076 8525
Banff Harbour Marina	01261 815544
Bangor Marina	028 91 453297
Beaucette Marina	01481 245000
Bedwells Boatyard	01255 675873
Bembridge Harbour Authority	01983 872828
Berthon Lymington Marina	01590 647405
Birdham Pool Marina	01243 512310
Blackwater Marina	01621 740264
Boston Gateway Marina	07480 525230
Bradwell Marina	01621 776235
Bray Marina	01628 623654
Brentford Dock Marina	020 8232 8941
Bridgemarsh Marine	01621 740414
Brighton Marina	01273 819919
Bristol Marina	0117 921 3198
Brixham Marina	01803 882929
Bucklers Hard Marina	01590 616200

Burnham Yacht Harbour Marina Ltd
01621 782150
BWML Glasson Basin 01524 751491
BWML Limehouse Marina
020 7308 9930
Cahersiveen Marina +353 66 947 2777
Caley Marina 01463 236539
0
Campbeltown Marina
Cardiff Marina 02920 396078
Carlingford Marina +353 42 9373072
Carrickfergus Marina 028 9336 6666
Castlepark Marina +353 21 477 4959
Chatham Maritime Marina
01634 899200
Chelsea Harbour Marina
07770 542783
Chichester Marina 01243 512731
Clyde Marina Ltd 01294 607077
Cobbs Quay Marina 01202 674299
Coleraine Harbour Town
Centre Marina 028 7034 2012
Coleraine Marina 028 703 44768
Conwy Quays Marina 01492 593000
Cork Harbour Marina
+353 87 3669009
Cowes Harbour Shepards Marina
01983 297821
Cowes Yacht Haven 01983 299975
Craobh Marina 01852 500222
Crinan Boatyard 01546 830232
Crosshaven Boatyard Marina
+353 21 483 1161
Dart Marina Yacht Harbour
01803 837161
Darthaven Marina 01803 752242
Dartside Quay 01803 845445
Deganwy Marina 01492 576888
Dingle Marina +353 (0)87 925 4115
Douglas Marina 01624 686627
Dover Marina 01304 241663
Dun Laoghaire Marina
+353 1 202 0040
Dunstaffnage Marina Ltd
01631 566555
East Cowes Marina 01983 293983
Emsworth Yacht Harbour
01243 377727
Essex Marina 01702 258531
Falmouth Haven Marina
01326 310991
Falmouth Marina 01326 316620
Fambridge Yacht Haven 01621 740370
Fambridge Yacht Station
01621 742911

Fenit Harbour & Marina
+353 66 7136231
Fleetwood Haven Marina
01253 879062
Fox's Marina & Boatyard
01473 689111
Foyle Port Marina 02871 860555
Gallions Point Marina 0207 476 7054
Galway Harbour Marina
+353 91 561874
Gillingham Marina 01634 280022
Gosport Marina 023 9252 4811
Hafan Pwllheli 01758 701219
Hamble Point Marina 02380 452464
Harbour of Rye 01797 225225
Hartlepool Marina 01429 865744
Haslar Marina 023 9260 1201
Heybridge Basin 07712 079764
Holy Loch Marina 01369 701800
Holyhead Marina 01407 764242
Howth Marina +353 1839 2777
Hull Marina 01482 609960
Humber Cruising Association
01472 268424
Hythe Marina Village 02380 207073
Inverness Marina 01463 220501
Ipswich Haven Marina 01473 236644
Island Harbour Marina 01983 539994
James Watt Dock Marina
01475 729838
Kemps Quay 023 8063 2323
Kilmore Quay Marina
+353 53 91 29955
Kilrush Marina +353 65 9052072
Kinsale Yacht Club Marina
+353 21 477 2196
Kip Marina 01475 521485
Kirkcudbright Marina 01557 331135
Kirkwall Marina 01856 871313
Lady Bee Marina 01273 593801
Lake Yard Marina 01202 674531
Largs Yacht Haven 01475 675333
Lawrence Cove Marina +353 27 75044
Littlehampton Marina 01903 713553
Liverpool Marina Bar & Grill
0151 707 6777
Lossiemouth Marina 01343 813066
Lowestoft Cruising Club 07810 522515
Lowestoft Haven Marina
01502 580300
Lymington Harbour Commission
01590 672014
Lymington Yacht Haven
01590 677071
Malahide Marina +353 1 845 4129

Mallaig Marina 01687 462406
Maryport Harbour and Marina
01900 814431
Mayflower International Marina
01752 556633
Melfort Pier & Harbour 01852 200333
Mercury Yacht Harbour
023 8045 5994
Milford Marina 01646 696312
Mylor Yacht Harbour 01326 372121
Nairn Marina 01667 456008
Neptune Marina Ltd 01473 215204
Newhaven Marina 01273 513881
Neyland Yacht Haven 01646 601601
Northney Marina 02392 466321
Noss Marina 01803 839087
Oban Marina & Yacht Services Ltd
01631 565333
Ocean Village Marina 023 8022 9385
Padstow Harbour 01841 532239
Parkstone Yacht Club Haven
01202 738824
Peel Marina 01624 842338
Penarth Quays Marina 02920 705021
Penton Hook 01932 568681
Peterhead Bay Marina 01779 477868
Plymouth Yacht Haven 01752 404231
Poole Quay Boat Haven 01202 649488
Port Bannatyne Marina 01700 503116
Port Edgar Marina 0131 331 3330
Port Ellen Marina
Port Hamble Marina 023 8045 2741
Port of Poole Marina 01202 649488
Port Pendennis Marina 01326 211211
Port Solent Marina 02392 210765
Port Werburgh 01634 252107
Portaferry Marina 07703 209780
Portavadie Marina 01700 811075
Portishead Quays Marina
01275 841941
Portland Marina 0345 430 2012
Preston Marina 01772 733595
Quay Marinas Rhu 01436 820238
Queen Anne's Battery 01752 671142
Ridge Wharf Yacht Centre
01929 552650
Royal Clarence Marina 02392 523523
Royal Cork Yacht Club Marina
+353 21 483 1023
Royal Harbour Marina, Ramsgate
01843 572100
Royal Harwich Yacht Club Marina
01473 780319
Royal Norfolk and Suffolk Yacht Club
01502 566726

Royal Northumberland Yacht Club	01670 353636
Royal Quays Marina	0191 272 8282
Ryde Leisure Harbour	01983 613879
Salterns Marina Ltd	01202 709971
Salve Engineering Marina	+353 21 483 1145
Sandpoint Marina (Dumbarton)	01389 762396
Saxon Wharf	023 8033 9490
Seaport Marina	01463 725500
Seaton's Marina	028 703 832086
Shamrock Quay	023 8022 9461
Shotley Marina	01473 788982
South Dock Marina	020 7252 2244
South Ferriby Marina	01652 635620
Southsea Marina	02392 822719
Sovereign Harbour Marina	01323 470099
Sparkes Marina	023 92463572
St Helier Marina	01534 447708
St Katharine Marina Ltd	0207 264 5312
St Peter Port Marinas	01481 720229
St Peter's Marina	0191 265 4472
Stornoway Marina	01851 702688
Stranraer Marina	01776 706565
Stromness Marina	01856 871313
Suffolk Yacht Harbour Ltd	01473 659240
Sunderland Marina	0191 514 4721
Sutton Harbour	01752 204702
Swansea Marina	01792 470310
Swanwick Marina	01489 884081
Tarbert Harbour	01880 820344
Titchmarsh Marina	01255 672185
Tobermory Harbour Association	01688 302876
Tollesbury Marina	01621 869202
Torquay Marina	01803 200210
Town Quay Marina	02380 234397
Troon Yacht Haven	01292 315553
Universal Marina	01489 574272
Victoria Marina	01481 725987
Waterford City Marina	+353 87 238 4944
Weymouth Harbour	
Weymouth & Portland BC	01305 838423
Weymouth Marina	01305 767576
Whitby Marina	01947 602354
Whitehaven Marina	01946 692435
Whitehills Marina	01261 861427
Wick Marina	01955 602030
WicorMarine Yacht Haven	01329 237112
Windsor Marina	01753 853911
Wisbech Yacht Harbour	01945 588059
Woolverstone Marina	01473 780206
Yarmouth Harbour	01983 760321

MARINE ENGINEERS

AAS Marine Aberystwyth	01970 631090
Allerton Engineering Lowestoft	01502 537870
APAS Engineering Ltd Southampton	023 8063 2558
Ardmair Boat Centre Ullapool	01854 612054
Arisaig Marine Inverness-shire	01687 450224
Arun Craft Littlehampton	01903 723667
ASL Auto Services Boston	01205 761560
Atlantis Marine Power Ltd Plymouth	01752 208810
Attrill & Sons, H Bembridge	01983 872319
Auto & Marine Services Botley	07836 507000
Auto Marine Southsea	023 9282 5601
Baker, Keith Brentford	07792 937790
BJ Marine Ltd Bangor	028 9127 1434
Bristol Boat Ltd Bristol	01225 872032
Browne, Jimmy Tralee	+353 87 262 7158
Buccaneer Ltd Macduff	01261 835199
Buzzard Marine Engineering Yarmouth	01983 760707
C & B Marine Ltd Chichester Marina	01243 511273
Caddy, Simon Falmouth Marina Falmouth	01326 372682
Caledonian Marine Rhu Marina	01436 821184
Caratek Hull	07957 922301
Cardigan Outboards Cardigan	01239 613966
Channel Islands Marine Ltd Guernsey	01481 716880
Channel Islands Marine Ltd Jersey	01534 767595

Cook's Diesel Service Ltd Faversham	01795 538553
Cragie Engineering Kirkwall	01856 874680
Wartsila Havant	023 9240 0121
Crinan Boatyard Ltd Crinan	01546 830232
Cutler Marine Engineering, John Emsworth	01243 375014
Dale Sailing Co Ltd Milford Haven	01646 603110
Davis Marine Services Ramsgate	01843 586172
Denney & Son, EL Redcar	01642 483507
DH Marine (Shetland) Ltd Shetland	01595 690618
Emark Marine Ltd Emsworth	01243 375383
Evans, Lyndon Brentford	07795 218704
Evans Marine Engineering, Tony Pwllheli	01758 703070
Felton Marine Engineering Brighton	01273 601779
Felton Marine Engineering Eastbourne	01323 470211
Ferrypoint Boat Co Youghal	+353 24 94232
Fettes & Rankine Engineering Aberdeen	01224 573343
Fleming Engineering, J Stornoway	01851 703488
Floetree Ltd Loch Lomond Marina Balloch	01389 752069
Fowey Harbour Marine Engineers Fowey	01726 832806
Fox Marine Services Ltd Jersey	01534 721312
Freeport Marine Jersey	01534 888100
French Marine Motors Ltd Colchester	01206 302133
French Marine Motors Ltd Titchmarsh Marina	01255 850303
GH Douglas Marine Services Fleetwood Harbour Village Marina, Fleetwood	01253 877200
Golden Arrow Marine Southampton	023 8071 0371
Goodchild Marine Services Great Yarmouth	01493 782301
Goodwick Marine Fishguard	01348 873955

Gosport Marina   023 9252 4811

Griffins Garage Dingle Marina,
Co Kerry   +353 66 91 51178

Hale Marine, Ron
Portsmouth   023 9273 2985

Hamnavoe Engineering
Stromness   01856 850576

Harbour Engineering
Itchenor   01243 513454

Hartlepool Marine Engineering
Hartlepool   01429 867883

Hayles, Harold
Yarmouth   01983 760373

Herm Seaway Marine Ltd
St Peter Port   01481 726829

HNP Engineers (Lerwick Ltd)
Lerwick   01595 692493

Hodges, T
Coleraine   028 7035 6422

Home Marine Emsworth Yacht
Harbour, Emsworth   01243 374125

Hook Marine Ltd Troon   01292 679500

Humphrey, Chris
Teignmouth   01626 772324

Instow Marine Services
Bideford   01271 861081

Jones (Boatbuilders), David
Chester   01244 390363

Keating Marine Engineering Ltd, Bill
Jersey   01534 733977

Kingston Marine Services
Cowes   01983 299385

Kippford Slipway Ltd
Dalbeattie   01556 620249

Lansdale Pannell Marine
Chichester   01243 512374

Lencraft Boats Ltd
Dungarvan   +353 58 68220

Llyn Marine Services
Pwllheli   01758 612606

Lynx Engineering
St Helens, Isle of Wight   01983 873711

M&G Marine Services
Mayflower International Marina,
Plymouth   01752 563345

MacDonald & Co Ltd, JN
Glasgow   0141 810 3400

Mackay Marine Services
Aberdeen   01224 575772

Mainbrayce Marine
Alderney   01481 722772

Malakoff and Moore
Lerwick   01595 695544

Marine Blast
Holy Loch   01369 705394

Mallaig Boat Building and Engineering
Mallaig   01687 462304

Marindus Engineering
Kilmore Quay   +353 53 29794

Marine Engineering Looe
Brixham   01803 844777

Marine Engineering Looe
Looe   01503 263009

Marine Engineering Services
Port Dinorwic   01248 671215

Marine General Engineers Beaucette
Marina, Guernsey   01481 245808

Marine Propulsion
Hayling Island   07836 737488

Marine & General Engineers
St. Sampsons Harbour, Guernsey
    01481 245808

Marine-Trak Engineering
Mylor Yacht Harbour
Falmouth   01326 376588

Marine Warehouse
Gosport   023 9258 0420

Marlec Marine
Ramsgate   01843 592176

Martin Outboards
Galgate   01524 751750

McQueen, Michael
Kilrush   +35 87 2574623

Meiher, Denis
Fenit   +353 87 958 4744

MES Marine Greenock   01475 744655

MMS Ardrossan   01294 604831

Mobile Marine Engineering Liverpool
Marina, Liverpool   01565 733553

Mount's Bay Engineering
Newlyn   01736 363095

MP Marine Maryport   01900 810299

New World Yacht Care
Helensburgh   01436 820586

North Western Automarine Engineers
Largs   01475 687139

Noss Marine Services Dart Marina,
Dartmouth   01803 833343

Owen Marine, Robert
Porthmadog   01766 513435

Pace, Andy Newhaven   01273 516010

**Penzance Dry Dock and Engineering
Co Ltd** Penzance   01736 363838

Pirie & Co, John S
Fraserburgh   01346 513314

Portavon Marine
Keynsham   01225 424301

Power Afloat, Elkins Boatyard
Christchurch   01202 489555

Powerplus Marine Cowes Yacht Haven,
Cowes   01983 290421

Pro-Marine Queen Anne's Battery
Marina, Plymouth   01752 267984

PT Marine Engineering
Hayling Island   023 9246 9332

R & M Marine
Portsmouth   023 9273 7555

R & S Engineering
Dingle Marina   +353 66 915 1189

Reddish Marine
Salcombe   01548 844094

RHP Marine Cowes   01983 290421

RK Marine Ltd
Hamble   01489 583585

RK Marine Ltd
Swanwick   01489 583572

Rossiter Yachts Ltd
Christchurch   01202 483250

Ryan & Roberts Marine Services
Askeaton   +353 61 392198

Salve Marine Ltd
Crosshaven   +353 21 4831145

Seamark-Nunn & Co
Felixstowe   01394 275327

Seapower Ipswich   01473 780090

Seaward Engineering
Glasgow   0141 632 4910

Seaway Marine
Gosport   023 9260 2722

Shearwater Engineering Services Ltd
Dunoon   01369 706666

Silvers Marina Ltd
Helensburgh   01436 831222

Starey Marine
Salcombe   01548 843655

Swordfish Marine Engineering
Holy Loch   01369 701905

Tarbert Marine
Arbroath   01241 872879

Thorne Boat Services
Thorne   01405 814197

Tollesbury Marine Engineering
Tollesbury Marina   01621 869919

Tony's Marine Services
Coleraine   07866 690436

TOR (Gerald Hales)
Stornoway   01851 871025

Vasey Marine Engineering, Gordon
Fareham   07798 638625

Volspec Ltd
Tollesbury   01621 869756

Wallis, Peter Torquay Marina,
Torquay   01803 844777

WB Marine Chichester   01243 512857

West Coast Marine
Troon   01292 318121

West Marine
Brighton   01273 626656

Weymouth Marina Mechanical Services
Weymouth   01305 779379

Whittington, G Lady Bee Marine,
Shoreham   01273 593801

Whitewater Marine
Malahide   +353 1 816 8473

Wigmore Wright Marine Services
Penarth Marina   029 2070 9983

Wright, M Manaccan   01326 231502

Wyko Industrial Services
Aberdeen   01224 246560

Ynys Marine
Cardigan   01239 613179

Youngboats
Faversham   01795 536176

1° West Marine Ltd
Portsmouth   023 9283 8335

MASTS, SPARS & RIGGING

JWS Marine Services
Portsmouth   02392 755155

A2 Rigging
Falmouth   01326 312209

Allspars Plymouth   01752 266766

Amble Boat Co Ltd
Morpeth   01665 710267

Arun Canvas & Rigging
Littlehampton   01903 732561

B+ St Peter Port   01481 726071

Buchanan, Keith
St Mary's   01720 422037

Bussell & Co, WL
Weymouth   01305 785633

Carbospars Ltd
Hamble   023 8045 6736

Cable & Rope Works
Bexhill-on-Sea   01424 220112

Clarke Rigging, Niall
Coleraine   07916 083858

Coates Marine Ltd
Whitby   01947 604486

Dauntless Boatyard Ltd
Canvey Island   01268 793782

Davies Marine Services
Ramsgate   01843 586172

Eurospars Ltd
Plymouth   01752 550550

Exe Leisure
Exeter   01392 879055

Fox's Marine Ipswich Ltd
Ipswich   01473 689111

Freeland Yacht Spars Ltd
Dorchester on Thames   01865 341277

Gordon, AD Portland   01305 821569

Hamble Custom Rigging Centre
Hamble   023 8045 2000

Harris Rigging Totnes   01803 840160

Heyn Engineering
Belfast   028 9035 0022

Holman Rigging
Chichester   01243 514000

Irish Spars and Rigging
Malahide   +353 86 209 5996

JWS Marine Services
Portsmouth   02392 755155

Kildale Marine Hull   01482 227464

Kilrush Marina Boatyard
Kilrush   +35 87 7990091

Lowestoft Yacht Services
Lowestoft   01502 585535

Laverty, Billy Galway   +353 86 3892614

Leitch, WB
Tarbert, Loch Fyne   01880 820287

Lewis, Harry
Kinsale   +353 87 266 7127

Marine Resource Centre
Oban   01631 720291

Martin Leaning Masts & Rigging
Hayling   023 9237 1157

Mast & Rigging
Crosshaven   +353 21 483 3878

Mast & Rigging Services
Largs   01475 670110

Mast & Rigging Services
Inverkip   01475 522700

MP Marine Maryport   01900 810299

Ocean Rigging
Lymington   01590 676292

Owen Sails Oban   01631 720485

Pro Rig S Ireland   +353 87 298 3333

Ratsey, Stephen
Milford Haven   01646 601561

Rigit Ardrossan   07593 220213

Rig Magic Ipswich   01473 655089

Rig Shop
Southampton   023 8033 8341

Ronstan Gosport   023 9252 5377

Salcombe Boatstore
Salcombe   01548 843708

Seldén Mast Ltd
Gosport   01329 504000

Silvers Marina Ltd
Helensburgh   01436 831222

Silverwood Yacht Services Ltd
Portsmouth   023 9232 7067

Spencer Rigging
Cowes   01983 292022

Storrar Marine Store
Newcastle upon Tyne   0191 266 1037

Tedfords Rigging & Rafts
Belfast   028 9032 6763

TJ Rigging Conwy   07780 972411

TS Rigging Malden   01621 874861

Windjammer Marine
Milford Marina   01646 699070

Yacht Rigging Services
Plymouth   01752 226609

Z Spars UK Hadleigh   01473 822130

NAVIGATION EQUIPMENT – GENERAL

Belson Design Ltd, Nick
Southampton   077 6835 1330

Brown Son & Ferguson Ltd
Glasgow   0141 429 1234

Cooke & Son Ltd, B
Hull   01482 223454

Diverse Yacht Services
Hamble   023 8045 3399

Dolphin Maritime Software Ltd
Lancaster   01524 841946

Dubois Phillips & McCallum Ltd
Liverpool   0151 236 2776

Garmin
Southampton   02380 524000

Geonav UK Ltd
Poole   0870 240 4575

Imray Laurie Norie and Wilson Ltd
St Ives, Cambs   01480 462114

Kelvin Hughes
Southampton   023 8063 4911

Lilley & Gillie Ltd, John
North Shields   0191 257 2217

Marine Chart Services
Wellingborough   01933 441629

Navico UK
Romsey   01794 510010

PC Maritime
Plymouth   01752 254205

Price & Co, WF Bristol   0117 929 2229

Raymarine Ltd
Portsmouth   023 9269 3611

Royal Institute of Navigation
London   020 7591 3130

Sea Chest Nautical Bookshop
Plymouth   01752 222012

Seath Instruments (1992) Ltd
Lowestoft   01502 573811

Smith (Marine) Ltd, AM
London   020 8529 6988

South Bank Marine Charts Ltd
Grimsby   01472 361137

Southcoasting Navigators
Devon   01626 335626

Stanford Charts
Bristol   0117 929 9966
London   020 7836 1321
Manchester   0870 890 3730

Todd Chart Agency Ltd
County Down   028 9146 6640

UK Hydrographic Office
Taunton   01823 337900

Warsash Nautical Bookshop
Warsash   01489 572384

Yachting Instruments Ltd
Sturminster Newton   01258 817662

PAINT & OSMOSIS

Advanced Blast Cleaning Paint
Tavistock   01822 617192
                        07970 407911

Herm Seaway Marine Ltd
St Peter Port   01481 726829

Gillingham Marina   01634 280022

Hempel Paints
Southampton   02380 232000

International Coatings Ltd
Southampton   023 8022 6722

Marineware Ltd
Southampton   023 8033 0208

NLB Marine
Ardrossan   01563 521509

Pro-Boat Ltd
Burnham on Crouch   01621 785455

Rustbuster Ltd
Peterborough   01775 761222

Smith & Son Ltd, EC
Luton   01582 729721

SP Systems
Isle of Wight   01983 828000

PROPELLERS & STERGEAR/REPAIRS

CJR Propulsion Ltd
Southampton   023 8063 9366

Darglow Engineering Ltd
Wareham   01929 556512

Propeller Revolutions
Poole   01202 671226

Sillette – Sonic Ltd
Sutton   020 8337 7543

Vetus Den Ouden Ltd
Southampton   02380 454507

RADIO COURSES / SCHOOLS

**Bisham Abbey Sailing
& Navigation School**
Bisham   01628 474960

**East Coast Offshore Yachting –
Les Rant** Perry   01480 861381

Hamble School of Yachting
Hamble   023 8045 6687

Pembrokeshire Cruising
Neyland   01646 602500

Plymouth Sailing School
Plymouth   01752 493377

Start Point Sailing
Kingsbridge   01548 810917

REEFING SYSTEMS

Atlantic Spars Ltd
Brixham   01803 843322

Calibra Marine International Ltd
Southampton   08702 400358

Eurospars Ltd
Plymouth   01752 550550

Holman Rigging
Chichester   01243 514000

Sea Teach Ltd
Emsworth   01243 375774

Southern Spar Services
Northam   023 8033 1714

Wragg, Chris
Lymington   01590 677052

Z Spars UK Hadleigh   01473 822130

REPAIR MATERIALS & ACCESSORIES

Akeron Ltd
Southend on Sea   01702 297101

Howells & Son, KJ
Poole   01202 665724

JB Timber Ltd
North Ferriby   01482 631765

Robbins Timber
Bristol   0117 9633136

Sika Ltd
Welwyn Garden City   01707 394444

Solent Composite Systems
East Cowes   01983 292602

Technix Rubber & Plastics Ltd
Southampton   01489 789944

Tiflex Liskeard   01579 320808

Timage & Co Ltd
Braintree   01376 343087

Trade Grade Products Ltd
Poole   01202 820177

Wessex Resins & Adhesives Ltd
Romsey   01794 521111

ROPE & WIRE

Cable & Rope Works
Bexhill-on-Sea   01424 220112

Euro Rope Ltd
Scunthorpe   01724 280480

Marlow Ropes
Hailsham   01323 444444

Mr Splice Leicester   0800 1697178

Spinlock Ltd Cowes   01983 295555

TJ Rigging Conwy   07780 972411

SAFETY EQUIPMENT

AB Marine Ltd
St Peter Port   01481 722378

Adec Marine Ltd
Croydon   020 8686 9717

Anchorwatch UK
Edinburgh   0131 447 5057

Avon Inflatables
Llanelli   01554 882000

Cosalt International Ltd
Aberdeen   01224 588327

Crewsaver Gosport   01329 820000

Glaslyn Marine Supplies Ltd
Porthmadog   01766 513545

Exposure Lights
Pulborough   01798 839300

Guardian Fire Protection
Manchester   0800 358 7522

Hale Marine, Ron
Portsmouth 023 9273 2985

Herm Seaway Marine Ltd
St Peter Port 01481 722838

KTS Seasafety Kilkeel 028 41762655

McMurdo Pains Wessex
Portsmouth 023 9262 3900

Met Office Bracknell 0845 300 0300

Nationwide Marine Hire
Warrington 01925 245788

Norwest Marine Ltd
Liverpool 0151 207 2860

Ocean Safety
Southampton 023 8072 0800

Polymarine Ltd
Conwy 01492 583322

Premium Liferaft Services
Burnham-on-Crouch 0800 243673

Ribeye Dartmouth 01803 832060

South Eastern Marine Services Ltd
Basildon 01268 534427

Suffolk Sailing
Ipswich 01473 604678

Whitstable Marine
Whitstable 01227 262525

Winters Marine Ltd
Salcombe 01548 843580

SAILMAKERS & REPAIRS

Allison-Gray
Dundee 01382 505888

Alsop Sailmakers, John
Salcombe 01548 843702

AM Trimming Windsor 01932 821090

Arun Canvas & Rigging
Littlehampton 01903 732561

Arun Sails Chichester 01243 573185

Bank Sails, Bruce
Southampton 01489 582444

Barrett, Katy
St Peter Port 07781 404299

Batt Sails Bosham 01243 575505

Bissett and Ross
Aberdeen 01224 580659

Boatshed, The
Felinheli, Bangor 01248 679939

Breaksea Sails Barry 01446 730785

Bristol Sails Bristol 0117 922 5080

Buchanan, Keith
St Mary's 01720 422037

C&J Marine Textiles
Chichester 01243 782629

Calibra Sails Dartmouth 01803 833094

Clarke Rigging, Niall
Coleraine 07916 083858

Coastal Covers
Portsmouth 023 9252 0200

Covercare Fareham 01329 311878

Covers + Stuff
Douglas, Isle of Man 07624 400037

Crawford, Margaret
Kirkwall 01856 875692

Crusader Sails Poole 01202 670580

Crystal Covers
Portsmouth 023 9238 0143

Cullen Sailmakers
Galway +353 91 771991

Dolphin Sails Harwich 01255 243366

Doyle Sails
Southampton 023 8033 2622

Downer International Sails & Chandlery
Dun Laoghaire +353 1 280 0231

Duthie Marine Safety, Arthur
Glasgow 0141 429 4553

Dynamic Sails
Emsworth 01243 374495

Flew Sailmakers
Portchester 01329 822676

Fylde Coast Sailmaking Co
Fleetwood 01253 873476

Freeman Sails
Padstow 07771 610053

Garland Sails Bristol 01275 393473

Goacher Sails
Cumbria 01539 488686

Gowen Ocean Sailmakers
West Mersea 01206 384412

Green Sailmakers, Paul
Plymouth 01752 660317

Henderson Sails & Covers
Southsea 023 9229 4700

Hood Sailmakers
Lymington 01590 675011

Hooper, A Plymouth 01752 830411

Hyde Sails
Southampton 0845 543 8945

Jackson Yacht Services
Jersey 01534 743819

Jeckells and Son Ltd (Wroxham)
Wroxham 01603 782223

Jessail Ardrossan 01294 467311

JKA Sailmakers
Pwllheli 01758 613266

Kemp Sails Ltd
Wareham 01929 554308/554378

Kildale Marine Hull 01482 227464

Lawrence Sailmakers, J
Brightlingsea 01206 302863

Leitch, WB
Tarbert, Loch Fyne 01880 820287

Leith UK
Berwick on Tweed 01289 307264

Le Monnier, Yannick
Galway +353 87 628 9854

Lodey Sails Newlyn 01736 719359

Lossie Sails
Lossiemouth 07989 956698

Lucas Sails Portchester 023 9237 3699

Malakoff and Moore
Lerwick 01595 695544

McCready and Co Ltd, J
Belfast 028 90232842

McKillop Sails, John
Kingsbridge 01548 852343

McNamara Sails, Michael
Great Yarmouth 01692 584186

McWilliam Sailmaker (Crosshaven)
Crosshaven +353 21 4831505

Sail Shape
Fowey 01726 833731

Montrose Rope and Sails
Montrose 01674 672657

Mountfield Sails
Hayling Island 023 9246 3720

Mouse Sails Holyhead 01407 763636

Nicholson Hughes Sails
Rosneath 01436 831356

North Sea Sails
Tollesbury 01621 869367

North West Sails
Keighley 01535 652949

Northrop Sails
Ramsgate 01843 851665

O'Mahony Sailmakers
Kinsale +353 86 326 0018

O'Sullivans Marine Ltd
Tralee +353 66 7129635

Owen Sails Benderloch 01631 720485

Parker & Kay Sailmakers –
East Ipswich 01473 659878

Parker & Kay Sailmakers –
South Hamble 023 8045 8213

Penrose Sailmakers
Falmouth 01326 312705

Pinnell & Bax
Northampton 01604 592808

Pollard Marine
Port St Mary 01624 835831

Quantum Sails
Ipswich Haven Marina   01473 659878

Quantum-Parker & Kay Sailmakers
Hamble   023 8045 8213

Quay Sails (Poole) Ltd
Poole   01202 681128

Ratsey & Lapthorn
Isle of Wight   01983 294051

Ratsey Sailmakers, Stephen
Milford Haven   01646 601561

Relling One Design
Portland   01305 826555

SO31 Bags
Southampton   023 8045 5106

Rig Shop, The
Southampton   023 8033 8341

Rockall Sails
Chichester   01243 573185

Sail Locker
Woolverstone Marina   01473 780206

Sail Style
Hayling Island   023 9246 3720

Sails & Canvas Exeter   01392 877527
Sail Register Ulceby   01469 589444

Saltern Sail Co
West Cowes   01983 280014

Saltern Sail Company
Yarmouth   01983 760120

Sanders Sails
Lymington   01590 673981

Saturn Sails Largs   01475 689933

Scott & Co, Graham
St Peter Port   01481 259380

Shore Sailmakers
Swanwick   01489 589450

SKB Sails Falmouth   01326 372107

Sketrick Sailmakers Ltd
Killinchy   028 9754 1400

Solo Sails Penzance   01736 366004

Storrar Marine Store
Newcastle upon Tyne   0191 266 1037

Suffolk Sails
Woodbridge   01394 386323

Sunset Sails Sligo   +353 71 62792

Torquay Marina Sails and Canvas
Exeter   01392 877527

Trident UK Gateshead   0191 490 1736

UK McWilliam Cowes   01983 281100

Underwood Sails
Queen Anne's Battery
Plymouth   01752 229661

W Sails Leigh-on-Sea   01702 714550

Warren Hall
Beaucette, Guernsey   07781 444280

Watson Sails Dublin   +353 1 846 2206

WB Leitch and Son
Tarbert   01880 820287

Westaway Sails
Plymouth Yacht Haven   01752 892560

Westsails.ie Kilrush   +35 876289854

Wilkinson Sails
Burnham-on-Crouch   01621 786770

Wilkinson Sails
Teynham   01795 521503

Yacht Shop, The
Fleetwood   01253 879238

SOLAR POWER

Ampair Ringwood   01425 480780

Barden UK Ltd Fareham   01489 570770

Marlec Engineering Co Ltd
Corby   01536 201588

SPRAYHOODS & DODGERS

A & B Textiles
Gillingham   01634 579686

Allison–Gray Dundee   01382 505888

Arton, Charles
Milford-on-Sea   01590 644682

Arun Canvas and Rigging Ltd
Littlehampton   01903 732561

Boatshed, The
Felinheli, Bangor   01248 679939

Buchanan, Keith
St Mary's   01720 422037

C & J Marine Textiles
Chichester   01243 785485

Covercare Fareham   01329 311878

Covercraft
Southampton   023 8033 8286

Crystal Covers
Portsmouth   023 9238 0143

Jeckells and Son Ltd
Wroxham   01603 782223

Jessail Ardrossan   01294 467311

Lomond Boat Covers
Alexandria   01389 602734

Lucas Sails Portchester   023 9237 3699

Poole Canvas Co Ltd
Poole   01202 677477

Sail Register Ulceby   01469 589444

Saundersfoot Auto Marine
Saundersfoot   01834 812115

Trident UK Gateshead   0191 490 1736

SURVEYORS AND NAVAL ARCHITECTS

Amble Boat Company Ltd
Amble   01665 710267

Ark Surveys East Anglia/South Coast
01621 857065/01794 521957

Atkin & Associates
Lymington   01590 688633

Barbican Yacht Agency Ltd
Plymouth   01752 228855

Battick, Lee St Helier   01534 611143

Booth Marine Surveys, Graham
Birchington-on-Sea   01843 843793

Byrde & Associates
Kimmeridge   01929 480064

Bureau Maritime Ltd
Maldon   01621 859181

Byrde & Associates
Kimmeridge   01929 480064

Cannell & Associates, David M
Wivenhoe   01206 823337

Cardiff Commercial Boat Operators Ltd
Cardiff   029 2037 7872

Clarke Designs LLP, Owen
Dartmouth   01803 770495

Connor, Richard
Coleraine   07712 115751

Cox, David Penryn   01326 340808

Davies, Peter N
Wivenhoe   01206 823289

Down Marine Co Ltd
Belfast   028 90480247

Evans, Martin
Kirby le Soken   07887 724055

Goodall, JL Whitby   01947 604791

Green, James Plymouth   01752 660516

Greening Naval Architect Ltd, David
Salcombe   01548 842000

Hansing & Associates
North Wales/Midlands   01248 671291

JP Services – Marine Safety & Training
Chichester   01243 537552

MacGregor, WA
Felixstowe   01394 676034

Mahoney & Co, KPO
Co Cork   +353 21 477 6150

Marinte Surveys UK
Emsworth   07798 554535

Marintec
Lymington   01590 683414

Norwood Marine
Margate   01843 835711

Quay Consultants Ltd
West Wittering   01243 673056

Scott Marine Surveyors & Consultants
Conwy   01492 573001

S Roberts Marine Ltd
Liverpool   0151 707 8300

Staton-Bevan, Tony
Lymington   01590 645755/
        07850 315744

Thomas, Stephen
Southampton   023 8048 6273

Towler, Perrin
Lymington   01590 718087

Victoria Yacht Surveys
Cornwall   0800 083 2113

Ward & McKenzie
Woodbridge   01394 383222

Ward & McKenzie (North East)
Pocklington   01759 304322

YDSA Yacht Designers & Surveyors Association Bordon   0845 0900162

TAPE TECHNOLOGY

CC Marine Services (Rubbaweld) Ltd
London   020 7402 4009

Trade Grade Products Ltd
Poole   01202 820177

UK Epoxy Resins
Burscough   01704 892364

3M United Kingdom plc
Bracknell   0870 5360036

TRANSPORT/YACHT DELIVERIES

Boat Shifters
        07733 344018/01326 210548

Convoi Exceptionnel Ltd
Hamble   023 8045 3045

Debbage Yachting
Ipswich   01473 601169

East Coast Offshore Yachting
        01480 861381

Hainsworth's UK and Continental
Bingley   01274 565925

Houghton Boat Transport
Tewkesbury   07831 486710

MCL Transboat   08455 201900

MJS Boat Transport
Alexandria, Scotland   01389 755047

Moonfleet Sailing
Poole   01202 682269

Performance Yachting
Plymouth   01752 565023

Peters & May Ltd
Southampton   023 8048 0480

Reeder School of Seamanship, Mike
Lymington   01590 674560

Seafix Boat Transfer
North Wales   01766 514507

Sealand Boat Deliveries Ltd
Liverpool   01254 705225

Shearwater Sailing
Southampton   01962 775213

Southcoasting Navigators
Devon   01626 335626

West Country Boat Transport
        01566 785651

Wolff, David   07659 550131

TUITION/SAILING SCHOOLS

Association of Scottish Yacht Charterers Argyll   07787 363562
        01852 200258

Bisham Abbey Sailing & Navigation School Bisham   01628 474960

Blue Baker Yachts
Ipswich   01473 780008

British Offshore Sailing School
Hamble   023 8045 7733

Coastal Sea School
Weymouth   0870 321 3271

Dart Harbour Sea School
Dartmouth   01803 839339

Dartmouth Sailing
Dartmouth   01803 833399

Drake Sailing School
Plymouth   01635 253009

East Anglian Sea School
Ipswich   01473 659992

East Coast Offshore Yachting – Les Rant Perry   01480 861381

Gibraltar Sailing Centre
Gibraltar   +350 78554

Glenans Irish Sailing School
Baltimore   +353 28 20154

Hamble School of Yachting
Hamble   023 8045 6687

Haslar Sea School
Gosport   023 9260 2708

Hobo Yachting
Southampton   023 8033 4574

Hoylake Sailing School
Wirral   0151 632 4664

Ibiza Sailing School   07092 235 853

International Yachtmaster Academy
Southampton   0800 515439

JP Services – Marine Safety & Training
Chichester   01243 537552

Lymington Cruising School
Lymington   01590 677478

Marine Leisure Association (MLA)
Southampton   023 8029 3822

Menorca Cruising School
        01995 679240

Moonfleet Sailing
Poole   01202 682269

National Marine Correspondence School Macclesfield   01625 262365

Pembrokeshire Cruising
Neyland   01646 602500

Performance Yachting & Chandlery
Plymouth   01752 565023

Plain Sailing
Dartmouth   01803 853843

Plymouth Sailing School
Plymouth   01752 493377

Port Edgar Marina & Sailing School
Port Edgar   0131 331 3330

Portsmouth Outdoor Centre
Portsmouth   023 9266 3873

Portugal Sail & Power   01473 833001

Safe Water Training Sea School Ltd
Wirral   0151 630 0466

Sail East
Felixstowe   01255 502887

Sail East
River Crouch   07860 271954

Sail East
River Medway   07932 157027

Sail East Harwich   01473 689344

Sally Water Training
East Cowes   01983 299033

Sea-N-Shore
Salcombe   01548 842276

Seafever
East Grinstead   01342 316293

Solaris Mediterranean Sea School
01925 642909

Solent School of Yachting
Southampton   023 8045 7733

Southcoasting Navigators
Devon   01626 335626

Southern Sailing
Southampton   01489 575511

Start Point Sailing
Dartmouth   01548 810917

Sunsail
Port Solent/Largs   0870 770 6314

Team Sailing Gosport   023 9252 4370

Workman Marine School
Portishead   01275 845844

Wride School of Sailing, Bob
North Ferriby   01482 635623

WATERSIDE ACCOMMODATION & RESTAURANTS

Abbey, The Penzance   01736 366906

Al Porto Hull Marina   01482 238889

Arun View Inn, The
Littlehampton   01903 722335

Baywatch on the Beach
Bembridge   01983 873259

Beaucette Marina Restaurant
Guernsey   01481 247066

Bella Napoli
Brighton Marina   01273 818577

Bembridge Coast Hotel
Bembridge   01983 873931

Budock Vean Hotel
Porth Navas Creek   01326 252100

Café Mozart Cowes   01983 293681

Caffé Uno Port Solent   023 9237 5227

Chandlers Bar & Bistro
Queen Anne's Battery Marina
Plymouth   01752 257772

Chiquito Port Solent   02392 205070

Cruzzo Malahide Marina
Co Dublin   +353 1 845 0599

Cullins Yard Bistro
Dover   01304 211666

Custom House, The
Poole   01202 676767

Dart Marina River Lounge
Dartmouth   01803 832580

Deer Leap, The
Exmouth   01395 265030

Doghouse Swanwick Marina,
Hamble   01489 571602

Dolphin Restaurant
Gorey   01534 853370

Doune Knoydart   01687 462667

El Puertos
Penarth Marina   029 2070 5551

Falmouth Marina
Marine Bar and Restaurant
Falmouth   01326 313481

Ferry Boat Inn West Wick Marina
Nr Chelmsford   01621 740208

Ferry Inn, The (restaurant)
Pembroke Dock   01646 682947

Fisherman's Wharf
Sandwich   01304 613636

Folly Inn Cowes   01983 297171

Gaffs Restaurant
Fenit, County Kerry   +353 66 71 36666

Godleys Hotel Fenit
County Kerry   +353 66 71 36108

Harbour Lights Restaurant
Walton on the Naze   01255 851887

Haven Bar and Bistro, The
Lymington Yacht Haven 01590 679971

Haven Hotel Poole   08453 371550

HMS Ganges Restaurant
Mylor Yacht Harbour   01326 374320

Jolly Sailor, The
Bursledon   023 8040 5557

Kames Hotel Argyll   01700 811489

Ketch Rigger, The Hamble Point
Marina Hamble   023 8045 5601

Kings Arms Stoborough   01929 552705

Kota Restaurant
Porthleven   01326 562407

La Cala Lady Bee Marina
Shoreham   01273 597422

Le Nautique
St Peter Port   01481 721714

Lighter Inn, The
Topsham   01392 875439

Mariners Bistro Sparkes Marina,
Hayling Island   023 9246 9459

Mary Mouse II Haslar Marina,
Gosport   023 9252 5200

Martha's Vineyard
Milford Haven   01646 697083

Master Builder's House Hotel
Buckler's Hard   01590 616253

Millstream Hotel
Bosham   01243 573234

Montagu Arms Hotel
Beaulieu   01590 612324

Oyster Quay
Mercury Yacht Harbour,
Hamble   023 8045 7220

Paris Hotel Coverack   01326 280258

Pebble Beach, The
Gosport   023 9251 0789

Philip Leisure Group
Dartmouth   01803 833351

Priory Bay Hotel
Seaview, Isle of Wight   01983 613146

Quayside Hotel Brixham 01803 855751

Queen's Hotel Kirkwall   01856 872200

Sails Dartmouth   01803 839281

Shell Bay Seafood Restaurant
Poole Harbour   01929 450363

Simply Italian Sovereign Harbour,
Eastbourne   01323 470911

Spinnaker, The
Chichester Marina   01243 511032

Spit Sand Fort
The Solent   01329 242077

Steamboat Inn
Lossiemouth   01343 812066

Tayvallich Inn, The
Argyll   01546 870282

Villa Adriana Newhaven Marina
Newhaven   01273 513976

Warehouse Brasserie, The
Poole   01202 677238

36 on the Quay
Emsworth   01243 375592

WEATHER INFORMATION

Met Office Exeter   0870 900 0100

WOOD FITTINGS

Howells & Son, KJ
Poole   01202 665724

Onward Trading Co Ltd
Southampton   01489 885250

Robbins Timber
Bristol   0117 963 3136

Sheraton Marine Cabinet
Witney   01993 868275

YACHT BROKERS

ABC Powermarine
Beaumaris   01248 811413

ABYA Association of Brokers & Yacht Agents
Bordon   0845 0900162

Adur Boat Sales
Southwick   01273 596680

Ancasta International Boat Sales
Southampton   023 8045 0000

Anglia Yacht Brokerage
Bury St Edmunds   01359 271747

Ardmair Boat Centre
Ullapool   01854 612054

Barbican Yacht Agency, The
Plymouth   01752 228855

Bates Wharf Marine Sales Ltd
01932 571141

BJ Marine Bangor   028 9127 1434

Boatworks + Ltd
St Peter Port   01481 726071

Caley Marina Inverness   01463 236539

Calibra Marine International Ltd
Southampton   08702 400358

Camper & Nicholsons International
London   020 7009 1950

Clarke & Carter Interyacht Ltd
Ipswich/Burnham on Crouch
01473 659681/01621 785600

Coastal Leisure Ltd
Southampton   023 8033 2222

Dale Sailing Brokerage
Neyland   01646 603105

Deacons Southampton   023 8040 2253

Exe Leisure Topsham   001392 879055

Ferrypoint Boat Co
Youghal   +353 24 94232

Gweek Quay Boatyard
Helston   01326 221657

**International Barge
& Yacht Brokers**
Southampton   023 8045 5205

Iron Wharf Boatyard
Faversham   01795 537122

Jackson Yacht Services
Jersey   01534 743819

Kings Yacht Agency
Beaulieu   01590 616316

Kippford Slipway Ltd
Dalbeattie   01556 620249

Lencraft Boats Ltd
Dungarvan   +353 58 68220

Liberty Yachts Ltd
Plymouth   01752 227911

Lucas Yachting, Mike
Torquay   01803 212840

Network Yacht Brokers
Dartmouth   01803 834864

Network Yacht Brokers
Plymouth   01752 605377

New Horizon Yacht Agency
Guernsey   01481 726335

Oyster Brokerage Ltd
Southampton   02380 831011

Pearn and Co, Norman
(Looe Boatyard) Looe   01503 262244

Performance Boat Company
Maidenhead   07768 464717

Peters Chandlery
Chichester   01243 511033

Portavon Marina
Keynsham   0117 986 1626

Retreat BY Topsham   01392 874720

SD Marine Ltd
Southampton   023 8045 7278

Sea & Shore Ship Chandler
Dundee   01382 202666

South Pier Shipyard
St Helier   01534 711000

South West Yacht Brokers Group
Plymouth   01752 401421

Sunbird Marine Services
Fareham   01329 842613

Swordfish Marine Brokerage
Holy Loch   01369 701905

Trafalgar Yacht Services
Fareham   01329 823577

Transworld Yachts
Hamble   023 8045 7704

Walton Marine Sales
Brighton   01273 670707
Portishead   01275 840132

Walton Marine Sales
Wroxham   01603 781178

Watson Marine, Charles
Hamble   023 8045 6505

Western Marine
Dublin   +353 1280 0321

Woodrolfe Brokerage
Maldon   01621 868494

Youngboats Faversham   01795 536176

YACHT CHARTERS & HOLIDAYS

Ardmair Boat Centre
Ullapool   01854 612054

**Association of Scottish Yacht
Charterers** Argyll   01880 820012

Camper & Nicholsons International
London   020 7009 1950

Coastal Leisure Ltd
Southampton   023 8033 2222

Crusader Yachting
Turkey   01732 867321

Dartmouth Sailing
Dartmouth   01803 833399

Dartmouth Yacht Charters
Kingswear   01803 883501

Doune Marine Mallaig   01687 462667

Four Seasons Yacht Charter
Gosport   023 9251 1789

Golden Black Sailing
Cornwall   01209 715757

Hamble Point Yacht Charters
Hamble   023 8045 7110

Haslar Marina & Victory Yacht Charters
Gosport   023 9252 0099

Indulgence Charters
Wendover   01296 696006

Liberty Yachts West Country, Greece,
Mallorca & Italy   01752 227911

Nautilus Yachting
Mediterranean & Caribbean
01732 867445

On Deck Sailing
Southampton   023 8063 9997

Patriot Charters & Sail School
Milford Haven   01437 741202

West Country Yachts
Plymouth   01752 606999
Falmouth   01326 212320

Puffin Yachts
Port Solent   01483 420728

Sailing Holidays Ltd
Mediterranean   020 8459 8787

Sailing Holidays in Ireland
Kinsale   +353 21 477 2927

Setsail Holidays
Greece, Turkey,
Croatia, Majorca   01787 310445

Shannon Sailing Ltd
Tipperary   +353 67 24499

Sleat Marine Services
Isle of Skye   01471 844216

Smart Yachts
Mediterranean   01425 614804

South West Marine Training
Dartmouth   01803 853843

Sovereign Sailingl
Kinsale   +353 87 6172555

Sunsail
Worldwide   0870 770 0102

Templecraft Yacht Charters
Lewes   01273 812333

TJ Sailing Gosport   07803 499691

Top Yacht Sailing Ltd
Havant   02392 347655

Victory Yacht Charters
Gosport   023 9252 0099

West Wales Yacht Charter
Pwllheli   07748 634869

39 North (Mediterranean)
Kingskerwell   07071 393939

YACHT CLUBS

Aberaeron YC
Aberdovey   01545 570077

Aberdeen and Stonehaven SC
Nr Inverurie   01569 764006

Aberdour BC   01383 860029

Abersoch Power BC
Abersoch   01758 712027

Aberystwyth BC
Aberystwyth   01970 624575

Aldeburgh YC   01728 452562

Alderney SC   01481 822959

Alexandra YC
Southend-on-Sea   01702 340363

Arklow SC   +353 402 33100

Arun YC Littlehampton 01903 716016

Axe YC Axemouth   01297 20043

Ayr Yacht and CC   01292 476034

Ballyholme YC Bangor   028 91271467

Baltimore SC	+353 28 20426
Banff SC	01464 820308
Bantry Bay SC	+353 27 51724
Barry YC	01446 735511
Beaulieu River SC Brockenhurst	01590 616273
Bembridge SC Isle of Wight	01983 872237
Benfleet YC Canvey Island	01268 792278
Blackpool and Fleetwood YC	01253 884205
Blackwater SC Maldon	01621 853923
Blundellsands SC	0151 929 2101
Bosham SC Chichester	01243 572341
Brading Haven YC Isle of Wight	01983 872289
Bradwell CC	01621 892970
Bradwell Quay YC Wickford	01268 890173
Brancaster Staithe SC	01485 210249
Brandy Hole YC Hullbridge	01702 230320
Brightlingsea SC	01206 303275
Brighton Marina YC Peacehaven	01273 818711
Bristol Avon SC	01225 873472
Bristol Channel YC Swansea	01792 366000
Bristol Corinthian YC Axbridge	01934 732033
Brixham YC	01803 853332
Burnham Overy Staithe SC	01328 730961
Burnham-on-Crouch SC	01621 782812
Burnham-on-Sea SC Bridgwater	01278 792911
Burry Port YC	01554 833635
Cabot CC	01275 855207
Caernarfon SC (Menai Strait) Caernarfon	01286 672861
Campbeltown SC	01586 552488
Island YC Canvey Island	01702 510360
Cardiff YC	029 2046 3697
Cardiff Bay YC	029 20226575
Carlingford Lough YC Rostrevor	028 4173 8604
Carrickfergus SC Whitehead	028 93 351402
Castle Cove SC Weymouth	01305 783708

Castlegate Marine Club Stockton on Tees	01642 583299
Chanonry SC Fortrose	01463 221415
Chichester Cruiser and Racing Club	01483 770391
Chichester YC	01243 512918
Christchurch SC	01202 483150
Clyde CC Glasgow	0141 221 2774
Co Antrim YC Carrickfergus	028 9337 2322
Cobnor Activities Centre Trust	01243 572791
Coleraine YC	028 703 44503
Colne YC Brightlingsea	01206 302594
Conwy YC Deganwy	01492 583690
Coquet YC	01665 710367
Corrib Rowing & YC Galway City	+353 91 564560
Cowes Combined Clubs	01983 295744
Cowes Corinthian YC Isle of Wight	01983 296333
Cowes Yachting	01983 280770
Cramond BC	0131 336 1356
Creeksea SC Burnham-on-Crouch	01245 320578
Crookhaven SC	+353 87 2379997
Crouch YC Burnham-on-Crouch	01621 782252
Dale YC	01646 636362
Dartmouth YC	01803 832305
Deben YC Woodbridge	01394 384440
Dell Quay SC Chichester	01243 514639
Dingle SC	+353 66 51984
Douglas Bay YC	01624 673965
Dovey YC Aberdovey	01213 600008
Dun Laoghaire MYC	+353 1 288 938
Dunbar SC Cockburnspath	01368 86287
East Antrim BC	028 28 277204
East Belfast YC	028 9065 6283
East Cowes SC	01983 531687
East Dorset SC Poole	01202 706111
East Lothian YC	01620 892698
Eastney Cruising Association Portsmouth	023 92734103
Eling SC	023 80863987
Emsworth SC	01243 372850
Emsworth Slipper SC	01243 378881

Essex YC Southend	01702 478404
Exe SC (River Exe) Exmouth	01395 264607
Eyott SC Mayland	01245 320703
Fairlie YC	01294 213940
Falmouth Town SC	01326 373915
Falmouth Watersports Association Falmouth	01326 211223
Fareham Sailing & Motor BC Fareham	01329 280738
Felixstowe Ferry SC	01394 283785
Findhorn YC Findhorn	01309 690247
Fishguard Bay YC Lower Fishguard	01348 872866
Flushing SC Falmouth	01326 374043
Folkestone Yacht and Motor BC Folkestone	01303 251574
Forth Corinthian YC Haddington	0131 552 5939
Forth YCs Association Edinburgh	0131 552 3006
Fowey Gallants SC	01726 832335
Foynes YC Foynes	+353 69 91201
Galway Bay SC	+353 91 794527
Glasson SC Lancaster	01524 751089
Glenans Irish Sailing School	+353 1 6611481
Glenans Irish SC (Westport)	+353 98 26046
Gosport CC Gosport	02392 586838
Gravesend SC	07538 326623
Greenwich YC London	020 8858 7339
Grimsby and Cleethorpes YC Grimsby	01472 356678
Guernsey YC St Peter Port	01481 725342
Hamble River SC Southampton	023 80452070
Hampton Pier YC Herne Bay	01227 364749
Hardway SC Gosport	023 9258 1875
Hartlepool YC	01429 233423
Harwich Town SC	01255 503200
Hastings and St Leonards YC Hastings	01424 420656
Haven Ports YC Woodbridge	01473 659658
Hayling Ferry SC; Locks SC Hayling Island	07870 367571
Hayling Island SC	023 92463768
Helensburgh SC Rhu	01436 672778
Helensburgh	01436 821234
Helford River SC Helston	01326 231006

Herne Bay SC	01227 375650
Highcliffe SC Christchurch	01425 274874
Holyhead SC	01407 762526
Holywood YC	028 90423355
Hoo Ness YC Sidcup	01634 250052
Hornet SC Gosport	023 9258 0403
Howth YC	+353 1 832 2141
Hoylake SC Wirral	0151 632 2616
Hullbridge YC	01702 231797
Humber Yawl Club	01482 667224
Hundred of Hoo SC	01634 250102
Hurlingham YC London	020 8788 5547
Hurst Castle SC	01590 645589
Hythe SC Southampton	02380 846563
Hythe & Saltwood SC	01303 265178
Ilfracombe YC	01271 863969
Iniscealtra SC Limerick	+353 61 338347
Invergordon BC	01349 893772
Irish CC	+353 214870031
Island CC Salcombe	01548 844631
Island SC Isle of Wight	01983 296621
Island YC Canvey Island	01268 510360
Isle of Bute SC Rothesay	01700 502819
Isle of Man YC Port St Mary	01624 832088
Itchenor SC Chichester	01243 512400
Keyhaven YC	01590 642165
Killyleagh YC	028 4482 8250
Kircubbin SC	028 4273 8422
Kirkcudbright SC	01557 331727
Langstone SC Havant	023 9248 4577
Largs SC Largs	01475 670000
Larne Rowing & SC	028 2827 4573
Lawrenny YC	01646 651212
Leigh-on-Sea SC	01702 476788
Lerwick BC	01595 696954
Lilliput SC Poole	01202 740319
Littlehampton Yacht Club Littlehampton	01903 713990
Loch Ryan SC Stranraer	01776 706322
Lochaber YC Fort William	01397 772361
Locks SC Portsmouth	07980 856267
Looe SC	01503 262559
Lossiemouth CC Fochabers	01348 812121
Lough Swilly YC Fahn	+353 74 22377
Lowestoft CC	07810 522515
Lyme Regis Power BC	01297 443788
Lyme Regis SC	01297 442373
Lymington Town SC	0159 674514
Lympstone SC Exeter	01395 278792
Madoc YC Porthmadog	01766 512976
Malahide YC	+353 1 845 3372
Maldon Little Ship Club	01621 854139
Manx Sailing & CC Ramsey	01624 813494
Marchwood YC	023 80666141
Margate YC	01843 292602
Marina BC Pwllheli	01758 612271
Maryport YC	01228 560865
Mayflower SC Plymouth	01752 662526
Mayo SC (Rosmoney) Rosmoney	+353 98 27772
Medway YC Rochester	01634 718399
Menai Bridge BC Beaumaris	01248 810583
Mengham Rythe SC Hayling Island	023 92463337
Merioneth YC Barmouth	01341 280000
Monkstone Cruising and SC Swansea	01792 812229
Montrose SC Montrose	01674 672554
Mumbles YC Swansea	01792 369321
Mylor YC Falmouth	01326 374391
Nairn SC	01667 453897
National YC Dun Laoghaire	+353 1 280 5725
Netley SC Netley	023 80454272
New Quay YC Aberdovey	01545 560516
Newhaven & Seaford SC Seaford	01323 890077
Newport and Uskmouth SC Cardiff	01633 271417
Newtownards SC	028 9181 3426
Neyland YC	01646 600267
North Devon YC Bideford	01271 861390
North Fambridge Yacht Centre	01621 740370
North Haven YC Poole	01202 708830
North of England Yachting Association Kirkwall	01856 872331
North Sunderland Marine Club Sunderland	01665 721231
North Wales CC Conwy	01492 593481
North West Venturers YC (Beaumaris) Beaumaris	0161 2921943
Oban SC Ledaig by Oban	01631 563999
Orford SC Woodbridge	01394 450997
Orkney SC Kirkwall	01856 872331
Orwell YC Ipswich	01473 602288
Oulton Broad Yacht Station	01502 574946
Ouse Amateur SC Kings Lynn	01553 772239
Paignton SC Paignton	01803 525817
Parkstone YC Poole	01202 743610
Peel Sailing and CC Peel	01624 842390
Pembroke Haven YC	01646 684403
Pembrokeshire YC Milford Haven	01646 692799
Penarth YC	029 20708196
Pentland Firth YC Thurso	01847 891803
Penzance YC	01736 364989
Peterhead SC Ellon	01779 75527
Pin Mill SC Woodbridge	01394 780271
Plym YC Plymouth	01752 404991
Poolbeg YC	+353 1 660 4681
Poole YC	01202 672687
Porlock Weir SC Watchet	01643 862702
Port Edgar YC Penicuik	0131 657 2854
Port Navas YC Falmouth	01326 340065
Port of Falmouth Sailing Association Falmouth	01326 372927
Portchester SC Portchester	023 9237 6375
Porthcawl Harbour BC Swansea	01656 655935
Porthmadog SC Porthmadog	01766 513546
Portrush YC Portrush	028 7082 3932
Portsmouth SC	02392 820596
Prestwick SC Prestwick	01292 671117
Pwllheli SC Pwllheli	01758 613343
Queenborough YC Queenborough	01795 663955
Quoile YC Downpatrick	028 44 612266
River Towy BC Tenby	01267 241755
RAFYC	023 80452208
Redclyffe YC Poole	01929 557227

Restronguet SC
Falmouth 01326 374536

Ribble CC
Lytham St Anne's 01253 739983

River Wyre YC 01253 811948

RNSA (Plymouth) 01752 55123/83

Rochester CC 01634 841350

Rock Sailing and Water Ski Club
Wadebridge 01208 862431

Royal Dart YC
Dartmouth 01803 752496

Royal Motor YC Poole 01202 707227

Royal Anglesey YC (Beaumaris)
Anglesey 01248 810295

Royal Burnham YC
Burnham-on-Crouch 01621 782044

Royal Channel Islands YC (Jersey)
St Aubin 01534 745783

Royal Cinque Ports YC
Dover 01304 206262

**Royal Corinthian YC
(Burnham-on-Crouch)**
Burnham-on-Crouch 01621 782105

Royal Corinthian YC (Cowes)
Cowes 01983 293581

Royal Cork YC
Crosshaven +353 214 831023

Royal Cornwall YC (RCYC)
Falmouth 01326 312126

Royal Dorset YC
Weymouth 01305 786258

Royal Forth YC
Edinburgh 0131 552 3006

Royal Fowey YC Fowey 01726 833573

Royal Gourock YC 01475 632983

Royal Highland YC
Nairn 01667 493855

Royal Irish YC
Dun Laoghaire +353 1 280 9452

Royal London YC
Isle of Wight 019 83299727

Royal Lymington YC 01590 672677

Royal Mersey YC
Birkenhead 0151 645 3204

Royal Motor YC Poole 01202 707227

Royal Naval Club and Royal Albert YC
Portsmouth 023 9282 5924

Royal Naval Sailing Association
Gosport 023 9252 1100

Royal Norfolk & Suffolk YC
Lowestoft 01502 566726

Royal North of Ireland YC
028 90 428041

Royal Northern and Clyde YC
Rhu 01436 820322

Royal Northumberland YC
Blyth 01670 353636

Royal Plymouth Corinthian YC
Plymouth 01752 664327

Royal Scottish Motor YC
0141 881 1024

Royal Solent YC
Yarmouth 01983 760256

Royal Southampton YC
Southampton 023 8022 3352

Royal Southern YC
Southampton 023 8045 0300

Royal St George YC
Dun Laoghaire +353 1 280 1811

Royal Tay YC Dundee 01382 477133

Royal Temple YC
Ramsgate 01843 591766

Royal Torbay YC
Torquay 01803 292006

Royal Ulster YC
Bangor 028 91 270568

Royal Victoria YC
Fishbourne 01983 882325

Royal Welsh YC (Caernarfon)
Caernarfon 01286 672599

Royal Welsh YC
Aernarfon 01286 672599

Royal Western YC
Plymouth 01752 226299

Royal Yacht Squadron
Isle of Wight 01983 292191

Royal Yorkshire YC
Bridlington 01262 672041

Rye Harbour SC 01797 223136

Salcombe YC 01548 842593

Saltash SC 01752 845988

Scalloway BC
Lerwick 01595 880409

Scarborough YC 01723 373821

Schull SC +353 28 37352

Scillonian Sailing and BC
St Mary's 01720 277229

Seasalter SC Whitstable 07773 189943

Seaview YC
Isle of Wight 01983 613268

Shoreham SC Henfield 01273 453078

Skerries SC
Carlingdford Lough +353 1 849 1233

Slaughden SC
Duxford 01728 689036

Sligo YC Sligo +353 71 77168

Solva Boat Owners Association
Fishguard 01437 721538

Solway YC
Kirkdudbright 01556 620312

South Caernavonshire YC
Abersoch 01758 712338

South Cork SC +353 28 36383

South Devon Sailing School
Newton Abbot 01626 52352

South Gare Marine Club - Sail Section
Middlesbrough 01642 505630

South Shields SC 0191 456 5821

South Woodham Ferrers YC
Chelmsford 01245 325391

Southampton SC 023 8044 6575

Southwold SC 01986 784225

Sovereign Harbour YC
Eastbourne 01323 470888

St Helier YC 01534 721307/32229

St Mawes SC 01326 270686

Starcross Fishing & CC (River Exe)
Starcross 01626 891996

Starcross YC Exeter 01626 890470

Stoke SC Ipswich 01473 624989

Stornoway SC 01851 705412

Stour SC 01206 393924

Strangford Lough YC
Newtownards 028 97 541202

Strangford SC
Downpatrick 028 4488 1404

Strood YC Aylesford 01634 718261

Sunderland YC 0191 567 5133

Sunsail Portsmouth 023 92222224

Sussex YC
Shoreham-by-Sea 01273 464868

Swanage SC 01929 422987

Swansea Yacht & Sub-Aqua Club
Swansea 01792 469096

Tamar River SC
Plymouth 01752 362741

Tarbert Lochfyne YC 01880 820376

Tay Corinthian BC
Dundee 01382 553534

Tay YCs Association 01738 621860

Tees & Hartlepool YC 01429 233423

Tees SC
Aycliffe Village 01429 265400

Teifi BC - Cardigan Bay
Fishguard 01239 613846

Teign Corinthian YC
Teignmouth 01626 777699

Tenby SC 01834 842762

Tenby YC	01834 842762
Thames Estuary YC	01702 345967
Thorney Island SC	01243 371731
Thorpe Bay YC	01702 587563
Thurrock YC Grays	01375 373720
Tollesbury CC	01621 869561
Topsham SC	01392 877524
Torpoint Mosquito SC -	
Plymouth	01752 812508
Tralee SC	+353 66 7136119
Troon CC	01292 311190
Troon YC	01292 315315
Tudor SC	02392 662002
Portsmouth	02392 664948
Tynemouth SC	
Newcastle upon Tyne	0191 2572167
Up River YC	
Hullbridge	01702 231654
Upnor SC	01634 718043
Vanguard SC	
Workington	01228 674238
Wakering YC Rochford	01702 530926
Waldringfield SC	
Woodbridge	01394 283347
Walls Regatta Club	
Lerwick	01595 809273
Walton & Frinton YC	
Walton-on-the-Naze	01255 675526
Warrenpoint BC	028 4175 2137
Warsash SC Soton	01489 583575
Watchet Boat Owner Association	
Watchet	01984 633736
Waterford Harbour SC	
Dunmore East	+353 51 383389
Watermouth YC	
Watchet	01271 865048

Wear Boating Association	
	0191 567 5313
Wells SC	
Wells-next-the-sea	01328 711190
West Kirby SC	0151 625 5579
West Mersea YC	
Colchester	01206 382947
Western Isles YC	01688 302371
Western YC Kilrush	+353 87 2262885
Weston Bay YC	
Portishead	07867 966429
Weston CC Soton	02380 466790
Weston SC Soton	02380 452527
Wexford HBC	+353 53 22039
Weymouth SC	01305 785481
Whitby YC	07786 289393
Whitstable YC	01227 272942
Wicklow SC	+353 404 67526
Witham SC Boston	01205 363598
Wivenhoe SC	
Colchester	01206 822132
Woodbridge CC	01394 386737
Wormit BC	01382 553878
Yarmouth SC	01983 760270
Yealm YC	
Newton Ferrers	01752 872291
Youghal Sailing Club	+353 24 92447

YACHT DESIGNERS

Cannell & Associates, David M	
Wivenhoe	01206 823337
Clarke Designs LLP, Owen	
Dartmouth	01803 770495
Giles Naval Architects, Laurent	
Lymington	01590 641777
Harvey Design, Ray	
Barton on Sea	01425 613492

Jones Yacht Design, Stephen	
Warsash	01489 576439
Wharram Designs, James	
Truro	01872 864792
Wolstenholme Yacht Design	
Coltishall	01603 737024

YACHT MANAGEMENT

Barbican Yacht Agency Ltd	
Plymouth	01752 228855
Coastal Leisure Ltd	
Southampton	023 8033 2222
O'Sullivan Boat Management	
Dun Laoghaire	+353 86 829 6625
Swanwick Yacht Surveyors	
Swanwick	01489 564822
Amble Boat Company Ltd	
Amble	01665 710267

YACHT VALETING

Autogleam	
Lymington	0800 074 4672
Blackwell, Craig	
Co Meath	+353 87 677 9605
Bright 'N' Clean	
South Coast	07789 494430
Clean It All	
Nr Brixham	01803 844564
Kip Marina Inverkip	01475 521485
Mainstay Yacht Maintenance	
Dartmouth	01803 839076
Mobile Yacht Maintenance	
	07900 148806
Shipshape Hayling Is	023 9232 4500